"THE WORLD'S EASIEST GUIDE"

TO

Family Relationships

Randy Southern is a freelance writer with more than 50 books to his credit. A former product developer for David C. Cook, he lives with his wife and two children in Mount Prospect, Illinois.

James S. Bell Jr. is Executive Editor for Moody Press. He has compiled and abridged numerous classics. He is also the general editor of *The World's Easiest Guide* series as well as co-author of *The Complete Idiot's Guide to the Bible* and *The Complete Idiot's Guide to Prayer.*

"THE WORLD'S EASIEST GUIDE"

— TO —

Family Relationships

GARY CHAPMAN

WITH RANDY SOUTHERN

NORTHFIELD PUBLISHING

Chicago

Scripture taken from the *Holy Bible, New International Version.*® NIV® Copyright © 1973, 1978, 1984 by International Bible Society. Used by permission of Zondervan Publishing House. All rights reserved.

Editors: James Bell Jr.
James Vincent

ISBN: 1-881273-40-7

Printed in the United States of America

Table of Contents

"THE WORLD'S EASIEST GUIDE"

Your Relationship

With Your Spouse

Before You Say, "I Do"

SNAPSHOT

"How are things going with Adele?" Owen asked as he put on his shirt.

Rich zipped open his gym bag and sighed. "OK, I guess."

"Then what's with the sigh?" Owen asked.

"I'm just starting to have second thoughts about the relationship, that's all," Rich said.

Owen groaned. "I thought you said Adele could be *the* one for you. You were even talking about buying a ring, weren't you?"

"Yeah," Rich admitted, "but I'm starting to see things in the relationship that I don't like."

"Here we go again," Owen mumbled.

"No, that's not it," Rich protested. "You say I'm too picky, but I'm not. Every time I've ended a

SNEAK PREVIEW

1. Purposeful dating is an excellent way to prepare for marriage.
2. Common interests, personal attractiveness, and parental involvement are all important ingredients in a successful dating relationship.
3. Since marriage is a process of two people becoming one, it's wise to date people with whom you can build unity.

relationship it was for a very good reason."

"Right," Owen said. "Like when you broke up with Sharon because she talked too much while you were playing mini-golf."

"Hey, she cost me at least three strokes that game," Rich said.

"Or when you dumped Erin because she asked you why you owned so many CDs," Owen continued.

"I'm telling you, that's how those control freaks work," Rich explained. "It started with an innocent question, but it would have ended with all of my disks in a garage sale someday. I just know it."

"And then there's the time you decided you couldn't see a future with Lori because she had a lower Social Security number than you have," Owen continued.

"Don't you think it was a little weird that hers started with 302 when both of ours start with 310?" Rich replied. "She said she was *younger* than I am, so how did she jump ahead eight million places in the Social Security line?"

"I'm not even going to dignify that with an answer," Owen replied. "So now what's the problem with Adele? She's beautiful, funny, and creative. She loves kids, just like you do. She loves golf, just like you do. She comes from a close family, just like you do. She's everything you've been looking for. So why are you having second thoughts about the relationship?"

"Her silverware," Rich replied.

"I beg your pardon."

"She invited me over for dinner on Saturday," Rich explained, "and just as I was about to take my first bite I noticed some dried gravy on my fork."

Owen stared at him.

"What did she want me to do?" Rich continued, oblivious to Owen's disbelieving gaze. "Prove my love through botulism? I was so disgusted I couldn't even look her in the eye during dinner."

"Yeah, well, in light of such a blatant utensil violation, I can't see much hope for your relationship, either," Owen said.

"Hey, you can make fun all you want," Rich said. "But you didn't have to look at that fork."

Owen closed his locker and started toward the door. "You're going to make some lucky woman very happy one day," he called over his shoulder. "By not marrying her."

* * * * * * * * * * * * * *

You're probably wondering what a chapter on dating is doing in a book about family relationships. But, hey, families have to start *somewhere,* don't they? The dating relationship is a logical beginning for a discussion of families because many of the patterns and dynamics of family relationships get their start in the courtship stage. So let's start at the very beginning . . . well, near the beginning for most couples who will say, "I do." If you've already said those words, this chapter's a good review of why and perhaps how you got together in this rewarding and challenging relationship.

Obviously the topic of dating is too immense to cover adequately in one chapter. What we're going to do is focus on four specific areas, as they relate to marriage (and, eventually, family relationships):

1. Why you should date

2. What you should avoid

3. What you should look for in a mate

4. What you should be working toward in your dating relationship

What Dating Can Do for You

Ask a dozen single people why they date, and chances are you'll get a dozen different answers. Some may be profound ("I want to find a soul mate"); others may be, well, less profound ("I don't like to go to movies by myself"). Dating means different things to different people. Some people treat it as a hobby or pastime; others treat it as a matter of life and death. Some people enjoy the thrill of the chase; others despise what they see as "games."

For those who are serious about dating—those who view it as something more than a way to kill time on a Friday night—we offer four reasons to continue making your way through laughable blind dates and overzealous paramours.

1. Dating gives you valuable experience with the opposite sex.

If marriage were a career, dating would be the internship. You'll find that socializing with members of the opposite sex will give you the "training" you need to become a desirable candidate for marriage (just as a good internship will give you the training you need to become a desirable job candidate). The more time you spend in social settings with guys or girls, the more comfortable you'll become around them. The more comfortable you are, the better date you'll be. The better date you are, the higher your stock will rise on the Potential Spouse Market.

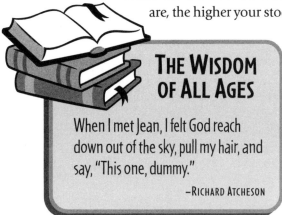

THE WISDOM OF ALL AGES

When I met Jean, I felt God reach down out of the sky, pull my hair, and say, "This one, dummy."

—RICHARD ATCHESON

If your knowledge of the opposite sex comes primarily from your years of trying to coexist with a brother or sister in your parents' house, dating will give you a whole new appreciation of the real differences a chromosome can make. By the same token, dating will also help you recognize that, in many areas, men and women are a lot more similar than you might imagine (or care to admit).

Spending time with members of the opposite sex in social settings is a good way to "demystify" them. In the absence of any real personal experience, guys and girls have a tendency to create stereotypes or idealized versions of the opposite sex in their heads. Interacting regularly with your chromosomal opposites is the best way to smash those stereotypes and idealized notions and replace them with views that are grounded in reality.

For example, Georgia had some very strong opinions about what men were like and what they wanted from women, based on the way her father treated her mother. As she began to date, she got to know guys who were nothing like her father. In fact, she found that some guys are even easier to talk to than her girlfriends are. She hasn't had a serious relationship yet, but at least now she knows she's capable of having one, whereas before she started dating, she wasn't so sure.

T. J. had a problem with fantasizing about some of the girls in his college classes. His mind would wander in class and he would start painting elaborate pictures in his mind of what some of his female classmates were like. Over time, T. J. had opportunities to date a few of those classmates. He discovered, for better or worse, that his "fantasy girls" were, in fact, real people, with the same kind of foibles, weaknesses, and unpleasant characteristics that everyone else has. He also discovered that it's much easier to talk to a real person than a fantasy figure.

Forget the notion of ever trying to understand the opposite sex completely. Some things were just not meant for us to know. What you can get from dating is a general sense of how guys or girls think, what's important to them, and how you can best communicate with them. All of this information will come in extremely handy if and when you decide to tie the knot. Call it a head start to marriage.

2. Dating helps you develop and improve your own personality.

If you're perfectly satisfied with every aspect of your personality, if you're convinced beyond all doubt that you don't need to change a thing about yourself, you might want to consider some alternatives to dating. The dating process, more than almost any other type of interaction, has a tendency to illuminate some of the, well, less-than-perfect aspects of our personalities.

If you're open to the idea of examining yourself—the way you talk, the way you listen, the way you conduct yourself in public, the way you treat others—you'll likely find a wealth of useful information in your dating relationships. The key is recognizing the signs your dates are giving you.

For example, Keith found his identity in being the life of every party. People loved him (or so he thought) because he was willing to say or do anything for a laugh. One night in a restaurant, while he was giving a waitress a hard time by pretending he couldn't read, he noticed his date squirming in embarrassment. His friends had always encouraged his outrageousness, so it was a shock for him to see someone he enjoyed spending time with get embarrassed by his behavior. In fact, it bothered him so much that, since that night, he has made a conscious effort to be more subdued—and tolerable—in social settings.

That's not to say that you should create an identity for yourself based solely on the preferences of the people you date. However, dating can give you a unique view of yourself, one that may answer a lot of questions about why people respond to you the way they do. That will be a good thing to know when you find yourself in a lifelong relationship with a spouse.

3. Dating gives you an opportunity to contribute to someone else's life.

Relax, it's not nearly as Oprah-ish as it sounds. We're not talking about the kind of contributions that inevitably lead to teary reminisces or surprise reunions twenty years down the line ("Next on *Oprah*: people who've made a difference in other people's lives"). We're talking about minor, everyday contributions that ultimately pave the way for major changes in a person's life.

Catherine was an introverted, gawky, self-conscious college sophomore when she started dating Darin. From the start of their relationship, Darin made a habit of telling Catherine how pretty she was. He listened with interest whenever she worked up the courage to say something. He laughed at her barely audible jokes. He made her feel important. Over the course of their eight-month relationship, Catherine's confidence increased dramatically. Darin helped Catherine come out of her shell and encouraged her to realize her potential. The relationship didn't last, but the results of it certainly have. Today Catherine is a vivacious, confident, and successful business owner.

The point that you shouldn't miss is that Catherine isn't the only one who benefited from that dating relationship. Darin saw how his comments and encouragement helped Catherine blossom and become a new person. As a result, he came away from the relationship with the confidence that he could help others and the desire to do so. Chances are, the woman Darin eventually marries will benefit tremendously from what he learned in his relationship with Catherine.

What it comes down to is this: You have something beneficial to offer the people you date and the people you date have something beneficial to offer you. And while those mutual offerings may not always lead to marriage, they can change lives in small ways.

4. Dating will help you discover what kind of person you want to marry.

Let's get this out of the way right now. Mr. Right does not exist. Neither does Ms. Right. There is no perfect person waiting for you on the observation deck of the

Empire State Building, à la *Sleepless in Seattle* or *An Affair to Remember*. In fact, if your notion of what your spouse will be like has any roots in Hollywood, do yourself a favor and rethink your spousal profile right now.

If your list of qualities you want in a spouse includes phrases like "breathtakingly gorgeous," "unfathomably rich," "devastatingly witty," or "unbelievably successful," you might want to hold off on making any honeymoon plans. You've got a long wait ahead of you.

There's nothing wrong with having high expectations for your future spouse, as long as they don't exclude everyone in the human gene pool. That's where dating comes in handy. If you interact with enough people in dating situations, you'll discover which qualities are really important to you and which ones don't matter quite as much. You'll find out what kind of personalities you click with and what kind you clash with. In short, you'll get a sense of what your nonnegotiables are.

The Wisdom of All Ages

Bridegroom: a man who is amazed at the outcome of what he thought was a harmless little flirtation.

—Anonymous

And, chances are, what you discover will surprise you. Very few people end up marrying the type of person they thought they would marry. Qualities that once seemed important have a way of fading from significance when you get to know people with other, more interesting, qualities.

For example, as *wealth* loses its importance to you, *honesty* may replace it on your list of must-have qualities for your spouse. Likewise, instead of wanting to marry someone who is success-oriented, you may find yourself instead preferring someone who is family-oriented. The more kinds of people you're exposed to in your dating relationships, the more informed decisions you can make about what you're looking for in a life partner.

Shana's father was a college football star, and Shana grew up wanting to marry the same type of guy. A cheerleader in high school and college, Shana dated only football and basketball players—until about midway through her senior year of college. That's when she realized that she was more interested in some of the guys in her photography and creative writing classes than in jocks. She discovered that creativity was a higher priority to her than popularity.

The dream of finding Mr. or Ms. Right is one that dies hard. No matter how cynical you claim to be, it's likely that in some corner of your brain, you're holding out hope for that one person who will sweep you off your feet, fulfill your every need, and meet your every criteria.

Fortunately, you'll find that the more people you date, the more you'll recognize just how widespread imperfection is. Once you come to the conclusion that no one could ever embody every attribute and quality you're looking for, you will be forced to determine what it is you want in the people with whom you spend time. And that's the first step toward a marital mind-set.

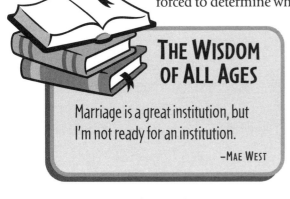

THE WISDOM OF ALL AGES

Marriage is a great institution, but I'm not ready for an institution.

—MAE WEST

Disclaimer: In the interest of full disclosure, we must also point out that there is at least one valid argument *against* dating. In some cultures, the idea of a guy and a girl seeing each other socially, with an eye toward developing a future relationship, is unheard of. Parents are the ones who do the matchmaking, and their decisions are final. In such societies, some spouses don't even meet until their wedding day. The process may seem outdated to us, but the fact is, it has produced many stable marriages. We bring this up not as an endorsement for parental matchmaking, but as a reminder that there is an alternative to the dating process.

If you're like most people, you'd probably rather try your luck at Singles' Night at the local penitentiary than allow your parents to choose your life partner. So that leaves dating, with all of its annoyances and imperfections, as the one viable option for finding that "special someone."

What to Watch Out For

No, this isn't the obligatory warning about why you should always date in groups or run a thorough background check on everyone you date. The purpose of this section is to highlight some dating mistakes that can affect your chances for a long-term relationship.

1. Don't let the physical aspects of your relationship dominate.

If you date long enough, chances are you'll hear more than a few reasons why exploring the physical areas of your relationship is a good idea. These reasons might include the following:

➤ "Sex is a natural way of expressing our love for one another."

➤ "We need to know if we're physically compatible or not."

➤ "It's the next logical stage of our relationship."

Allow us to offer one reason why you may want to put your exploration plans on hold: Sex will overwhelm every other area of your relationship.

We're not even going to get into the moral arguments against a sexual dating relationship. We're not going to dwell on matters such as pregnancy or sexually transmitted diseases. We're not going to hammer home issues such as the lowered self-image problems that plague people who are sexually active before marriage. (Of course, there's no reason you shouldn't take those issues into consideration the next time you're tempted to expand the boundaries of your physical relationship.)

The point we want to emphasize is that once physical intimacy is introduced into a relationship, things like get-to-know-you questions, meaningful discussions, and fun for fun's sake become much less important. The relationship often becomes unbalanced as sex begins to occupy more and more of the couple's time together.

Unfortunately, this usually isn't a mistake couples can learn from. You can't undo a physical encounter, even if you realize that it was a mistake. After certain boundaries have been crossed once, there's a very good chance that they will be crossed again. And again. And again.

If you've already introduced physical intimacy into your current dating relationship, or if you see your boundaries rapidly approaching, you need to reevaluate your relationship and set some serious rules and guidelines to abide by. That might mean changing the places you go or the things you do on your dates. It might mean cutting way back on the time you spend alone with your date. It might mean changing the way you and your date express yourselves physically— eliminating caresses and deep kisses, for example. It might mean doing more things with other couples or groups.

Whatever you need to do to keep the physical part of your relationship in check is what you should do.

2. Don't limit your dating experience unnecessarily.

You've probably heard your share of heartwarming "love at first sight" testimonials ("My husband and I met in sixth grade, dated each other exclusively in junior high and high school, and got married in college. Neither one of us has ever dated anyone else in our entire lives. We've been happily married for twenty-two years and blah, blah, blah"). What you probably haven't heard are the less romantic counterparts to those testimonials ("I was so worried about finding a spouse that I married the first person I dated. I've been married five years now, and even though I love my spouse, I often wonder whether I could have found someone better").

We mentioned earlier in the chapter that dating can give you valuable experience in interacting with the opposite sex. If, however, you choose to limit your dating to one or two serious relationships, all you're getting is experience in interacting with a specific individual. And you won't know what you're missing until it's too late to do anything about it.

Usually fear and insecurity are what drive people into committed relationships too early in their dating "careers." They're afraid that if they don't hook up with someone right away, they may never get another chance to hook up again. And while a committed relationship may give you some sense of security, it will also reduce your chances of meeting and interacting with other really interesting members of

GLAD YOU ASKED

How can I avoid sexual situations when the temptation is so strong?

Set guidelines at the beginning of your relationship and stick to them. Make sure the person you're dating knows exactly where your boundaries are. Any time you sense that a line is about to be crossed, call it a night and go your separate ways. If you want a starting point for setting boundaries, here are three rules to consider: (1) never take your clothes off in each other's presence, (2) never put your hands under each other's clothes, and (3) never lie down together.

the opposite sex—people who, given a chance, may open your eyes to deeper and more fulfilling relationship opportunities.

We're not suggesting that your "little black book" should be the size of a Stephen King novel or that quantity should be job one when it comes to dating. What we are suggesting is that you take advantage of the full array of opportunities that dating offers.

3. Don't get blinded by romance.

For those of you who have already committed to long-term dating relationships, this is the part of the book where we remove your rose-colored glasses and smash them to bits right before your eyes.

Let's look at three givens that come into play in every dating relationship:

1. We all have our strengths and weaknesses when it comes to appearance, talents, background, personality, and character.

2. When we get romantically involved with someone, it's easy to overestimate his or her strengths and overlook his or her weaknesses. ("I can't believe that some of Barbara's coworkers think she's obnoxious. They don't realize that she's only trying to help them when she tells them they're wrong." "Bob's not dumb; he's just not interested in stuff that you have to think about.")

3. Overlooking a person's weaknesses will ultimately prove costly. (Unfortunately, this is a mistake that's usually most obvious in hindsight.)

If you believe you're above being blinded by romance, try this exercise. With your sweetie pie, make a list of everything you like about each other. Chances are, you two lovebirds will be writing for hours about the myriad qualities that make you so special to each other. When you're finished with that, make a list of the things you don't like about each other or things that could become problems in your relationship.

That's right, put it all on paper—the good, the bad, and the ugly.

How did it feel to write down some of the less-than-flattering aspects of your special someone? Did you have a hard time finding chinks in the armor? Were you uncomfortable with the whole exercise? If so, you may be blinded by romance.

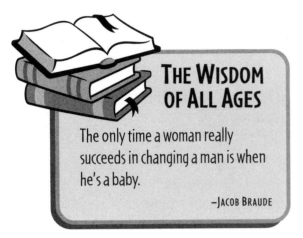

THE WISDOM OF ALL AGES

The only time a woman really succeeds in changing a man is when he's a baby.

–JACOB BRAUDE

In the early stages of dating, romantic blindness isn't necessarily a bad thing. In fact, it's kind of cute and endearing. In the later stages of dating, though, it can be dangerous. Sooner or later, you're going to have to accept the fact that your sweetie is not perfect and, in fact, may be capable of making your life miserable over the course of a decade or so.

The sooner you come to grips with the many strengths *and* weaknesses of your loved one, the better chance you have of maintaining your relationship over the long haul. Though you'll probably never see such sentiments on a greeting card, the fact is, cold-eyed reality is often more beneficial to a relationship than starry-eyed romance.

4. Don't convince yourself that love conquers all.

How many times have you heard someone defend his or her relationship by saying, "As long as we love each other, that's all that really matters." Ask any engaged couple why they're getting married and they'll tell you, "Because we love each other."

But what is *love?* Is it that breathtaking feeling you get when you lock eyes with a certain someone? Is it a general sense of being happier with someone in your life than you would be without him or her? Is it a feeling so deep that it can't be described?

These are questions you'll need to consider sooner or later, because if you don't you may end up committing yourself to someone for the rest of your life based on a physical reaction that turns out to be a heart murmur or an ulcer.

The fact is, feelings are fickle. (Say that ten times fast.) They come and go like moods. What happens when you stop experiencing physical sensations in the presence of your sweetheart? Does that mean you've fallen out of love? Should you ditch the relationship and start looking for the next person who causes you intestinal discomfort?

Don't misunderstand; this isn't an anti-love diatribe. Physical sensations play a very important role in any romantic relationship. The key, however, is not to give those sensations and feelings too prominent a role in your relationship. In other words, don't simply follow your heart into a romantic commitment. Use your head, too. Let your emotions and rational decision making work together in shaping your relationship.

What to Look for in a Mate

If you're absolutely certain that you don't want your parents to choose your spouse, the responsibility falls to you. So how do you find a prospective partner? While we may not be able to tell you exactly what your spouse should be like, we can give you a few principles to consider as you search.

Mutuality (Common Interests)

The old saying goes that when two people get married, they become one. That means if you're going to build a life with someone, you need to start with a large, strong foundation. Ideally, that foundation will be made from the things the two of you have in common—from a spiritual, intellectual, social, physical, moral, and cultural perspective.

Without common ground, the oneness that is required for a successful marital relationship can't exist. It would be like trying to build a structure using a combination of Legos and Lincoln Logs. You may be able to jerry-build something, but it wouldn't be very pretty or secure.

Your task during the dating process is to discover what you have in common with your partner and then determine whether it's enough to build a foundation for a lifetime relationship on. For example, the fact that you and the person you're dating both love Cherry Garcia ice cream and think Woody Allen is an overrated filmmaker is not enough to build a relationship on. On the other hand, the

FAMILY TIES

How well do you know the details of your parents' courtship? For a fun and insightful evening, take your parents on a date–treat them to banana splits or milk shakes at a local ice cream parlor. Then proceed to fatten them up with questions about their dating days. (Prepare eight to ten questions.) Questions can include: What attracted you to the other person? What differences did you discover about the other during courtship? How did you deal with those differences?

fact that you both come from close-knit families, you both enjoy traveling and outdoor sports, you both prefer quiet evenings at home to an active social life, and you both are extremely committed to your Christian faith may provide an excellent foundation for a lifetime relationship.

That's not to say you and your partner should match up exactly in every personality category. The differences between the two of you will ultimately prove to be just as important to the success of your relationship as your similarities. From the beginning of your relationship, your primary concern should be finding common ground to build on.

Beauty

You want to marry someone who is attractive to you. On the surface, that may seem like an obvious statement, along the lines of "You want to find a job that pays money." But the two words you need to keep in mind are "to you."

Don't hold out for a supermodel or one of the "ten most eligible bachelors" in your city. Find someone that *you* feel good about. Remember, attractiveness can grow over time—and so can ugliness. Character, attitude, intelligence, and other inner qualities can make even the most plain person attractive. They can also make even the most gorgeous person unattractive.

Other people may try to convince you that you can "do better," but why should that matter to you? What should matter to you is that *you* find the person attractive—not just in a surfacy way, but inside and out. Remember, if all goes well, this is someone you're going to be staring at forty years from now. You want to make sure that you find someone who will still look and seem pleasing to you at that time.

Morality

Common moral ground between partners is absolutely essential to a long-term relationship. The ideal scenario would have you and your future mate coming together as virgins to explore the wonderful mysteries of sex as husband and wife. Unfortunately, we don't live in an ideal world. Statistics indicate that there's a good chance you, your spouse, or both of you will have had at least some sexual experience before marriage.

If the ideal scenario is out of the question for you, your next goal should be full disclosure. That means emptying your closet and bringing your skeletons out into the open. During the engagement, share your sexual history with your future spouse. Trust him or her to forgive and accept you as you are, and not as he or she wishes you were. If your partner has a difficult time providing that acceptance, it should send up a few red flags concerning your relationship.

Of course, this should be a reciprocal process. Your potential spouse should share his or her sexual history with you, giving you a chance to extend the same kind of forgiveness and acceptance that you're looking for. And if you can't provide that acceptance, you might want to consider taking a few steps back in your relationship.

THE WISDOM OF ALL AGES

The odds of meeting a single guy are 1 in 19. The odds of meeting a good-looking, single guy are 1 in 393. The odds of meeting an intelligent, good-looking, single guy are 1 in 136,040. The odds of meeting an intelligent, good-looking, single guy on a great hair day are 1 in 1,753,000.

—JACOB BRAUDE

Admittedly, this sharing process is as risky as it is necessary. There's always the chance that you or your partner will be overwhelmed by what you hear or share ("You did what, with whom?"). There's also the problem of "keeping score." If one person's sexual "résumé" is significantly longer than the other's, it may create some tension in the relationship. At the very least, these are issues and problems that must be dealt with before you make lifetime plans with someone.

In addition to getting forgiveness and acceptance from your potential mate, you must also get it from yourself. You must learn to overcome your own past. If you have a negative attitude toward sex because of past experiences, you will have to deal with that before you get married. Otherwise, it may poison your physical relationship with your husband or wife. Marriage is challenging enough under ideal circumstances. The last thing you need is a strike against you going into it. Face your attitude toward sex and deal with it, using a professional counselor or local minister if necessary. It's *that* important.

Parents

For better or worse, you would not be who you are today—the person your sweetie fell in love with—without your parents. Neither would your sweetie be

GLAD YOU ASKED

Does the whole idea of "two becoming one" mean that I won't have any individual characteristics after I get married?

Not at all. It's not the kind of unity that wipes out a person's personality. Rather, it's the kind of unity that frees you to express your own diversity, yet experience complete oneness with your mate. You are free to be all you were meant to be and to experience all you were meant to experience as a male or female.

the person you fell in love with without his or her parents. That's why, when it comes to marriage, it's very important that you seek the blessing and guidance of your parents and your partner's parents. Make them an integral part of your relationship.

We're not just talking about doing the old "I would like to marry your daughter" routine that all prospective grooms dread. We're talking about sharing your plans with your parents from step one. We're talking about keeping them abreast of your relationship as it develops. We're talking about sharing your future plans with them. We're talking about explaining to them what you see in each other that makes you think you could spend a lifetime together. We're talking about sharing your financial vision with them (just as soon as you come up with one). We're talking about sharing your spiritual commitments with them. We're talking about telling them exactly why the relationship feels right to you.

If all goes smoothly, both sets of parents will be glad to get rid of you . . . uh, give you their blessing. But if they don't, you owe it to them, to yourself, and to your partner to listen to what they have to say. Their objections may seem like a slap in the face, but their words should be carefully considered. As we mentioned earlier, love can blind even the most levelheaded people. If your parents or your partner's parents throw up a red flag, it may be because they can see something in the relationship that you can't.

Remember what we said earlier about how past sexual experiences, if not properly resolved, can start you off with one strike against you in your relationship? Well, problems with parents can be like having two strikes against your relationship. Parents can provide much-needed support, encouragement, and direction during critical times in your marriage. That's why it's a really bad idea to alienate them from the start.

One Is the Happiest Number

If marriage is the ultimate purpose of dating, what is the ultimate purpose of marriage? Seems like an obvious question, doesn't it? Try answering it. Then ask your partner to answer it, then your parents, then your spouse's parents, and so on. Chances are, you'll end up with a variety of answers, including sex, companionship, love, a family, social acceptance, economic advantage, and security.

Yet most, if not all, of those things can be attained outside of marriage. So there has to be something more—some basic, all-encompassing need that can only be fulfilled by a marital relationship.

We mentioned earlier that marriage is an institution in which two people become one. Therein lies the ultimate purpose of marriage. Whether we realize it or not, we are created with a need for unity. Marriage is the way that we fulfill that need.

This unity that marriage brings encompasses all areas of life. It's not simply a physical relationship. It's not simply a matter of giving and receiving emotional support. It is the complete uniting of two lives on every level—intellectual, social, spiritual, emotional, and physical.

Unfortunately, many couples discover too late that the process of two people becoming one isn't something that happens automatically on your wedding day. Unity is something you have to work hard and persistently to achieve.

If you're considering marriage, the question you have to ask your spouse-to-be is, "What reasons do we have for believing that we could become one?" That question should then send you on a quest to explore the intellectual, social, physical, and spiritual areas of your lives to see if you have enough in common to build a suitable foundation for your future. Here are some tips for exploring each of those areas with your partner.

Intellectual Unity

Set aside time during your dates to talk about major issues of the day and major areas of your lives. Discuss with each other some books or magazine articles you've read lately. Talk about some of your favorite TV shows and movies and explain what you like about them. Such discussions should give you an idea of where the two of you stand in your intellectual pursuits. For example, if Jane explains that she chose the last book she read because of the author's track record of creating memorable characters through elliptical narrative structures and Steve explains that he chose the last book he read because it was short and he had an oral report due the next day in his high school English class, it's safe to say that they don't share the same intellectual tastes.

And while that may not necessarily drive a stake through the heart of the relationship, it is an obstacle that should be considered.

It's possible to find happiness with someone who has a GPA two points lower than yours. But there's a lot to be said for being able to communicate with your spouse on a common intellectual plane. To put it bluntly, you don't want to always have to "dumb down" your remarks in order to be understood.

If you're unsure about how to compare intellects with your spouse-to-be, try reading the same book together and discussing it afterward. Or read one newspaper article a day and discuss its implications together. These exercises will reveal a great deal regarding your present intellectual unity and your potential for future growth in that area.

Social Unity

We all have different social interests. The question is, how different is too different? Here are some questions to ask each other to discover where your social interests lie.

➤ "How important are sports to you?" "How many sports leagues do you participate in?" "How much of your time is spent competing or preparing to compete?"

➤ "How many hours a week do you spend in front of the tube?"

FAMILY TIES

A great way to become aware of your own strengths and weaknesses is to ask others to point them out. One night each family member should write about two strengths and one weakness of each family member on separate slips of paper (three slips for one person); include the person's name. After gathering and sorting the slips, have the person on the subject's left read the strengths, then the weaknesses. This exercise will help you remember that both you and the people you date will have strengths you appreciate and weaknesses you will need to accept if a long-term relationship is to continue.

➤ "What kind of music do you like?"

➤ "What are your hobbies?"

➤ "Do you enjoy parties or other social gatherings? If so, what kind?"

➤ "How do your tastes compare with mine?"

These are questions that cannot afford to go unanswered, because most people don't change their tastes or interests much after marriage.

You and your partner can set the stage for social unity by growing together socially *before* you get married. When you're dating, make it a point to stretch yourself—and ask your partner to do the same. Try things that you've never been interested in before. See if you can learn to enjoy some of your partner's interests. If you find yourself unable to get into your partner's ideas of fun, that may be a sign that you're not meant to be together. Remember, the goal of marriage is oneness. At some point, you have to ask the question, "If he or she never changes his or her present social interests, will I be happy to live with him or her the rest of my life?"

Keep in mind that marriage will not erase any social problems between you and your partner. It will only magnify them.

Spiritual Unity

This is one of the least explored, but most important, areas in which common ground is a must. The spiritual aspects of you and your partner affect every other area of your life—from the way you spend your money to your attitude toward pain and suffering to your expectations for the future.

This isn't just a matter of church attendance or believing in a higher power. We're not talking about lip-service spirituality. This is a matter of striving for the same goal and being guided by the same spiritual principles. Does your heart and your partner's heart beat together when it comes to spiritual matters? Do you encourage each other in spiritual growth, or is one of you pulling gently but consistently in the opposite direction?

If you answered "No" to either of the previous questions, you should reevaluate your marital priorities. The spiritual aspect of your life (and of your partner's life) is the bedrock on which your entire relationship should be based. Perhaps you and your partner come from different religious faiths; keep in mind those different faith perspectives will impact how you want to rear children (what church? what beliefs?) and a future family's religious traditions. Be honest with each other (and yourself) about how important the spiritual dimension is.

GLAD YOU ASKED

Should Christians marry people who don't share their beliefs?

Nope. The fact that a person identifies himself or herself as a Christian usually means that he or she has made honoring Jesus Christ the most important thing in his or her life. A spouse who doesn't share those priorities may eventually get tired of coming in second place to Christ. The tensions that are created as a result of the ensuing jealousy can do serious damage to the relationship.

Physical Unity

Developing a physical unity with your partner probably doesn't seem like much of a problem. (In fact, *restraining* from developing physical unity before marriage is probably more of a problem for most couples.) The fact is if you and your partner are physically attracted to each other, you have a basis for physical unity.

The problem you need to concern yourself with is building on the foundation of physical unity. To address that concern, we refer you back to the other "unity" sections in this chapter. Physical (or sexual) unity can never be separated from emotional, spiritual, and social unity. The problems that develop in the sexual aspect of marriage almost always have their root in one or more of these other areas. In fact, physical incompatibility between a couple in a marriage-bound relationship is almost nonexistent. The problem lies in other areas; it is only expressed in the sexual area.

Of course, there can be actual physical limits in marriage. To ensure that you encounter no physical problems later in your relationship, you and your partner should make it a point to reveal any physical disabilities or disfigurements that are not readily apparent. If you have a bond strong enough to be considering a permanent relationship, such information should be irrelevant to both of you. You and your spouse-to-be should be willing to accept each other as you are ("I think it's cute that you have a mole in the shape of North Carolina on your back").

Before you actually *get* married, you should probably consider a refresher course on the physical aspects of intimacy. Remember, eighth grade health class was a long time ago. Since then, you've probably picked up a great deal of misinformation about sex. You'll want to double-check the facts against a resource you can trust. (If you're looking for a recommendation, try *Intended for Pleasure* by Ed and Gaye Wheat, available from Baker Books.) It is important that you understand your own body and how it functions, as well as the sexual nature of your spouse-to-be.

Purposeful Dating Made Easy

Not everyone is born with dating skills. If you're a little unsure about how to develop purposeful and meaningful dating relationships, here are five tips to get you started.

1. Make yourself available.

If you're looking to connect with guys or girls, you've got to put yourself in places where you can have contact with them. If you're not a social animal by nature, this may take some effort on your part. Remember, playing hard to get is one thing; playing impossible to find is quite another.

Instead of going the "traditional," and often depressing, route of singles' bars and nightclubs, you might want to try a more casual approach. Parks, ball games, church activities, and (believe it or not) libraries are all great places for meeting and interacting with members of the opposite sex. That's not to say that you should start prowling the stacks in your local periodical section, looking for prey. Being in the right place at the right time and maintaining a friendly smile and an approachable demeanor is usually enough to get the ball rolling.

2. Lose your desperation.

If you've been to college, you're probably familiar with the term "senior panic"— the nervousness that afflicts unmarried coeds when they realize they are about to leave the most convenient spouse pool they will ever have access to. As a reaction to the panic, they start going out with men they never would have considered dating a year earlier, all in a last-ditch effort to find someone with whom to face an uncertain future.

That same panicky feeling can strike at any age. Any number of things can trigger it, from a friend's wedding to a romantic movie on TV. You start to wonder if you'll ever find anyone. The resulting depression can cause you to make some decisions that you will regret later.

Another problem is that desperation is usually pretty obvious—and rarely attractive. People tend to shy away from others who seem a little too intent on finding someone to marry.

Dating or finding a mate should never become the sole focus of your life. Keep your interests rounded. Make yourself available by spending time in places populated by the opposite sex, but don't target people for relationships. Let things happen naturally, and they usually will.

3. Analyze your relationship periodically.

When you find yourself in a dating relationship, take advantage of opportunities to assess it from time to time. You can't open a magazine these days without stumbling onto some compatibility test for couples. Start taking them with the person you're dating. The goal is not necessarily to determine once and for all whether the two of you are compatible or not, but to give you some things to talk about. Any discussions or debates that arise regarding the results of a test should prove to be very beneficial to your relationship.

GLAD YOU ASKED

What is the best way to end a relationship?

With directness and honesty. Don't beat around the bush or twist the truth in order to spare the person's feelings. If you care about the person at all, you owe it to him or her to explain exactly why you believe your relationship has no future.

4. Talk to trusted loved ones and friends.

Prospective spouses may be able to blind you with romance, but they won't be able to fool the people who know you best. Give your friends and family permission to speak freely about the person you're seeing. Take their comments to heart, without accusing them of having ulterior motives for wanting to end your relationship. Listen to what they have to say. Don't spend the entire discussion trying to explain away your partner's behavior or making excuses for him or her.

5. End the relationship when it's time.

As the song says, you've got to know when to hold

'em and know when to fold 'em. When you come to the realization that there's no future for you and the person you're dating, remember that sooner is better than later when it comes to breaking up.

Family Practice

Think you're an expert on dating? Here's a quiz to see how much you know.

1. Which of the following is not a good reason to date?
    a. To learn how to interact with members of the opposite sex
    b. To contribute to the lives of other people
    c. To add variety to your weekends
    d. To develop and refine your own personality

2. Which of the following will negatively affect a dating relationship?
    a. Spending too much time talking to each other about what's important to you
    b. Allowing the physical aspects of the relationship to take center stage
    c. Trying to do a variety of things together
    d. Introducing spiritual elements into the relationship

3. Which of the following is most important when it comes to finding a mate?
    a. Common interests
    b. Cooking skills
    c. Combined household earnings
    d. Genetic makeup

4. Which of the following is not an example of marital unity?
    a. Being able to carry on an intellectual conversation with each other
    b. Looking forward to a weekly doubles tennis game with another couple
    c. Serving in a church program together
    d. Eating the same leftovers

5. Which of the following strategies is most likely to improve your dating life?
    a. Adding or subtracting a few years when you tell people your age, depending on who you're talking to

b. Wearing a T-shirt that reads "Single and Extremely Available"

c. Bringing your parents along on all first dates

d. Spending time at parks, church activities, ball games, and other social settings

Answers: (1) c, (2) b, (3) a, (4) d, (5) d

CHAPTER 2

Trouble in Paradise

SNAPSHOT

Gwen answered the phone on the first ring.

"Hey, Sis, it's Liz," came the familiar chirpy voice. "I was just calling to check on the domestic bliss of my favorite newlywed."

"What a coincidence," Gwen said. "I was wondering where that went, too."

"Uh-oh," Liz said. "What's the problem?"

"Well," Gwen explained, "either we've been invaded by body snatchers from space or Phil has a secret twin brother who took his place in our house right after we got back from our honeymoon."

"It's only been four months," Liz said. "Has Phil changed that much?"

"It's unbelievable," Gwen explained. "It's like hiring someone for a job and finding out that he faked most of his résumé."

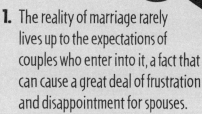

SNEAK PREVIEW

1. The reality of marriage rarely lives up to the expectations of couples who enter into it, a fact that can cause a great deal of frustration and disappointment for spouses.
2. People speak different love languages–that is, they find fulfillment in some expressions of love, but not others.
3. The key to keeping love alive in your marriage is learning to speak the love language of your spouse.

"What are you talking about?"

"He's nothing like I thought he was," Gwen explained. "For instance, when we were dating, Phil used to tell me all the time that he loved sports. I thought that meant he and I would be playing tennis or racquetball a couple times a week when we got married. I didn't realize he was talking about sitting in the basement with his brother every night, playing computer football and watching Brazilian tractor pull competitions or whatever else they show on ESPN at three o'clock in the morning."

"Yikes."

"You said it," Gwen replied. "And do you remember how, when we were dating, he used to stand behind me and rub my back or hold my hand when we walked?"

"Yes."

"Good, then I wasn't just imagining it," Gwen said. "I wasn't sure, because that whole part of the relationship seems like a dream to me."

"Have you talked to him about it?" Liz asked.

"Oh, yeah," Gwen replied. "We had a big argument a couple of days ago about whose needs were being ignored more."

"What did he say?" Liz asked.

"He said I never show any 'appreciation' for the things he does around the house," Gwen replied. "But what does he want, a standing ovation every time he changes a lightbulb?"

"Do you ever talk to any of your married friends about your problem?" Liz asked.

"Oh, yeah," Gwen replied. "Most of them, actually."

"And what do they say?"

"They say, 'Welcome to married life.'"

* * * * * * * * * * * * * * *

"What happened?" That's the common refrain of many married couples after a few months or so of what they thought would be wedded bliss. For them, the reality of married life—or what they've experienced of it—turns out to be far less glamorous, romantic, and fulfilling than they expected it to be. It's a common problem, and one that can turn serious if no action is taken.

The bad news is that the feelings of disappointment and frustration that result from unmet premarital expectations can do long-term damage to a young, vulnerable relationship. The good news is that those feelings are usually temporary. Couples who are committed to making their relationship work *can* get beyond the disappointment and frustration and create a mutually fulfilling life together.

Expectations, Schmexpectations

The first step in dealing with disappointment and frustration in your relationship is recognizing where those feelings come from. What happens in many relationships is that from the time dating turns serious and throughout their engagement period, couples tend to point to "being together" as the end-all goal of their relationship. This attitude is expressed in phrases like . . .

➤ "Things will be different after we're married."

➤ "I can't wait until we can be together all the time."

➤ "Won't it be great when we don't have to say good-bye every night?"

The assumption is that physical closeness equals relational closeness. In other words, living together will automatically bring a couple closer together. But that's like saying that spending time in a school building will make you smarter. It only works if you put the effort into making it work.

Things Change

People who ask, "What happened to the way things were when we were dating?" don't realize that that initial rush of being "in love" is the exception, and not the rule, when it comes to relationships. Swooning feelings and constant, starry-eyed proclamations of devotion are fine for the la-la land that is dating. Real life, however, has a way of smacking us in the back of the head and waking us from our romantic reveries.

If you're in a marriage and asking "What happened?" here are three possibilities for you to consider:

1. You didn't get to know each other well enough before you got married.

Fill in the blanks:

"If I'd known my spouse was so _____, I would have had second thoughts about going through with the wedding."

"I can't believe the way my spouse _____. He or she never did anything like that when we were dating."

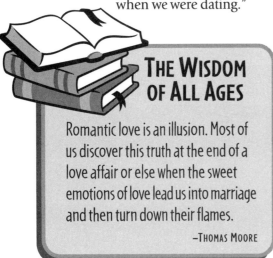

THE WISDOM OF ALL AGES

Romantic love is an illusion. Most of us discover this truth at the end of a love affair or else when the sweet emotions of love lead us into marriage and then turn down their flames.

—THOMAS MOORE

Seem familiar? If you've been blindsided by characteristics or personality traits that you didn't know your spouse had, you've got to ask yourself some questions:

➤ While we were dating and engaged, was I blinded by romance to my spouse's faults and weaknesses? Did I allow my "love" to override my common sense?

➤ Did my spouse trick me into believing that he or she was a different person than he or she really is? If so, how could I have been so gullible as to fall for it?

➤ Were there any clues in my spouse's behavior while we were dating that I should have picked up on? If so, why did I dismiss them at the time?

➤ What would my spouse say or do about the fact that I'm disappointed and frustrated by our relationship?

The thing is, people's personalities don't change overnight. It's likely that your spouse really isn't much different from the way he or she was when you were dating. Any characteristics or traits you've noticed that have changed the way you relate to your spouse were probably there long before you got married. That means you either missed the signs or chose to ignore them.

And that's all we'll say about that. The purpose of this chapter is not to browbeat you for making dumb dating choices before you were married. So after you've considered these questions, go ahead and file them under "Woulda, Shoulda, Coulda" and forget about them. There's no need to dwell on your past mistakes—especially if you're committed to making your relationship work now and in the future. Knowing what you did wrong will give you a starting point in addressing the problem, but it won't change your situation. The fact is, you're still married to someone who has caused you disappointment and frustration.

The key to getting past those letdowns is setting your sights forward, and not backward. Instead of pining for the person you *thought* you married (a person who, by the way, may have existed only in your hopeful mind), learn to love and accept the person you *actually* married.

That's not to say you should excuse the inexcusable (such as physical or emotional abuse) or overlook ugly character flaws (such as racism). But instead of trying to remake your spouse into the person you thought he or she would be after marriage, a better strategy would be to learn to live (and communicate) with the person he or she *is*.

Chances are, your spouse still possesses some lovable qualities, despite his or her raging imperfections. Focus on those qualities. Show your appreciation for them. Rebuild your relationship around the positive characteristics you see in your spouse. Leave the past in the past.

2. You're underestimating the difficulty of living together.

If you entered your marriage believing that you could merge lives effortlessly with your spouse, the first thing you need to do is adjust your expectations. The truth is, living together (after marriage) often *creates* as many problems as it solves. Learning to coexist under one roof is difficult enough. (Remember, your luggage isn't the only "baggage" you and your spouse bring to the marital relationship.) This is especially true if you or your

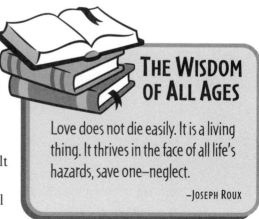

THE WISDOM OF ALL AGES

Love does not die easily. It is a living thing. It thrives in the face of all life's hazards, save one—neglect.

–JOSEPH ROUX

spouse have lived on your own for a while. The more time you have to develop your own patterns and preferences for everyday life, the more difficult it is to accommodate the patterns and preferences of someone else—even if that someone is your spouse.

THE WISDOM OF ALL AGES

Love dies only when growth stops.

–PEARL S. BUCK

Add to that the responsibility of *building a life together* with your spouse, and you're putting a tremendous amount of pressure on a newly formed, still-unsteady relationship. Remember, this isn't like trying to put up with a college roommate or the person splitting the rent in your apartment, where you can choose to ignore minor irritations or strange habits until the end of the semester or the end of the lease agreement. This is your life partner we're talking about, the one you vowed to stay tight with *until death.*

Like it or not, you're going to have to find a way to live together until that time. Obviously, that's easier said than done, especially when . . .

➤ he snores like a lumberjack with a head cold.

➤ she squeezes the toothpaste tube in the middle.

➤ he thinks Burger King and laser tag are key ingredients in a romantic night out.

➤ she sings the wrong lyrics to every song on the radio—at the top of her lungs.

➤ he clips his toenails in front of the TV and leaves the evidence on the table in the family room.

➤ she serves Hamburger Helper at least twice a week for dinner.

The key to working through such irritations is to keep them in their proper perspective. Don't let small things become big problems in your relationship. Remind yourself that it's not really the condition of a toothpaste tube, unimaginative meals, or any other household issue causing the problem; it's your poor communication with your spouse. (Fortunately for you, the next five chapters of this book are devoted to specific ways to improve your one-on-one communication with your spouse.)

3. You're neglecting to grow your relationship beyond marriage.

Too many couples view marriage as the finish line of their relationship. They work and work to make it to their wedding day with their relationship intact, then sit back and wait for "happily ever after" to begin.

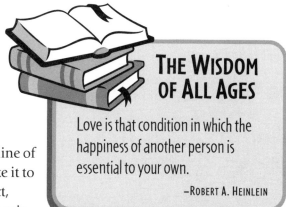

THE WISDOM OF ALL AGES

Love is that condition in which the happiness of another person is essential to your own.

—ROBERT A. HEINLEIN

That's not how marriage works. If doing nothing is your strategy for keeping love alive in your relationship, you're in trouble. Remember, the wedding is the *first* step, not the final one. To make your relationship work over the long haul, you need to put the same kind of time, energy, and effort into it after marriage that you did when you were still dating.

The best way to keep love alive is to learn to communicate and demonstrate your feelings for your spouse in a way that is meaningful to him or her.

Where Did Our Love Go?

You wouldn't think people in our self-help-obsessed, media-saturated society would have a problem keeping love alive in their relationships. After all, there's certainly no shortage of places to turn for advice. Flip through the channels of daytime television. Check out the "Relationships" section of your local bookstore. Work your way through a well-stocked magazine rack. Chances are you'll find more strategies, tips, methods, rules, dos, and don'ts than you could apply in ten lifetimes' worth of relationships.

➤ "How to Play Hard to Get—and Make Your Spouse Love It!"

➤ "Aromatherapy: Smell Your Way to a Better Relationship"

➤ "Separate Vacations Can Do Wonders for Your Marriage"

➤ "Renew Your Vows, Renew Your Love"

➤ "From the Mouths of Babes: Letting Your Children Tell You What's Wrong with Your Relationship"

➤ "Plastic Surgery: Let Your Husband Fall in Love with a Whole New You"

That's not to say that some relationship strategies and advice won't improve certain areas of your marriage. The problem, though, is that most of the tips and suggestions you find in books or magazines make one fundamental mistake in their approach that prevents them from initiating real change in a relationship.

Their fatal flaw is that they tend to assume that "love" means the same thing to everyone. More specifically, they assume that everyone prefers love to be expressed in one specific way. Everyday experience would suggest that's not the case at all. In real life, people express love in different ways. What's more, the type of expression that works for one person may not work at all for another. We all have individual tastes when it comes to cars, movies, and music. Why shouldn't that individuality extend to love?

> **THE WISDOM OF ALL AGES**
>
> 'Tis not love's going hurts my day,
> But that it went in little ways.
>
> —EDNA ST. VINCENT MILLAY

Say What?

The fact is, people speak different "love languages." To help you understand what we're talking about, let's review some of the basics of linguistics (the study of human speech). Most of us grow up speaking the language of our parents and family, whether it's English, Spanish, German, or something else. That language, then, becomes our "mother tongue," the one we feel most comfortable speaking. When we encounter someone else who speaks the same primary language, we can communicate easily with no barriers to hinder us.

On the other hand, if we encounter someone who speaks a different primary language from ours—say, Chinese to our English—communication becomes much more difficult. In worst-case scenarios, we may be reduced to pointing, nodding, pantomiming, or drawing pictures to make ourselves known.

Communication can take place in such circumstances, but not without a lot of awkwardness, frustration, and misunderstandings.

The same principle holds true when speaking a love language. A love language (we'll soon learn there are five of them) is a way we communicate love to another person. The love language you use (and respond to) may be as different from your spouse's love language as Chinese is from English. So no matter what you try to communicate in your language, your spouse may understand something different in his or her language.

Unfortunately, even sincerity and honesty can't do much to change that. It doesn't really matter how good your intentions are when you communicate with your spouse; if your message isn't spoken in a language your spouse can understand, it isn't going to do much good.

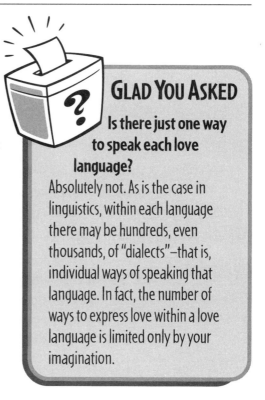

GLAD YOU ASKED

Is there just one way to speak each love language?

Absolutely not. As is the case in linguistics, within each language there may be hundreds, even thousands, of "dialects"—that is, individual ways of speaking that language. In fact, the number of ways to express love within a love language is limited only by your imagination.

The Big Five: A Sneak Preview

Love languages can be divided into five categories: (1) words of affirmation; (2) quality time; (3) receiving gifts; (4) acts of service; and (5) physical touch.

We will explore each of these love languages individually in chapters 3–7. For the purposes of this chapter, though, here's a quick overview of each one:

➤ **Words of Affirmation.** Some people prefer to express their love—and have love expressed to them—through verbal compliments and affirming statements. Comments such as "Wow! You look like a model" or "I love the way you make people laugh" would fall into this category.

➤ **Quality Time.** Some people find and give love through undivided attention. That means when they are with their spouses they are *completely* with them—in mind, body, and spirit. It also means that they feel loved when their spouses give them their undivided attention, even if it's for just twenty minutes at a time.

➤ **Receiving Gifts.** Some people express and receive love through presents. That doesn't mean they're gold diggers; the gifts don't necessarily have to be expensive. What they want is a visual symbol of love, something they can hold in their hands, evidence that their spouse was thinking of them.

➤ **Acts of Service.** Some people communicate their love by doing things to make life easier for their spouse. By the same token, they prefer to have love expressed to them in the same way. Cooking a meal, cleaning a bathroom, and fixing a broken railing are all examples of acts of service.

➤ **Physical Touch.** Some people prefer to express love and have love expressed to them through physical contact, whether it's kissing, caressing, hugging, holding hands, or high-fiving. (If you're wondering where sexual intercourse is on this list, keep reading.)

We need to point out that none of these languages is better or more desirable than another. The fact that you're a "quality timer" doesn't make you any more or less loving than, say, a "physical toucher." All five languages are legitimate expressions of love. That means none of us has the right to look down on another form of expressing love simply because it's foreign to us.

More important is the fact that none of these languages is unlearnable. The gap between *any* two of the languages can be bridged. That means if your preferred method of communicating love is receiving gifts and your spouse's is acts of service, there is hope for your relationship. You *can* overcome your communication barrier. All it takes is a little work . . . . OK, maybe a *lot* of work.

THE WISDOM OF ALL AGES

When you love you wish to do things for. You wish to sacrifice for. You wish to serve.

—ERNEST HEMINGWAY

Language Arts

The first step in bridging the language barriers in your relationship is to identify your primary love language. When you saw the list of the five love languages, did any of them jump out at you or seem extremely familiar? If so, there's a good chance that may be your primary love language.

If none of the languages on the list struck a chord with you right away, here are three questions for you to consider that may help you identify your love language: (1) What does your spouse do or fail to do that hurts you most deeply? (2) What have you most often requested of your spouse? (3) In what way do you regularly express love to your spouse?

Let's take a look at what each question can tell you about your "native tongue," when it comes to love.

1. What does your spouse do or fail to do that hurts you most deeply?

Sometimes looking at the negative use of love languages is helpful in identifying a person's primary love language. If, for example, you find yourself devastated whenever your spouse offers critical or judgmental comments about you, then your primary love language may be "words of affirmation."

Here's how it works. If your spouse uses your primary love language in a negative way—if he or she gives you the exact opposite of what you want—it will hurt you more deeply than it otherwise might. It's extremely hard to come to grips with the fact that not only is your spouse neglecting to use your love language to build you up, he or she is actually using it against you to hurt you.

For example . . .

> ➤ If you feel rejected because your spouse insists on watching TV during meals instead of talking to you, "quality time" may be your primary love language.

GLAD YOU ASKED

Is my love language physical touch if I greatly enjoy sexual expression and yearn for physical intimacy?

Many people, guys in particular, mistake their desire for sex for an emotional need. For the male of our species, the strong desire for sexual intercourse has a physical root. But since a physical need is not the same as an emotional need, guys shouldn't automatically assume that physical touch is their primary love language. For a quick litmus test to determine whether this is your love language, read items under "Physical Touch: What It Is and What It Isn't" in chapter 7.

➤ If it tears you up inside—or you feel jealous—when you see other people in your office receive cards, flowers, and other presents from their spouses, "receiving gifts" may be your primary love language.

➤ If you're having problems with the fact that your spouse considers most areas of housework to be *your* responsibility and refuses to lift a finger to help you, "acts of service" may be your primary love language.

➤ If you feel like a leper because your spouse refuses to show you any physical affection, "physical touch" may be your primary love language.

If your spouse hasn't done anything to hurt or upset you lately, you might want to consider another question in your search for your primary love language.

2. What have you most often requested of your spouse?

Your primary love language may be showing itself in the things you ask of your spouse. For example, if you ask questions like, "How do you like the way I rearranged the furniture in the living room?" or "What did you think of the cleaning and waxing I gave your car?" you may be looking for words of affirmation.

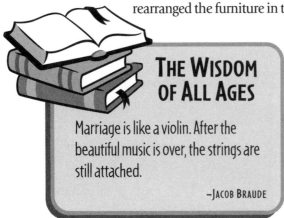

THE WISDOM OF ALL AGES

Marriage is like a violin. After the beautiful music is over, the strings are still attached.

—Jacob Braude

If you find yourself asking your spouse to leave work a few minutes early, to turn off the TV during dinner, or to take walks with you at night, you may be craving quality time.

If you drop hints about wanting something special from your spouse on your anniversary or some other special occasion, "receiving gifts" might be your primary love language.

If you regularly ask your spouse to lend a hand with the dishes, laundry, or yard work, you may be in need of acts of service.

If you find yourself asking for back rubs or grabbing your spouse's hand when you walk, you may be requesting love through physical touch.

Make a mental note to keep track of the things you request of your spouse to see if you can discover your primary love language. If that doesn't work, try looking at it from another point of view. Consider this question: What does your spouse accuse you of nagging him or her about?

You know that if you repeat a request enough times, eventually it's going to wear on your spouse's nerves. That's just human nature. So think about the last time you and your spouse argued. Do you remember phrases similar to any of the following getting tossed around?

"If I hear about _____ one more time, I'm gonna go crazy."

"_____, _____, _____! That's all you ever talk about!"

"Why can't you ever focus on the good things in our relationship, instead of always focusing on things like _____?"

Fill in those blanks, and you may be on your way to discovering your primary love language. If something is important enough to you to risk being called a nag, it may very well be the key to your preferred love language. (After you discover your love language, you can marvel at the irony of learning what you really need from your spouse from the things he or she complains most bitterly about.)

If you and your spouse haven't had any helpful arguments lately, or if you can't recall making any specific requests of him or her, here's another question that might help you identify your primary love language.

3. In what way do you regularly express love to your spouse?
Chances are the way you show love to your spouse is the way you would like love to be shown to you. For example, if you're quick to offer compliments and encouragement to your spouse, you may be looking for words of affirmation yourself.

If you make it a point to find time to spend with your spouse, regardless of your schedule, you may have a desire to have love expressed to you through quality time.

If you enjoy buying small but meaningful presents for your spouse—things that remind you of him or her or things that you know he or she would appreciate— "receiving gifts" may very well be your primary love language.

If you're committed to working to make life easier for your spouse—whether it's by preparing the kind of meals he or she likes, maintaining the condition of his or her car, or keeping a clean, organized home—there's a good chance that you would respond well to love that is expressed through acts of service.

If you enjoy placing a hand on your spouse's shoulder, offering silent encouragement through caresses and meaningful physical contact, or holding hands when you walk, it's likely that physical touch is your primary love language.

Opening Up

Once you discover your primary love language, your next step should be to talk to your spouse about it. Write your preferred love language on a piece of paper, then list the other four languages in order of their importance to you. When you're finished with that, write down what you think your spouse's primary love language is. (If you're feeling really ambitious, list the other four categories according to how important you think they are to your spouse.)

Set aside some time to discuss your primary love languages with your spouse. Share the lists you made and ask your spouse to tell you how close your guesses for him or her were. Spend some time talking specifically about what your love language says about you and how you would like your spouse to express his or her love for you.

FAMILY TIES

If you're the father of a young child and you want to perform an act of service for your wife, offer to watch the baby for a day. Give your spouse some much-needed alone time. Give her a chance to relax and do something for herself for a change.

Learning a New Language

What about learning your spouse's love language? Have him or her answer the above three questions as well. If your spouse is unavailable or unwilling to do that, there's still a way to identify your mate's likely love language, so you can convey love in the clearest way possible. Ask questions two and three of your spouse: What does my husband (wife) most often request of me? In what way does my husband (wife) regularly express love to me? Those are signs of their own love language being reflected back to you. In addition, read the sections in chapters 3–7 that give clues as to your spouse's love language. (For example, read pages 102-103 ["How to Tell If You're Married . . ."]

for clues on the person whose primary love language is receiving gifts.)

After you and your spouse have identified each other's love languages, the work really begins. Somehow you have to learn to *speak* those languages. Chapters 3–7 will give you the information you need to do that. Before you get to those chapters, though, we would like to emphasize once more the importance of becoming fluent in the love language of your spouse.

The most popular objection to this learning process goes something like this: "Giving words of affirmation [or speaking any of the primary love languages] isn't something that comes naturally to me." It's not hard to see the logic in that objection. If you've never had any practice expressing love in a certain way, you're bound to be a little wary of actually trying it for the first time.

But there's an obvious response to this objection that may help you overcome your initial wariness. If expressing love in a certain way isn't something that comes naturally to you . . . *so what?*

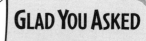

GLAD YOU ASKED

I'm afraid my relationship is too dysfunctional to yield any clues about my primary love language. Is there anything else I can do to discover what it is?

Try picturing your ideal spouse. Forget about looks for now; this isn't about creating a fantasy. Instead, ask yourself, "How would my ideal spouse treat me? What would he or she do to make me happy?" The answers you come up with will likely point the way to your primary love language.

If we all restricted ourselves to things that come naturally to us, things we're comfortable with, or things that are familiar to us, we would never stretch, never risk, never learn, and never grow. Inexperience or unfamiliarity is never a legitimate excuse for inaction. Learning your spouse's love language will be a challenge. You can either rise to that challenge or shrink from it.

You also need to understand that this isn't rocket science we're talking about. You don't need an advanced degree in psychiatry (or linguistics) to learn to express love to your spouse in the language that is most meaningful to him or her.

If your spouse's primary love language is words of affirmation, give him or her a sincere compliment.

If your spouse's primary love language is quality time, turn off the TV and give him or her your full attention for a half hour or so.

If your spouse's primary love language is receiving gifts, go shopping for something he or she would like.

GLAD YOU ASKED

What can I do if my spouse isn't interested in discovering my primary love language?

Lead by example. Find out everything you can about your spouse's love language and then let him or her know how you plan to express your love, using that language, in your relationship. Sooner or later, your spouse will notice the radical change in your approach to your relationship and may choose to reciprocate.

If your spouse's primary love language is acts of service, clean the bathroom.

If your spouse's primary love language is physical touch, give him or her a back rub.

That's how you take the first step in communicating to your spouse through his or her primary love language.

It may not feel comfortable to you at first. It may make you a little self-conscious. It may not always work out as well as you hope. That's fine. Just do it.

Four to Grow On

Chapters 3 through 7 will give you the information you need to learn to speak each of the five love languages. Once you determine your spouse's primary love language, read just the chapter that deals with it; this is a reference guide, so no need to read all five chapters. Then go on to chapter 8.

Perhaps you've narrowed his or her love language down to two but aren't sure which one communicates love to your spouse. In that case, it's possible your mate is bilingual; he hears love in two languages. Or maybe he has just one primary love language, but you aren't clear which it is among two languages. In either case, read two chapters—the ones on those two languages.

In the meantime, here are four tips for keeping your love alive after the "honeymoon" is over.

1. Keep talking.

There will come a point in your relationship (actually, there will come many points in your relationship) where, instead of sharing your feelings with your spouse or trying to resolve your differences, you'll be tempted to ask yourself, "Why bother?" and keep your thoughts and emotions to yourself. Don't make that mistake. Once communication lines are down, you'll find that it's extremely difficult to restore them.

Maintaining communication with your spouse will take a boatload of patience and persistence. There will be times when you'll feel like you're beating your head against a brick wall as you try to make yourself understood. Take some aspirin and keep pounding. Eventually your work will pay off.

Never assume that silence or indifference is preferable to conflict. It's not. As long as you and your spouse are interacting and actively trying to resolve your differences, there's hope for your relationship.

2. Keep your relationship off the back burner.

With all of the things going on in your busy life, you may be tempted to put your relationship with your spouse on the "back burner" in order to free up time and energy for other things. The thinking that leads to that type of decision goes something like this: I know my relationship with my spouse is strong enough to survive a little neglect. *After I _____, I'll make my spouse my number one priority again.*

You really need to resist that mind-set. For one thing, neglect can poison a relationship a lot faster than you might think. When you're ready to turn your attention back to your spouse, he or she may not be interested in it anymore. For another thing, putting something on a back burner once makes it that much easier to put it there again. And again. And again.

3. Find new things to love in your spouse.

Earlier in the chapter we discussed the problem of discovering after you're married that your spouse isn't the person you thought he or she was. But we only covered the negative aspects of it. The flip side is that your spouse may have positive characteristics, noteworthy attributes, or hidden talents that you knew nothing about. Seek out those qualities. Look beyond the imperfections and minor annoyances. Find the goodness in your spouse.

4. *Get rid of potential wedges in your relationship.*

A relationship wedge is anything that has the potential to drive you and your spouse apart. The first and most dangerous wedge that you need to rid yourself of is pride. Specifically, you need to eliminate the kind of pride that keeps you from apologizing to your spouse or making the first move in resolving conflict with him or her. Pride is what turns simple misunderstandings into long-term problems. Eliminating pride from your interactions with your spouse can do wonders for your relationship.

Other potential wedges that you'll want to look out for include negative input from friends and family, an overbooked schedule, and indifference. You probably won't be able to remove all of the wedges from your relationship, but you can remove enough to give your love a chance to grow.

Family Practice

Think you're an expert on keeping love alive? Here's a quiz to see how much you know.

1. What happens when couples look to marriage as the ultimate goal of their relationship?
   a. They spend three times as much on their wedding as couples who identify something else as the ultimate goal of their relationship do.
   b. They usually live happily ever after.
   c. They neglect to put the necessary work into their relationship after they're married.
   d. They usually end up canceling their honeymoon plans.

2. What does it mean that people speak different love languages?
   a. No one should expect to have his or her "love needs" met by another person.
   b. True intimacy is unattainable.
   c. A relationship can work only if the two people have the same primary love language.
   d. Something that expresses love to one person may not necessarily express love to another.

3. Which of the following is *not* one of the five primary love languages?
   a. Complete obedience
   b. Words of affirmation
   c. Acts of service
   d. Receiving gifts

4. Which of these methods would be most helpful in discovering your primary love language?
   a. Interviewing your parents about what you were like as a child
   b. Identifying the things you most often request of your spouse
   c. Watching *Oprah* (or reading *O* magazine)
   d. Asking your spouse which language he or she would prefer to use

5. What is the best strategy for communicating in a love language you're unfamiliar or uncomfortable with?
   a. Don't try it until you're absolutely sure you can do it.
   b. Test it on a friend or family member before you try it on your spouse.
   c. Make sure your spouse knows just how uncomfortable you are.
   d. Just do it.

Answers: (1) c, (2) d, (3) a, (4) b, (5) d

Increase Your Word Power

LOVE LANGUAGE #1: WORDS OF AFFIRMATION

SNAPSHOT

"Did you notice how Ralph kept complimenting Karen all night?" Julie asked.

"They were hosting a dinner party," Mark reminded her as he backed out of the Fife's driveway. "They had to put on a good show. It's the law. If you don't, the authorities will take away your party-hosting license and impound your barbecue grill."

"It didn't look like a show to me," Julie said. "Karen acted like she was used to it. Must be nice."

"I'm telling you, you can't draw any conclusions from one night," Mark emphasized. "We don't know what Ralph did wrong or what he was trying to make up for."

"I heard him telling Brent what a great cook Karen is," Julie continued. "Then later I heard him telling Sue what a great mother she is."

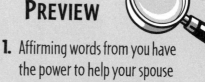

SNEAK PREVIEW

1. Affirming words from you have the power to help your spouse realize his or her potential.
2. Affirmation can be expressed through kindness in your everyday interactions with your spouse—especially during times of conflict and confrontation.
3. Making requests of your spouse, as opposed to telling him or her what to do, is a powerful way to affirm his or her worth to you.

"And after that, I saw him walk across the water of the swimming pool to get more charcoal," Mark added.

"I'm not saying he's perfect," Julie snapped. "I'm just saying it must be nice to get compliments and encouragement from your spouse sometimes."

"You look really nice in that dress," Mark offered.

Julie just stared at him.

"What?" Mark protested. "I'm serious. I've been meaning to tell you all night; I just never got the chance."

Julie placed her hand next to his face to block his peripheral vision. "All right, Mr. Sincerity, what color is this dress that looks so nice on me?"

Mark froze, but only for a second. "Um . . . bluish?"

"It's green."

"Oh," Mark said. "Well . . . your hair looks really nice."

"Give it up, Junior," Julie said. "You're in over your head."

* * * * * * * * * * * * * *

Imagine that you're a lifelong, die-hard Chicago Cubs fan sitting in Wrigley Field, just behind the Cubs' dugout, for the seventh game of the World Series. (If you actually happen to be a lifelong Cubs fan, we apologize if this illustration rubs salt in old wounds.)

The Cubs are trailing by three runs in the bottom of the ninth. But they have the bases loaded, and their most dangerous slugger, Sonny Sayso, is up. (The characters in this illustration are fictional. Any resemblance to actual persons, living or dead, is purely coincidental.)

"Come on, Sonny, hit one out of the park!" you shout as he walks to the plate. Sayso smiles a little as he digs in and waits for the first pitch.

"Strike one!" the umpire yells.

Sayso steps out of the batter's box. His smile is gone.

"You can do it, Sonny," you scream. "I know you can!"

Sayso looks in your direction and nods. Then he steps back into the batter's box for the next pitch.

"Strike two!" the umpire calls.

Sayso steps away from the plate and takes a couple of practice swings. His movements are tense and jerky. He seems unsure of himself.

THE WISDOM OF ALL AGES

I can live for two months on a good compliment.

—MARK TWAIN

"Sonny, you're the best home-run hitter in the league!" you yell. "You've already hit three round-trippers off this guy this season!"

Sayso suddenly snaps to attention. He takes a couple of steps toward your seat, smiles broadly, and tips his cap. Then he walks back to the batter's box.

The next pitch is a hanging curveball, and Sayso is all over it. CRACK!

The ball sails in a majestic arc over the heads of the left field Bleacher Bums. Sonny Sayso has hit perhaps the most dramatic home run in World Series history.

As he rounds the bases, Sayso points in your direction and then places his hand over his chest. *Thank you from the bottom of my heart.*

The Cubs win the World Series, all because you said the right thing at the right time.

How absurd is it to believe that a few words from you could produce such dramatic results? In the context of this illustration, it's pretty absurd. (So don't get your hopes up, Cubs fans.) However, in the context of your relationship with your spouse, the notion isn't absurd at all. Words of affirmation or encouragement from you, spoken at the right time, have the potential to change your spouse's life.

Parlez Vous Amour?

Before we tackle the topic of encouragement, let's take a step back and look at the big picture of healthy marital relationships. You need to know that there are five major love languages that people speak, five ways that they demonstrate and understand emotional love.

Words of affirmation make up one of those languages. The others are . . .

➤ Quality time

➤ Receiving gifts

➤ Acts of service

➤ Physical touch

We'll cover each of these languages in detail in the chapters that follow. For the purposes of this chapter, though, you should be aware of the fact that not everyone speaks and responds to the same language. What you have to do is figure out which language your spouse responds to and become fluent in that language.

This chapter is for people whose spouses respond most strongly to affirmation and encouragement. If your spouse falls into that category, you'll find in here the information you need to start speaking his or her language.

How to Tell if Your Spouse Loves Affirming Words

Notice the verb in the above heading. Every adult—and every spouse—*enjoys* and *needs* to hear encouraging words. But if words of affirmation are your spouse's primary love language, he or she will *love* to hear words of affirmation, encouragement, and kindness. Your mate may even *crave* those words. Such words convey the thought "I love you" simply yet elegantly. They are a loving embrace to your spouse's soul.

Clues that words of affirmation are the main language of love for your spouse include the following:

➤ Your spouse has an outward, positive response to your words—perhaps a big smile, words of heartfelt thanks, or even occasional tears of gratefulness.

➤ Your spouse regularly supports, affirms, or compliments you. She (or he) may be using her love language, thinking it's yours, too.

➤ Your spouse seems very hurt when you are sarcastic or cutting. She may either withdraw or show no interest in physical or emotional intimacy for long periods after "minor" (as you see them) slights.

➤ Your spouse reacts strongly and regularly to critical, judgmental words.

Remember, all spouses will respond to and need words of affirmation. But if such words are your spouse's main love language, you'll want to give extra helpings whenever possible.

Where Often Is Heard an Encouraging Word . . .

The word *encourage* means "to inspire courage." All of us, no matter how "together" or confident we may seem, have areas in which we feel insecure. We lack courage, and that lack of courage often hinders us from accomplishing what we would like to do—and sometimes what we *need* to do.

That's where an encouraging spouse comes in handy. The right words of affirmation, spoken at the right time, can give your spouse the courage he or she needs to take important and meaningful steps in his or her life.

That's a pretty heady thought, to realize that *you* have the ability to inspire your spouse to accomplish or overcome things that he or she may not have considered possible otherwise. And it's not something to take lightly.

Here are a couple of examples of how the right words of affirmation and encouragement can help a spouse reach his or her potential.

Nancy's Story

For Nancy, writing is more of a passion than a hobby. She briefly considered pursuing journalism as a career when she graduated from college. But when her first few articles were rejected by a couple of different magazines, she gave up on the idea. The years passed, and Nancy concentrated on raising her kids with her husband Elliot. As the kids got older, though, she began to think more and more about writing again. Whenever she had a few

THE WISDOM OF ALL AGES

A pat on the back, though only a few vertebrae removed from a kick in the pants, is miles ahead in results.

–ROYAL NEIGHBOR

hours to herself, she would hole up in a spare bedroom and write things for her own enjoyment.

One night, Elliot, who hadn't paid much attention to Nancy's writing years earlier, found one of the pieces she'd been working on. After he finished reading it, he rushed into the kitchen, where she was working. "Nancy, you are an excellent writer!" he said. "This piece ought to be published! Your words paint pictures that I can visualize. You have a fascinating style. You have to submit this to a magazine."

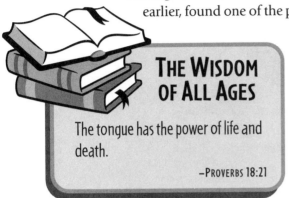

THE WISDOM OF ALL AGES

The tongue has the power of life and death.

—PROVERBS 18:21

Nancy managed to say, "Thank you," then turned back to the dishwasher, her heart swelling with pride and her mind filling with determination. In the years since Elliot gave Nancy her first critique, she's had one book and several articles published. All she needed was a little push, a few words of encouragement, to start her on the road to personal fulfillment.

Rita's Story

One day Rita asked her husband, "What would you think if I enrolled in a weight-loss program this fall?"

Patrick, her husband, considered the question for a moment and said, "If you decide to do it, I can tell you one thing: you'll be a success. When you set your mind to something, you do it. If enrolling in this program is what you want to do, I'll do everything I can to help you. Don't worry about the cost. If this means a lot to you, we'll find the money."

With Patrick's words echoing in her ears, Rita called the weight-loss center. Today she's fifty-five pounds lighter, thanks to her determination and willpower—and a few encouraging words from her spouse.

Rita's example brings up an important point. You can't claim to be encouraging your spouse if you're simply trying to pressure him or her into doing something that you want. For example, let's say Patrick had come to Rita and said, "I think you'd be really good at losing weight. In fact, I'll bet you could lose at least fifty pounds by next summer if you wanted to."

Do you think Rita would have heard encouragement in his words? Probably not. More than anything else, she would have heard dissatisfaction. ("You need to drop fifty pounds before you start wearing summer clothes, Tubby.") So instead of assuring her, Patrick's words in this case might actually have unsettled her.

Encouraging your spouse means helping him or her develop an interest that he or she already has. You can't decide for yourself what you want your spouse to do and then concentrate on pumping him or her up in those areas. That's called *manipulation*, not encouragement.

Only when your spouse *wants* to lose weight (or do anything else, for that matter) can you give him or her encouragement. Until the desire is there, your words will sound like nagging. Instead of motivating your spouse to action, they might simply make him or her feel guilty. In the end, those words will express rejection, not love.

> **FAMILY TIES**
>
> Why not enlist your kids in your affirmation efforts? It's a good bet that they see qualities and characteristics in your spouse that you've overlooked. A little input from your children may open an entirely new batch of affirmation possibilities.

A Firm Foundation

In order to encourage your spouse, you first have to learn what's really important to him or her. You can't just guess at what areas your spouse needs encouragement. And you can't make your spouse do all of the work for you, either. ("Just tell me where you need affirmation, and I'll give it.") You need to actively involve yourself in your spouse's life in order to develop an empathy for his or her feelings. You have to learn to see the world from your spouse's perspective.

Genuinely encouraging words are ones that communicate the idea, *I know who you are; I care about you, and I'm here to help you.* Encouragement is a way of showing that you believe in your spouse and in his or her abilities. It's a way of giving your spouse credit and praise.

If the past few paragraphs have read like a touchy-feely handbook to you, or if

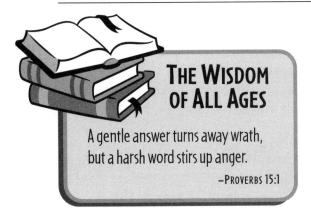

THE WISDOM OF ALL AGES

A gentle answer turns away wrath, but a harsh word stirs up anger.

—PROVERBS 15:1

you're feeling a little embarrassed because you haven't thought to provide this kind of encouragement to your spouse in the past, don't give up just yet. We're not suggesting for a moment that encouraging words should come naturally to you. If you grew up without a lot of encouragement yourself, you may not be comfortable offering encouraging words to other people, even your spouse. And if you're used to exchanging critical words with your spouse, making that transition will be even more difficult.

The good news is that any effort you put into encouraging your spouse will be well worth any temporary discomfort it might cause. The results you'll see will be dramatic and relationship-changing.

The Marrying "Kind"

Ideally, affirmation should be the rule, and not the exception, in your relationship with your spouse. You can't treat encouragement like a fire extinguisher, pulling it out only when you really need it and then putting it away again. You can't toss out a few encouraging words, call yourself an affirmer, and forget about it.

Words of affirmation, the first love language, can (and should) be spoken in a variety of ways and a variety of settings. Affirmation comes not only in the specific encouragement you offer, but also in the way you interact with your spouse every day.

We're talking about creating an atmosphere in your home in which affirmation and encouragement can be expressed freely. It's simply a matter of being consistent. If most of your communication with your spouse is marked by pettiness, complaining, and cutting remarks, you'll probably have a hard time being taken seriously by him or her when you suddenly shift into "affirmation mode."

One of the keys to creating an affirming spirit in your marriage is kindness—not only in the words you speak, but also in the way you speak them. For example, take a look at this statement: "I hope you have a good time with your friends tomorrow."

If you were to say that with a sneer on your face or an undercurrent of sarcasm in your voice, your words would probably not be taken as an expression of love and sincerity. The reason is simple: There would be no kindness behind the words.

By the same token, it is possible to share even the most negative sentiments—your hurt, your pain, even your anger—with kindness. A statement such as, "I felt disappointed and a little hurt because you made plans for the weekend without telling me," when it's said in an honest, kind manner, can be an expression of love.

A person who says something like, "I felt disappointed and hurt," wants to be known by his or her spouse. That person is taking steps to build intimacy by sharing his or her feelings. That person is asking for an opportunity to discuss a hurt in order to find healing.

Kindness is not a tool for avoiding conflict; it's a tool for working through it. Conflict that is dealt with in a loving, kind way can actually be healthy for a relationship. After all, if two people bring the same opinions, beliefs, and priorities to a partnership, one of those people is probably unnecessary.

Do the Right Thing

What it comes down to is making the right choice at the right time in the midst of conflict. When your spouse has reached the boiling point and is lashing out in anger, you can respond in one of two ways. (Actually, there are probably thousands of different ways you could respond, but for the purposes of this chapter, we've narrowed them down to two.) You can either stoke the flames with your own fiery words, turning the conflict into a pressure-cooker situation, or you can offer your spouse a kind voice and a listening ear.

Choose the Second Option

It's not an easy thing to do, especially if you have a competitive nature or are convinced that you're right and your spouse is wrong. Get over the notion that there is a winner and a loser in every conflict. When it comes to your relationship with your spouse, there should always be two winners in every conflict.

Instead of listening defensively while your spouse vents, waiting for him or her to say something wrong so that you can jump all over it like Johnnie Cochran going after a witness in a courtroom, try listening empathetically. Treat your spouse's words as important information about his or her emotional feelings. Let your spouse talk freely and uninterrupted about his or her hurt and anger. Do what you can to put yourself in your spouse's position and look at the situation through his or her eyes. Share with your spouse what you see. Explain your perception of how he or she is feeling and get feedback as to how close to reality your perception is.

When your spouse recognizes that you're making a real effort to understand him or her, the whole tone of the conflict will change. Instead of seeing each other as adversaries, each trying to win the argument or make a final point, you'll be able to look at each other as teammates, working together to improve your relationship.

Past, Present, and Past

Kindness also works hand in hand with forgiveness. Here's a news flash for you: Married couples don't always do the right thing for their relationship or what's best for each other. In fact, sometimes they say and do some pretty hurtful things. The problem is, barring any dramatic breakthroughs in time travel, those hurtful things can't be erased.

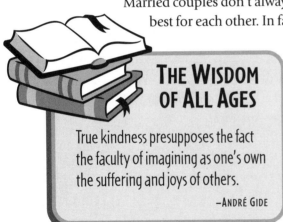

THE WISDOM OF ALL AGES

True kindness presupposes the fact the faculty of imagining as one's own the suffering and joys of others.

—ANDRÉ GIDE

If you're the one responsible for causing the hurt, all you can do is confess it to your spouse and agree with him or her that it was wrong. After that, you can ask for forgiveness and commit yourself to not repeating the hurtful action in the future. Beyond that, the situation lies in your spouse's hands.

The same holds true in reverse. If your spouse has hurt you and then confessed and asked forgiveness for it, you have the option of forgiving your spouse or seeking justice for your hurt. If you choose justice, you'll end up plotting ways to get even or make your spouse pay for the wrongdoing. In that case, you make yourself judge and your spouse the felon.

Obviously, with this type of arrangement, intimacy becomes impossible. Only when you choose to forgive your spouse completely can you restore intimacy.

It's amazing how many people choose to mess up every new day with yesterday. They insist on bringing the failures of the past into the present. In the process, they end up polluting 365 potentially wonderful days a year (366 each leap year).

The pollution usually begins with words like these:

➤ "I still can't believe you did that."

➤ "I'll never forget the way you . . . "

➤ "I don't know how you can sit there like nothing's wrong."

➤ "I don't know if I can ever forgive you."

Do you see much love in any of those statements? Do you see anything in them that can improve a marital relationship?

Bygones

The best thing you can do with failures of the past is to let them be history. Whatever happened, happened. It hurt. It may *still* hurt. But enough is enough. You can't hold your relationship hostage while you or your spouse tries to pay off an endless ransom. At some point, you have to let go of past hurts—for good.

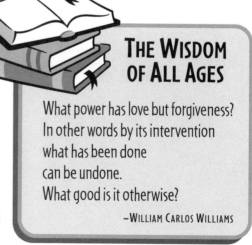

You can't erase the past, but you can accept it as history. You can *choose* to live free from the failures of yesterday. Forgiveness isn't something you feel; it's something you commit to. Forgiveness is a choice to show mercy and to refuse to hold an offense against your spouse. Forgiveness is an expression of love—if you do it right.

Remember, empathy, kindness, and affirmation are what you're shooting for. When it comes to forgiving your spouse, a heavy sigh followed by an irritated "I forgive you" isn't what you'd call a model of encouragement.

THE WISDOM OF ALL AGES

What power has love but forgiveness?
In other words by its intervention
what has been done
can be undone.
What good is it otherwise?

–WILLIAM CARLOS WILLIAMS

Here's a better alternative: "I love you. I care about you, and I choose to forgive you. Even though my feelings of hurt may linger, I will not allow what happened to come between us. I hope that we can learn from this experience. You are my spouse, and together we'll go on from here."

What better way is there to resolve a conflict than with a supersize order of affirmation and encouragement?

By Request

Earlier in this chapter, we suggested that in order to encourage your spouse, you first have to learn what is really important to him or her. The question is, how do you get that information and how do you share it with each other?

In order to maintain an affirming atmosphere in your relationship, you and your spouse have to find the right way to communicate your wants and desires. For best results, you'll want to make sure that you don't allow those wants and desires to come across as demands or manipulation.

GLAD YOU ASKED

If affirmation and encouragement are so important in a relationship, why do so many married couples neglect to use them?

It's usually a matter of habit. Once you establish a pattern of communication with your spouse, it's very difficult to change. And the longer people have to get comfortable in their routines, the less motivated they are to try new patterns of communication.

You see, when you demand something from your spouse or use manipulation to get what you want, you change the dynamics of your relationship. No longer are the two of you equal partners. Instead, you become a parent and your spouse becomes a child. When you start to assume those roles, you and your spouse will find yourselves drifting further and further apart.

If, on the other hand, you learn to express your desires as requests and to give your spouse guidance instead of orders, you'll find that it works better for both of you. For example, compare these two approaches:

"A guy at work was telling me that his wife makes a pie from scratch every Sunday. I told him to invite me over sometime, since that's the only way I'd ever get a homemade pie."

"Do you know what I have a craving for? One of your unbelievable apple pies. Do you think you could find time to make one for me this week?"

In the first approach, the husband uses a sarcastic and insulting tone to make his desires known. The unspoken demand in the statement is for his wife to be more like his coworker's wife. That's not what you'd call a good way to build intimacy.

In the second approach, the man gives his wife guidance on how to show him love. He risks rejection and embarrassment to share his desire with her—all in an effort to build intimacy with her.

Here are two more approaches to compare:

"Are you going to clean the gutters this weekend or should I just schedule an appointment to have new ones put on when these collapse under the weight of the leaves?"

"Could I ask you to take time out of your busy schedule to clean the gutters this weekend?"

> ### THE WISDOM OF ALL AGES
>
> Correction does much, but encouragement does more. Encouragement after censure is as the sun after a shower.
>
> —JOHANN WOLFGANG VON GOETHE

In the first approach, the wife expresses her desires through nagging sarcasm, without much thought of intimacy or affirmation. In the second approach, she shows her love by making a request. She gives her husband the chance to demonstrate where his priorities lie by fitting her request into his "busy" schedule.

Tyrants and Lovers

When you make a request of your spouse, you're actually affirming his or her worth and abilities. You're communicating the fact that he or she has the potential to do something that's meaningful and worthwhile to you.

When you make demands, you become a tyrant, not a lover. Your spouse will feel belittled, not affirmed, by your attitude. A request gives your spouse a choice. He or she may decide to respond to it or deny it. That's what ultimately makes it meaningful.

By responding to your request, your spouse communicates that he or she cares about you, respects you, admires you, and wants to do something to please you. You can't get emotional love from a demand. Your spouse may obey your demand, but it won't be an expression of love. More likely, it will be an expression of fear, guilt, or some other emotion.

Affirmation Made Easy

Not everyone is a born encourager. If you're a little unsure about how to incorporate words of affirmation into your relationship with your spouse, here are ten tips to get you started.

1. Keep it simple.

You may be tempted to "decorate" your affirmation with flowery language and poetic sentiments. (It's a compulsion some people call Hallmarkitis.) Unless you're naturally flowery or poetic, you should try to resist the temptation. No matter how plain and ineffective your words may seem, your spouse will recognize them as coming from your heart. And they will mean all the more to him or her because of it.

You'll also want to focus on one area of affirmation at a time. Once you see the effect your encouragement has on your spouse, you may be tempted to pile on the affirmation in as many different areas of your spouse's life as you can think of. Ultimately, though, that might prove to be more harmful than helpful.

You don't want to overwhelm your spouse with possibilities. Let him or her focus on one area of self-improvement at a time. Once your spouse has reached that goal, you can start looking and listening for another area in which to affirm him or her.

2. Mean what you say.

Most couples who have been together for any length of time can tell when their spouses are being sincere

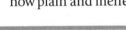

GLAD YOU ASKED

Is there anything I can do to become a better encourager?

Try keeping an affirmation notebook. When you read an article or book about love, write down some of the things that stand out to you. When you overhear someone say something positive about another person, jot it down. In time, you'll collect quite a list of ways to communicate love to your spouse.

and when they're just blowing smoke. So if you're serious about affirming your spouse, you've got to find an honest and sincere way to do it.

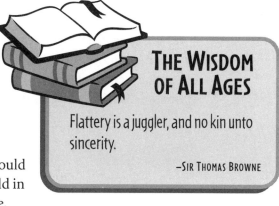

Affirming does not mean lying or exaggerating to make your spouse feel better about himself or herself ("If you started training right now, you could be the first person over forty to win Olympic gold in the 100-meter dash"). If you're not being sincere, you'll know it and your spouse will know it, so what's the point?

Careful thought and consideration are vital to providing quality affirmation. Not only do you need to know what your spouse's desires are, you also need to have a good idea of what his or her potential is. Your words of affirmation should encourage and inspire your spouse; they shouldn't set an impossible standard for him or her to achieve.

One more thing: Meaning what you say includes following through on your commitments. If you tell your spouse that you're going to support him or her every step of the way, you'd better be prepared to make the journey. Affirmation isn't just a one-time pep talk; it's a commitment to help your spouse achieve his or her potential—on a daily basis.

3. *Keep the focus on your spouse and not yourself.*

If your spouse is uncomfortable with receiving attention, he or she may try to deflect the spotlight by returning your compliments or words of affirmation. Or, if your spouse is surprised or overwhelmed by your encouragement, he or she may go on and on about how considerate and wonderful you are.

And, while there may be a time and place to consider your wonderfulness, this isn't it. The affirmation process isn't about you; it's about your spouse. If you notice your spouse trying to shift the focus of your discussion to you, gently turn it around again so that you're talking about his or her potential.

If you keep things casual and low-key, you'll help your spouse work through his or her initial discomfort and accept what you're saying.

4. Don't give backhanded encouragement.

If you're uncomfortable with the idea of giving encouragement (or even with the idea of being sincere), you may be tempted to joke your way through the affirmation process or to smother your comments in sarcasm or irony.

➤ "It took you almost two whole days to finish that bag of Oreos. I admire your willpower."

➤ "I think you should pursue scrapbooking as a hobby. It can't be any worse than your cake-decorating phase."

➤ "Going back to school is a great idea—anything to get you off the couch and out of the house for a while."

Comments like these may seem harmless, but they're not. They can actually do more damage than good. If you insist on including cheap jokes or "zingers" in your words of affirmation, your spouse won't be able to fully embrace what you say. Remember, the response you're looking for is a warm smile, not a self-conscious chuckle, from your spouse.

5. Keep your motives pure.

If you have any ulterior personal motives for affirming your spouse, you'd probably be better off keeping your mouth shut. Any encouragement you offer should come from your desire to see your spouse happy and fulfilled; period! You should not expect anything in return.

You should never use affirmation as a tool for manipulating your spouse. Remember, this isn't about what *you* want or what *you* think your spouse needs to do. It's about your spouse and what he or she is capable of.

THE WISDOM OF ALL AGES

Some fellows pay a compliment like they expect a receipt.

—KIN HUBBARD

6. Don't get upset if your spouse's response doesn't live up to your expectations.

Remember, everyone responds to compliments and encouragement in different ways. Sure, it would be great if your spouse responded to your affirmation with a swooning, teary-eyed "movie moment," complete with a swelling orchestral score in the background. But don't be disappointed if you get a confused look or a suspicious "What are you talking about?" instead.

This is especially important if you and your spouse are new to this affirmation business. If giving encouragement to your spouse is out of character for you, you can hardly blame your spouse for being confused by it at first. The good news is that the more he or she gets used to it, the better response you'll see.

7. Go public with your feelings.

Why should you be the only one who knows how great your spouse is or what you think he or she is capable of being? Spread the word around to your family, friends, and neighbors. In fact, let your spouse "catch" you saying good things about him or her. Or let him or her hear it through the grapevine.

Find people you know who are incapable of keeping a secret and share your affirmation and encouragement for your spouse with them. ("I know that with Dan's business savvy and work ethic he would be a great success if he ever decided to go into business for himself.") Obviously you don't want to share anything that would embarrass your spouse. You also don't want to make it seem as though you're enlisting other people to pressure him or her into doing something. With those issues aside, you'll find that "affirming gossip" can be a very powerful tool for encouragement.

If you have the chance, you might also consider affirming your spouse in front of others when he or she is present. For example, if you're ever honored in a public forum for an accomplishment in business or your community, take a few minutes to share the credit with your spouse and acknowledge how he or she has helped and supported you every step of the way.

8. Keep your eyes and ears open.

You never know when you'll have a perfect opportunity to affirm your spouse, so it's important to be prepared when you spot one. Pay attention to any verbal clues or hints that your spouse may be interested in pursuing a longtime goal or even just venturing beyond his or her comfort zone.

For example, let's say your spouse mentions something like this over dinner: "My sister's trying to talk me into signing up for a creative writing class at Harper College with her, but I told her she was crazy." That's a pretty strong verbal clue. If you're ready with some affirmation of your own, you could jump on that clue and explain to your spouse why you think he or she would do well in a writing class.

If you're serious about affirming your spouse, you should always be prepared to offer encouragement at a moment's notice.

THE WISDOM OF ALL AGES

Nothing is unthinkable, nothing impossible to the balanced person, provided it arises out of the needs of life and is dedicated to life's further developments.

—LEWIS MUMFORD

9. Keep a list.

Spontaneous affirmation—encouragement that pours unprompted from the very depths of your soul—may seem like the romantic ideal, but it's not a terribly practical concept. The unfortunate truth is that as you get caught up in the pressures and busyness of day-to-day life, you may not recognize opportunities to encourage and affirm your spouse.

That's why you should consider keeping a list of affirmation possibilities. As ideas for encouraging your spouse come to you, write them down, along with any specific things you want to say. Refer to your list every couple of days or so to keep the ideas fresh in your mind.

10. Put your thoughts into writing.

Give your spouse written evidence of your affirmation and encouragement. We're not talking about letting some freelance Hallmark hack express your feelings for you in an impersonal card. We're talking about writing a personal letter to your spouse, sharing your thoughts about his or her strengths and potential. We're talking about giving your spouse something he or she can refer to over and over again, as needed.

The obvious objection to this idea is, "I'm not a good writer." The even more obvious solution is, practice. Write, rewrite, and re-rewrite your sentiments until you get them just right. Put the same kind of effort into creating a permanent record of your love and appreciation for your spouse that you would put into creating an annual business report or an important presentation for a client.

On second thought, put *more* effort into your letter than that. After all, business reports will be thrown away and client presentations will be forgotten, but the right words of affirmation from you will change your spouse's life.

Where to Start?

If you're an affirmation rookie, you may be experiencing severe information overload right now. More than anything else, you may be wondering what to do with what you've learned. For example, let's say you've decided that (1) your spouse could benefit from some encouragement, and (2) you're the right person to give it.

Now what?

What areas should you affirm? What should you say? What can you do to lessen the awkwardness and discomfort of your first few attempts at encouraging your spouse?

Obviously there is no one strategy that will work for all couples. What inspires teary-eyed joy in one spouse may inspire nausea in another. The specifics of your affirmation will depend on your unique circumstances and your unique relationship with your spouse.

However, there are some common places to begin your search for things to affirm in your spouse. In this section we'll look at four of the most popular ones. We'll also look at some examples of affirming statements, models of conversation that you can use or adapt to fit your own situation.

The four areas that are most ripe for affirmation are . . .

1. Appearance

2. Attitude

FAMILY TIES

The best way to affirm your kids is to "catch" them doing something right and tell them how much it means to you. For example, let's say you spot your teenage daughter helping her younger brother with his homework. When the time is right, pull your daughter aside and say something like, "Your brother doesn't know how lucky he is to have a sister like you. I'm proud of the way you help him when he needs it."

3. Intelligence

4. Skills

Let's take a quick look at each one of them.

Appearance

The politically correct among us may suggest that it's shallow and superficial to focus attention on a person's outward appearance. But do you really think your spouse would be offended by a sincere compliment from you on the way he or she looks?

Here are some examples of "appearance affirmation":

➤ "Wow." (That's right, just "Wow." You may be surprised by how effective a single-word exclamation of appreciation can be when it's given at just the right time—like when you see your spouse dressed for a formal occasion.)

➤ "You have incredible eyes. That was the first thing I noticed about you when we met, and I still notice it every day." (Depending on your spouse's physical features, feel free to substitute "nose," "smile," "teeth," "hair," "biceps," or anything else for "eyes" in your words of affirmation.)

➤ "How much weight have you lost? You look great!" (This is an especially effective approach when you see your spouse wearing something that previously had been too small for him or her. But don't even think about using this line if your spouse hasn't lost weight.)

Attitude

This is probably the least obvious of the four categories. But if you're married to someone with a great outlook on life, someone who loves to have a good time and wants to help others do the same, why not affirm those qualities?

Here are some ways to do it:

➤ "I don't know what I would do if I didn't have you to come home to. No matter how bad my day has been, it seems like you always know how to make things better."

➤ "I hope our kids love life as much as you do."

➤ "A guy at work asked me if I wanted to join his golf foursome. They have a standing tee time every Saturday morning. But I told him there's nobody I'd rather spend my Saturdays with than you. It just wouldn't be as much fun to hang out all day with other people when you and I could be doing something together." (Obviously this would work with any invitation you decline, from joining a bowling league to shopping with friends.)

Intelligence

Your spouse doesn't have to be "book smart" to be intelligent. Some of the smartest and wisest people who ever lived had very little formal education. If your spouse is a "go to" person for people who need advice or answers, try affirming that quality in him or her.

Here are some examples for you to consider:

➤ "Would you explain _____ to me?" (You could fill in the blank with anything that falls within your spouse's area(s) of expertise. Asking your spouse to help you understand something is a powerful way to affirm his or her intelligence—assuming, of course, that you really want to learn from him or her. Remember, blowing smoke does not qualify as affirmation.)

➤ "I can see it now. All of our kids' friends will be lined up around the block, waiting to ask you questions about their homework."

➤ "You could do some serious damage as a contestant on *Jeopardy!* or *Who Wants to Be a Millionaire?* You ought to apply to become a contestant."

Skills

Everyone is good at something. Many people are good at several different things. If you take the time to observe your spouse, you may be surprised by how many different things he or she is good at. That's great for you, because it gives you plenty of affirmation ammunition.

Here are some examples of how to affirm a spouse's skills:

➤ "It's amazing to me that someone who is so good at _____ can also be so good at _____." (Find two different skills your spouse has mastered and double your affirmation effectiveness.)

➤ "I was watching you at church this morning and I noticed how good you are at making visitors seem welcome and treating complete strangers like old friends."

➤ "I don't know how you manage to stay so cool under pressure. I really admire that in you."

Remember, these are just *suggestions,* things to consider while you come up with your own encouragement strategies. The affirmation you ultimately give your spouse should be unique and should come straight from your heart.

Family Practice

Think you're an expert on affirmation and encouragement now? Here's a quiz to see how much you remember from chapter 3.

1. Which of the following is *not* a love language?
   a. Words of affirmation
   b. Quality time
   c. Physical touch
   d. Mind games

2. What is the most important thing that words of affirmation accomplish in a marital relationship?
   a. They inspire courage and determination and communicate love and appreciation.
   b. They force your spouse to be positive all of the time.
   c. They impress in-laws.
   d. They establish a pattern of spouses "owing" each other compliments and favors.

3. Which of the following suggestions is most likely to help you work through a conflict with your spouse?
   a. Maintaining an attitude of kindness can diffuse even the most intense confrontations.
   b. Laughing at everything your spouse says will help him or her understand the humor of the situation.
   c. Taking your problems to *The Jerry Springer Show* will give you the healing you need.
   d. Name-calling is the quickest route to resolving your problems.

4. Which of the following is *not* a good idea when it comes to affirming and encouraging your spouse?
   a. Keep your affirmation simple and straightforward.
   b. Don't expect a dramatic response at first.
   c. Put your thoughts into writing.
   d. Hire a professional to do it.

5. What should you do if your spouse seems uncomfortable with your words of affirmation?
   a. Contact a divorce lawyer.
   b. Save your encouragement for your kids or other family members who will appreciate it.
   c. Continue to offer encouragement, perhaps using a more low-key approach.
   d. Say something extremely critical or insulting to your spouse so that he or she understands the need for affirmation and encouragement.

Answers: (1) d, (2) a, (3) a, (4) d, (5) c

Quality Is Job One

LOVE LANGUAGE #2: QUALITY TIME

S N A P S H O T

"Do you ever feel like we're just roommates who wave to each other as we come and go?" Mindy asked.

Alan sighed from behind his newspaper. "If this is going to be another one of those 'We don't spend any time together' discussions, please tell me now so that I can catch an earlier train to work."

"It's not about just spending time together," Mindy corrected. "It's about spending *quality* time together."

"*Quality* time," Alan scoffed. "Another one of those psychobabble catchphrases that make self-help authors rich and everyone else feel guilty."

"What's your problem with spending quality time together?" Mindy asked.

"It's too subjective," Alan replied. "I mean, who determines whether the time we spend together is 'quality' or not? Are there written guidelines? I'd

SNEAK PREVIEW

1. Spending quality time with your spouse can go a long way toward meeting his or her deepest needs.
2. Spending quality time with your spouse may involve anything from playing a board game to going on a weekend camping trip–anything that gives the two of you some one-on-one time together.
3. Postponing or canceling a previous engagement in order to be with your spouse is one of the most powerful ways to express your love through quality time.

like to know, because what I consider quality time may be meaningless to you, and vice versa."

"Why do you have to make things so complicated?" Mindy sighed. "Quality time is when couples do things together. Period."

"No, that's not *all* there is to it," Alan said. "There's always some catch. You always have a reason for why the time we spend together isn't really 'quality time.'"

"When was the last time we spent any time together?" Mindy asked.

"Well, if you'll recall," Alan said, "we spent a good twenty minutes of quality time together yesterday evening."

Mindy tried to recall the previous evening, then rolled her eyes when she realized what Alan was talking about. "Looking for the remote control doesn't count as quality time together!" she yelled.

"See what I mean?" Alan protested. "There's always a catch!"

* * * * * * * * * * * * * * *

Many people, particularly the nonromantics among us, cringe when they hear the words "quality time." They envision a scene straight out of an old Cary Grant movie, complete with a candlelight dinner, soft violin music, witty repartee, and long, meaningful gazes. Frankly, it freaks them out.

So when their partners start clamoring for more "meaningful" time together, their first reaction is to recoil and protest. They're not exactly sure what "quality time" entails, and they're not terribly anxious to find out.

That's unfortunate, because, in reality, quality time doesn't necessarily have to involve anything more romantic than doing a crossword puzzle with your spouse. If that comes as a surprise to you, keep reading. You may just find that quality time is the accelerant you need to rekindle the fire in your relationship with your spouse.

The Second Language of Love

Quality time is one of the five primary love languages that people speak, one of the five ways people express and receive emotional love. (The concept of love

languages is explained in detail in chapter 2.)
The other four love languages are . . .

THE WISDOM OF ALL AGES

Our costliest expenditure is time.

–THEOPHRASTUS

➤ Words of affirmation

➤ Receiving gifts

➤ Acts of service

➤ Physical touch

The fact is, not everyone responds to the same love language. The type of expressions that demonstrate love to you may do zilch for your spouse, and vice versa. So if a healthy, growing marital relationship is a high priority for you, you need to figure out what your spouse's primary love language is and then learn to speak it.

Which brings us to quality time. Remember, you can't choose your spouse's love language for him or her. And you can't talk your spouse into choosing a different love language. That means if quality time is your spouse's primary love language, you've got to bite the bullet and learn how to give him or her quality time.

How to Tell If Your Spouse Is a "Quality Timer"

Obviously, at some point, it would be a good idea for you and your spouse to sit down and talk specifically about each other's primary love language. In the meantime, if you suspect that quality time may be your spouse's primary love language, there are some things you can look for to help you confirm your suspicions.

For example, if your spouse asks you point-blank to spend more time with him or her, that's probably a pretty good indication that quality time is his or her primary love language. Unfortunately, most spouses aren't that direct in expressing their needs, so you have to look for other clues.

If, for instance, your spouse gets particularly upset or angry about the number of hours you work or the way you spend your time in the evenings or on the weekends, he or she may be indicating a need for more quality time with you.

Here's another possibility to consider. Is your spouse always available and willing to give you quality time when you need it? If so, that may be his or her way of letting you know that he or she needs the same thing from you.

Again, there's no substitute for a frank conversation with your spouse about his or her love language. But if you notice one or more of these "clues" in your relationship, you might want to explore your quality time options.

Popular Excuses...

Let's get this out of the way right now. Meeting your spouse's need for quality time is going to require more than a little time, energy, sacrifice, and diligence on your part. This is especially true if you don't share your spouse's love language.

If quality time isn't a pressing need for you, you can probably find some good reasons to file your spouse's needs under "Retirement Plans" and get on with business as usual in your life. Allow us to get you started by listing a few of the most popular excuses for not spending quality time with your spouse.

1. *Time is tight.*
Sometimes it seems that there aren't enough hours in the day to finish your work in the office, get your kids where they need to be, do the things that need to be done around the house, and fulfill your church and social responsibilities—not to mention eat, sleep, shower, and shave.

With such a busy schedule, the idea of finding an extra twenty or thirty minutes may seem about as likely as finding an extra $100 in your coat pocket. So while you may be all for the idea of spending more time with your spouse, your calendar simply won't allow it.

2. *Things are OK as is.*
If you don't feel a particular need for quality time in your own life, it's easy to underestimate your spouse's urgency for it. Couple that with the natural resistance most of us have when it comes to changing our habits and behavior, and it's easy to lock yourself into a particular way of interacting with your spouse. Once you're locked in, it becomes very difficult to change.

What's more, if you're getting along with your spouse—that is, if you're not fighting every night of the week—you may not notice a problem in your relationship. You may just go on assuming that your marital communication is "hunky-dory"—especially if *your* needs are being met by your spouse.

3. Every minute we spend together is "quality time."

"Why do we have to make such a big deal of this?" you may be tempted to ask. "If my spouse and I are in the same room, we're together. And if we're together, it's quality time. Why should we spoil what we have by trying to force togetherness unnaturally?"

At first glance all three seem like pretty solid arguments for maintaining the status quo in your relationship. So let's take a second glance.

. . . and Why You Shouldn't Use Them

If you think your reasons for not spending quality time with your spouse are legitimate, you need to think again. Here's why.

1. There's no such thing as a booked-solid schedule.

Unless a military band plays "Hail to the Chief" every time you walk into a social gathering, you can't legitimately claim to have a *full* schedule. You may very well have a busy schedule—perhaps even an overbooked one—but not a full one.

Do you watch the news, or anything else on TV? Do you read the newspaper? Do you work out? Do you play or coach in any sports leagues? Do you eat meals? If you answered yes to any of these questions, you have time for quality activities with your spouse. No one is so in demand that he or she can't carve out twenty to thirty minutes regularly from his or her daily schedule. That means you aren't too busy for quality time with your spouse.

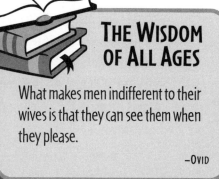

THE WISDOM OF ALL AGES

What makes men indifferent to their wives is that they can see them when they please.

—OVID

2. A change will do you good.

Remember what your relationship with your spouse was like back when you were dating and every day brought a new revelation—one that made you love

THE WISDOM OF ALL AGES

Constancy in love is a perpetual inconstancy, which makes the heart attach itself successively to all the qualities of the person we love, giving preference now to one and presently to another.

—François de La Rochefoucauld

each other even more? That same sense of discovery can be had again, through a commitment to regular quality time with your spouse.

Think about the way you approached your relationship back in those days. If you were like most people in the throes of romantic delirium, you probably used any excuse you could think of to spend time with your beloved.

The question you have to ask yourself is, "What happened?" Did you discover everything there is to know about your spouse? Did he or she become less important to you? If the answer to both of those questions is no, that means you still have some things to discover about, and demonstrate to, your spouse. And quality time is the way to do it.

3. More often than not, you give your spouse less than your best.

If you could view your relationship with your spouse from an outsider's perspective, you might be alarmed at what you saw. The fact is, it's easy to take your spouse for granted. After all, if you're OK with the relationship, you might automatically assume that he or she is, too. The idea of your spouse's needs being unmet may not even occur to you.

As a result, you may be with your spouse but are listening less than you should when he or she talks. Or you may allow your work responsibilities and your social engagements to interfere with your home life. You may lose interest in getting to know your spouse better. And while you may not mean to let these things happen, that won't change the negative impact they will have on your relationship.

The problem is a lack of focus on your spouse, and such disregard is wrong for a whole bushel of reasons. Let's start with the three most obvious:

➤ *It's rude.* Answer this question: If you wanted to offend, ignore, or take for granted someone on a regular basis, why would you choose your life partner as that person? What's more, if you know your spouse craves and thrives on quality time with you, isn't it more than a little mean to ignore that need?

➤ *It demonstrates some seriously weird priorities.* If watching reruns of *Friends* or playing on-line computer games is more engrossing to you than spending an evening enjoying your spouse's company, you need to ask yourself why. If you find yourself pursuing diversions more intensely than you pursue your commitment to your relationship, it's time for a major reevaluation of what's important to you.

➤ *It's ultimately damaging to your relationship.* Your spouse knows when he or she is being tuned out or listened to half-heartedly. (Don't you?) Do you think he or she finds it amusing or takes it in stride? Of course not. Every instance of being disregarded is like a slap in the face to your spouse—not to mention a blow to your relationship. And while one or two such blows aren't likely to make a big difference in the relationship, a repeated pattern of blows can weaken, and ultimately destroy, your relationship.

Now that you know *why* quality time is so important to your relationship, let's talk about some of the *hows*.

What You Should Know About Quality Timers

First, people whose primary love language is quality time experience love in togetherness. We're not just talking about proximity, physical closeness; we're talking about physical and emotional closeness. Being in a house together, or even sitting down for a meal together, isn't necessarily what quality timers are looking for.

Second, real togetherness can only be found in focused attention. Nils and Lara, for example, play mixed doubles racquetball together every Tuesday evening. They don't win many games, but the competition isn't the point. What matters to them is that they are spending time together, playing as a team, and cheering each other on. For them, pursuing a common interest like racquetball is a way of communicating that they care about each other, that they enjoy being with each other, and that they like to do things together.

On the flip side, people whose primary love language is quality time often experience feelings of rejection when their spouses . . .

➤ make plans to do things with other people during off-work hours.

➤ keep one eye on the TV during discussions.

➤ postpone dates or cancel plans for getting together because "something came up."

Finally, people who enjoy quality time above everything else from their spouse usually prefer equal parts of quality conversation and quality activities.

Quality Conversation and You

Some of the best and most meaningful quality time you ever spend with your spouse will involve nothing more than talking to each other. But in order to make your conversation good and memorable, you have to know what you're doing.

Quality conversation is a dialogue in which you and your spouse share your experiences, thoughts, feelings, and desires in a friendly, uninterrupted context. If your spouse's primary love language is quality time, this is the kind of conversation he or she is craving. It's crucial to his or her sense of fulfillment.

The first step in facilitating this type of communication has less to do with starting conversations than with encouraging them. Focus your energies on drawing your spouse out and listening sympathetically. Ask questions, not in an irritating or challenging manner, but in a genuine desire to understand what your spouse is saying and feeling.

You'll also want to steer clear of bad conversational habits that can suck the quality right out of any dialogue. If you're not sure what we're talking about, here are a few examples:

FAMILY TIES

If you have kids, enlist them in your quest for quality time with your spouse. Ask them to help you find a half hour here and twenty minutes there to spend with your spouse. Ask older siblings to baby-sit, if possible. Chances are, your kids will be excited to be included in your plans.

1. Advice giving

If you're the type of person who has a need to "fix" problems, you're going to have to work doubly hard to maintain quality conversations. You're going to have to hold your natural tendencies in check.

> ## THE WISDOM OF ALL AGES
>
> Good communication is as stimulating as black coffee, and just as hard to sleep after.
>
> —ANNE MORROW LINDBERGH

In the course of your quality conversations, your spouse will likely share some frustrations, hurts, questions, and doubts. That is not—repeat, *not*—your cue to come swooping in with all of the answers like some weird superhero advice columnist. Most of the times when your spouse shares personal frustrations, he or she is looking for sympathy and understanding, and not answers. Whether you know what you're talking about or not, your spouse will probably not appreciate your advice.

Of course, if your spouse *invites* your input by asking something like, "What do you think I should do?" then, by all means, share your thoughts and opinions. Let your brilliance shine in all of its glory. If you don't get that invitation, keep your mouth shut and your ears open.

2. One-word responses

At the risk of sounding like your ninth-grade English teacher, one of the best conversational habits you can develop is answering every question with a complete sentence. Responses like "Yep," "Nope," and "Fine" do nothing to further conversation. They're dialogue dead ends. ("I don't know," while technically a complete sentence, also falls into the latter category.)

For example, compare the following two brief exchanges:

Tricia: How was work today?
Shane: Fine.
Tricia: How was work today?
Shane: It started out really good, but then got worse as the day went on.

In the first exchange, the conversation was DOA (dead on arrival). Shane's one-word response left Tricia with nowhere to go with the conversation ("Fine . . . in

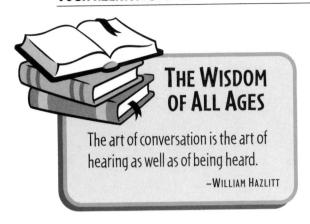

THE WISDOM OF ALL AGES

The art of conversation is the art of hearing as well as of being heard.

–WILLIAM HAZLITT

what way?"). In the second exchange, however, Shane left Tricia several follow-up possibilities ("What happened this morning?" "When did things start going downhill?" "How are you feeling now?").

3. Inappropriate humor

No, we're not referring to off-color jokes (although they, too, have been known to kill a conversation or two). We're talking about ill-timed wisecracks, thoughtless sarcasm, absurd non sequiturs, and obscure pop culture references that only serve to hijack a dialogue and carry it off somewhere else.

Humor is certainly welcome and appreciated when the conversation calls for it. But humor for the sake of being humorous is self-serving and contrary to the spirit of quality conversation.

Once you've mastered the art of quality conversation, you'll find that you can turn almost any situation into quality time with your spouse.

On Becoming a Quality Listener

For many people, listening is a learned behavior. It's not a skill that comes naturally to them. That doesn't necessarily make those people self-centered jerks, but they may very well appear to be that way.

Learning to listen is like learning to speak a foreign language. You have to practice. If listening doesn't come naturally to you, here are several practical tips to help get you started.

> ➤ *Maintain eye contact.* Keeping your eyes locked on your spouse's while he or she is talking not only will communicate the fact that he or she has your undivided attention, but also will help keep your mind from wandering.

> ➤ *Stop whatever else you're doing.* Remember, quality time is about undivided attention. If you're watching TV, reading the newspaper, or doing something else while your spouse is talking, you won't be able to focus on

what he or she is saying—no matter how good of a multitasker you consider yourself to be.

If you're doing something that you can't just drop, tell your spouse the truth. Let him or her know that what he or she has to say is important to you—so important to you, in fact, that you don't want to be distracted by whatever else is demanding your attention. Give your spouse an estimate as to when your full attention will be available and ask if the two of you can talk about it later. If your request is presented in those terms, it's likely that your spouse will be happy to accommodate it.

➤ *Learn to spot feelings.* Look beyond your spouse's words to find the emotions behind them. When you think you have a handle on those emotions, ask your spouse to confirm them. For example, you might say something like, "It sounds to me like you're angry at your boss because he expects more of you than he does your coworkers." This gives your spouse a chance to clarify his or her feelings ("No, I'm not so much angry as I am frustrated"). It also gives you a chance to offer proof of your listening skills.

➤ *Pay attention to body language.* If you pay attention only to your spouse's words, you will miss at least 50 percent of his or her communication. Body language—the physical motions we make when we talk—can tell as much about a person as his or her words. If the words you receive seem positive, but are accompanied by a clenched fist, trembling hands, or rolling eyes, you'd probably be better off giving the edge to the body language.

GLAD YOU ASKED

What if I'm not really interested in what my spouse is talking about? Should I fake an interest or tell my spouse the truth?

If something is of interest to your spouse, somehow you have to make it of interest to you. That's where questioning comes in. Ask enough questions, put in enough effort to understand something, and it will become interesting to you–with no acting required.

➤ *Refuse to interrupt.* Bite your tongue, hold your breath, do whatever you have to do in order to resist the urge to add your two cents to your spouse's comments. Remember, the goal of quality listening is not to show how wise or witty you are or to give you a chance to demonstrate your breadth of knowledge on a subject. Your goal is to discover your spouse's thoughts and feelings. The best way to do that is to offer him or her your undivided attention. (And, remember, talking always divides your attention.)

On Becoming a Quality Talker

In addition to listening carefully to what your spouse has to say, there's one more element of quality conversation that you'll need to master: self-revelation. The fact is, sphinxes don't make for quality conversationalists.

If your natural tendency is to play your cards close to the vest, to keep your thoughts and feelings to yourself, you're going to have to take some steps to start opening up to your spouse. Remember, intimacy and oneness are the hallmarks of a thriving relationship. And you can't achieve intimacy and oneness if your spouse is always wondering what you're thinking or feeling.

The first step in becoming a quality talker is to get in touch with your feelings. And the best way to do that is to get into the habit of writing them down. If expressing your feelings isn't something that comes naturally to you, you may not even be aware of when you're experiencing different emotions.

To remedy that situation, here's what you can do. Carry a small notebook around with you during the day and set your watch for every three hours or so. When you hear the alarm, stop and ask yourself, "What feeling or emotion have I experienced in the past three hours and what, specifically, brought on that emotion?" Write down in your notebook the emotion, as well as the circumstances that caused you to experience it.

Do that three times during the day, and when you and/or your spouse gets home from work, you'll have three emotions to talk about. Some emotions

THE WISDOM OF ALL AGES

Much unhappiness has come into the world because of bewilderment and things left unsaid.

−FYODOR DOSTOYEVSKY

may be simple and obvious ("I got mad at the idiot in the SUV who cut me off in traffic"); others may be much more complex ("I started feeling guilty and anxious about my relationship with my dad when I heard about a woman at work whose father suddenly dropped dead of a heart attack").

After a few weeks or so, as you start to get more and more in touch with your feelings, you may find that you no longer need "training wheels" and can dispense with the notebook.

The great thing about self-revelation is that not only will it put you in touch with the feelings and emotions that drive your everyday life, thus better equipping you to make important decisions, it will also make your spouse feel loved to hear you share those thoughts and feelings.

Quality Activities and You

Quality conversation is important, but it's not the only element of quality time of which you should be aware. There's also the matter of quality activities. We mentioned a few such activities earlier in the chapter. Let's expand our definition.

> **GLAD YOU ASKED**
>
> **Is there a minimum number of minutes required in order for an activity or conversation to qualify as quality time?**
>
> No, as long as your priorities are straight. If, say, you're in all-day meetings at work and the only free time you have available is a ten-minute afternoon break, you could make your spouse feel really special by asking him or her to meet you for a quick walk or a cup of coffee during that time. The fact that you're thinking of your spouse in that situation is what's meaningful, and not how much time you actually spend together.

Quality activities may include anything in which you or your spouse has an interest. If you're a newcomer to the quality time scene, it would probably be best to stick with your spouse's interests at first. That way, you'll resist the temptation of having your spouse simply "tag along" on the things you want to do ("You can ride in the cart while I play a round of golf!").

Along those same lines, you'll also want to avoid the temptation of dictating what's going to happen during your quality time. Don't make your spouse accept your terms in order to receive quality time from you ("If you want to spend time with me, let's go to a ball game or something. I'm not going to sit around the house all night trying to make small talk").

This is important. If you allow your spouse to choose a quality activity, make sure you follow through with it. No matter how distasteful you find his or her suggestions, give them a shot. And when you decide to do something, commit yourself to it. Don't do it halfheartedly, begrudgingly, or with an eye on the clock. Don't give your spouse the impression that he or she is lucky to be able to spend time with you. Don't make it seem like you're sacrificing more important things to pacify him or her. Make your spouse understand that you enjoy spending time with him or her and that you'd like to find ways to spend even more time together.

Of course, there's always the possibility that your spouse won't have any particular quality activities in mind (or that he or she will be hesitant to tell you about them because of your likely response). Your spouse may also prefer that you plan your own activities—at least, in the beginning of this new phase of your relationship. In that case, you'll need to come up with some quality activities yourself— perhaps with a little help from this book.

So Many Quality Activities, So Little Time

We've already mentioned a few quality activity possibilities in this chapter, but here are seven more for you to consider, use, or discard. Keep in mind that these are just starting points, ideas to spark your own creativity. If any of these seven suggestions work for you, great! If not, they may inspire some ideas that *will* work for you and your spouse. And that's even better.

1. *Plant a vegetable or flower garden together.* The periodic weeding, watering, and harvesting required to maintain the garden will give you and your spouse regular opportunities for soil-based quality time together.

2. *Tackle a home-improvement project together.* Wallpaper your kitchen, remodel your bathroom, install a closet organizer, or do something else around your house— as a team. If neither you nor your spouse will ever be confused with Bob Villa, keep your sense of humor intact throughout the process and, at the very least, you'll have some amusing anecdotes and memories to share from the experience.

3. *Play a board game.* Scrabble, Boggle, and any number of other board games can be used to foster togetherness. The excitement of competition, coupled with the natural opportunities for conversation, make board games a natural fit when it comes to quality time.

4. *Wash your car.* While you work, talk about some of your most memorable experiences with cars in the past. When you're finished, start a water fight and put your hose and buckets to really good use.

5. *Go antique shopping.* If genuine antiques are out of your price range, try a flea market or garage sale. You may be surprised at the fun you can have digging through treasures (and garbage) from the past. At the very least, the "Hey, I used to have something like this" factor can make for some interesting reminisces and conversations.

GLAD YOU ASKED

How can I tell if something is a "quality" activity or not?

There are three essential elements to a quality activity:

1. At least one of you wants to do it.
2. The other is willing to do it.
3. Both of you know why you are doing it—to express love by being together.

6. *Start a two-member book club.* Take turns choosing books to read and set realistic deadlines to finish them. Afterward, discuss each book together, giving each other a chance to explain what you liked about it and why.

7. *Shop for groceries together.* You may be surprised at the bonding you can do in the bread aisle or the conversations you can have in frozen foods. For example, the two of you may be inspired to reminisce and talk about the foods you liked and disliked as kids.

If some of these ideas seem a little, well, pedestrian or common, there's a reason for it. Quality activities don't always have to be super-exciting or creative. If you expand your definition of quality activities, you'll find that almost anything can fit the criteria.

Remember, it's not necessarily *what* you're doing that's important. What's important is *why* you're spending time together. The purpose is to share an experience together and to let your spouse know that you want to spend time with him or her.

Memory Makers

One of the fringe benefits of spending quality time together is a shared memory bank with your spouse. Years from now, you and your spouse can look back on the things you did together and find a renewed sense of joy and togetherness.

The words "Do you remember the time we . . ." followed by a description of a shared adventure or experience, such as . . .

➤ stumbled onto a bear cub and its mother during a mountain hike.

➤ tried to wallpaper the bathroom without knowing exactly what we were doing.

➤ spent an entire afternoon listening to 45s on an old turntable.

➤ walked the beach after a thunderstorm and found dozens of sea horses and other aquatic critters.

➤ rode the Vomit Comet together at the local amusement park.

. . . can stir old embers of emotion and provide loving warmth for you and your spouse for the rest of your days. (Of course, your kids and grandkids will get sick of hearing those stories after a dozen or so retellings, but that's their problem.) As an added bonus, your shared memory bank can provide you with conversation fodder at boring dinner parties for years to come.

THE WISDOM OF ALL AGES

The best of life is conversation, and the greatest success is confidence, or perfect understanding, between two people.

–RALPH WALDO EMERSON

Quality Versus Quantity

Before we wrap up this chapter, we'd like to offer a final warning. If time is in short supply for you, you may be tempted to give your spouse your schedule "leftovers" and justify it by claiming that quality, not quantity, is what's important.

But quantity is important, too. Yes, twenty minutes of uninterrupted interaction with your spouse is great—but thirty minutes is even better. Don't spend your day trying to decide how much quality time you can afford to give up to your spouse; spend it thinking of ways you can enjoy your spouse's company.

Tips for Maximizing Your Quality Time

If you're serious about dedicating more time to your spouse, you have a world of possibilities at your disposal. Here are five final tips and reminders to help you do it right.

1. Start slowly.

If you're new to the idea of quality time, don't try to do too much too soon. Start out with ten minutes a day, perhaps in the form of a morning walk together. Work your way up to twenty minutes (perhaps with an additional walk in the evening). If it's been a long time since you and your spouse have enjoyed concentrated time together, you may need to spend a day or so getting reacquainted and comfortable in each other's presence again.

2. Eliminate the pressure.

The reason some spouses tend to shy away from quality-time situations is that they feel a pressure to "perform," to be super-romantic or at least to say and do the right things. Consequently, quality-time situations feel unnatural and uncomfortable to them.

If you and your spouse can remove that pressure and set realistic expectations for your time together, you'll go a long way toward guaranteeing success.

3. Keep things surprising.

Don't allow yourself to get into a rut of doing the same thing over and over again for your spouse.

Take turns surprising each other by going to "mystery places" (whether they be bowling alleys or painting classes), engaging in odd, but interesting, conversations ("If you could have a superpower for a

FAMILY TIES

If you have kids, they will be a natural topic of conversation when you and your spouse get together for quality time. That's fine, to a certain extent. Be careful, however, that you don't focus your attention entirely on them. Try talking about things that are important or interesting to your spouse outside of his or her role as a parent.

day, what would it be and why?"), or doing other unusual (but nonembarrassing) things together.

4. Occasionally try to outdo yourself.

You won't always have time to plan extensively for some quality time with your spouse, but occasionally you will. Take advantage of those occasions. Think of questions to ask your spouse to get him or her talking. Make reservations at a special restaurant. Let your spouse know through your actions that quality time is important to you.

The key to successful quality time, whether it's conversation or activities, is comfort. And comfort develops with time. The more time you spend with your spouse in meaningful, one-on-one interaction, the more comfortable—and enjoyable— your quality time will become.

Family Practice

Think you're an expert on giving your spouse quality time? Here's a quiz to see how much you know.

1. Which of the following statements is not necessarily an indication that your spouse's primary love language is quality time?
   a. "We ought to find a baby-sitter this weekend and do something together— just the two of us."
   b. "Would you mind telling me how long you're going to keep putting in these eighty-hour workweeks?"
   c. "Do these pants make me look fat?"
   d. "I cleared my schedule all day for Saturday to give you a hand remodeling the bathroom."

2. Which of the following is actually welcome in a quality conversation?
   a. Follow-up questions
   b. Inappropriate humor
   c. One-word answers
   d. Advice giving

3. Which of the following is *not* a recommended strategy for becoming a good listener?
   a. Maintaining eye contact
   b. Paying attention to body language
   c. Stopping whatever else you're doing
   d. Repeating everything your spouse says

4. Which of the following is not a hallmark of a quality talker?
   a. Getting in touch with your feelings
   b. Making your feelings known to your spouse
   c. Giving your spouse a tongue-lashing for not sharing your feelings
   d. Wanting to make your spouse feel special—and loved—by revealing your feelings

5. Which of the following is not true of quality activities?
   a. They will create memories that you and your spouse can draw on for the rest of your lives.
   b. The quicker you finish them, the more meaningful they will be.
   c. They should involve things that either you or your spouse—or, preferably, both of you—want to do.
   d. Their purpose is to help you demonstrate love to your spouse by spending one-on-one time with him or her.

Answers: (1) c, (2) a, (3) d, (4) c, (5) b

Tokens of Affection

Love Language #3: Receiving Gifts

SNAPSHOT

"Stephanie came back to work today," Tammy said as she opened her carton of sweet-and-sour chicken. "You wouldn't believe how tan she is."

"In February?" Charlie asked.

"Yeah," Tammy said. "Remember, I told you her husband took her to Hawaii for their anniversary?"

"Oh, yeah," Charlie replied in a suddenly flat, emotionless voice.

"Steph was wearing the most beautiful diamond tennis bracelet I've ever seen," Tammy continued.

"Is that right?" Charlie asked in the same flat tone.

"She said her husband gave it to her while they were on a helicopter tour of some of the volcanoes on the island," Tammy said.

SNEAK PREVIEW

1. Many people have their deepest needs for love met by gifts or other tokens of affection.
2. The spirit in which a gift is given is more important to the receiver than the actual gift itself.
3. In order to give a gift that is meaningful to your spouse, you have to pay attention to his or her needs and desires.

"How about that," Charlie mumbled.

"And when they got back from the trip, Stephanie said her kitchen had been completely remodeled and a deck had been put on her house."

Charlie rolled his eyes in disgust, being careful not to let Tammy see. "What was it, some kind of special anniversary?" he asked. "Like their twenty-fifth or something?"

"No," Tammy replied. "Actually, they got married two weeks after we did."

Neither of them said anything as Tammy's reply hung in the air like a bad smell.

After a minute or so, Charlie reached into the food bag. "I got you an extra order of fried rice and an almond cookie," he offered hopefully.

"Thank you, Diamond Jim Brady," Tammy mumbled.

* * * * * * * * * * * * * * *

In every circle of acquaintances, it seems there's always one couple (like Stephanie and her husband) who ruin things for everybody else by setting the bar ridiculously high with the gifts they give one another. You know the type—the husband who makes sure his spouse is well-supplied in all manners of extravagance, and the wife who shows her appreciation by parading every new acquisition around like a Thanksgiving Day float.

Depending on your frame of mind, you may find yourself happy about, repulsed by, jealous of, or indifferent to each new flaunted possession. Regardless of how you feel about such conspicuous consumption, the fact is that some of these couples may very well have discovered something important about their primary love languages. (If you want to speculate about possible ulterior motives on the part of extragenerous spouses, you're on your own.)

There's no getting around the fact that many people find meaningful expressions of love in the presents they get from their spouses. Receiving gifts is their primary love language.

Love for Sale?

If receiving gifts isn't your primary love language, the idea of giving presents to express your love may offend your sensibilities and send up all kinds of red flags regarding your relationship. If it's particularly bothersome to you, you might even be able to find some moral high ground to stand on while you object. Arguments such as "My spouse's love isn't for sale!" or "My spouse loves me for who I am, not for what I buy" can sound pretty convincing if they're delivered with enough nobility and moral outrage.

However, all of the objections in the world ultimately don't matter if you happen to be married to someone who finds expressions of love in gifts received. Like it or not, his or her love language is every bit as legitimate as yours.

The gifts that we're talking about in this chapter aren't "love bribes"; they are simply evidence of the fact that you're thinking of your spouse. They are symbolic of the fact that you care enough about your spouse to make, secure, or buy something that you know will make him or her happy.

Whether you care to admit it to yourself or not, the impulse to give gifts is wired into our systems at an early age. Think about it. Did you ever pick flowers for your mother when you were a kid? Where did that impulse come from? Chances are you didn't have any ulterior motives in mind. You simply wanted to make your mom happy. (The fact that your mom probably didn't want the flowers picked from her garden is beside the point.) That same kind of spirit is what should guide your giving to your spouse.

GLAD YOU ASKED

How can I let my spouse know that receiving gifts is my primary love language without sounding like a mercenary?

Make it a point to acknowledge every small gift your spouse gives you, even if it's just a pizza or an anniversary card. Let him or her know how much even inexpensive presents mean to you. Do that often enough and pretty soon your spouse will start to connect the dots between tangible expressions of love and your fulfillment and happiness.

The Basics of the Love Languages

Receiving gifts is one of the five basic love languages that people speak. What that means is that people express and receive love in different ways. In addition to receiving gifts, the other languages are . . .

➤ Words of affirmation

➤ Quality time

➤ Acts of service

➤ Physical touch

GLAD YOU ASKED

What's the difference between someone whose primary love language is receiving gifts and a "gold digger," someone who's only in the relationship for the gifts?

A person whose love language is receiving gifts cares primarily about the love that inspired the gift. A gold digger cares primarily about the price of the gift. A person whose love language is receiving gifts would be thrilled to get something small, but meaningful, such as a homemade card. A gold digger, on the other hand, would ask, "What am I supposed to do with this?"

The whys and hows of love languages are covered in chapter 2. For the purposes of this chapter, all you really need to know is that not everyone speaks the same primary love language. In fact, there's a good chance that you and your spouse have different primary love languages. Things that get you all warm and fuzzy inside may leave your spouse cold. That doesn't make you incompatible, but it does present an obstacle to your communication.

How to Tell If You're Married to a Gift Lover

Showering presents on someone whose primary love language isn't "receiving gifts" can be a fairly costly waste of time. In order to avoid making such an expensive mistake, we've compiled a list of four questions for you to consider. These questions will help you determine whether or not your spouse finds expressions of love in receiving gifts.

1. How does your spouse react to the gifts he or she receives?

If your spouse responds with genuine excitement every time you give him or her a present—whether it's for Christmas, a birthday, an anniversary, or something else—it may be an indication that he or she is finding something more than material satisfaction in those presents.

2. How often does your spouse talk about gifts that other people receive?

We're not necessarily referring to expressions of envy here. ("I wish someone would treat me to a weekend in Aspen.") We're talking about the attitude your spouse demonstrates toward the gifts that his or her friends and family receive. If your spouse gets genuine pleasure from hearing about presents that other people have been given, it may be a sign that he or she has a special sensitivity to gifts.

3. How often does your spouse give you gifts?

If your spouse is especially generous with you—if he or she makes special efforts to find and acquire things that you like—it may be an indication that he or she is looking for the same consideration from you.

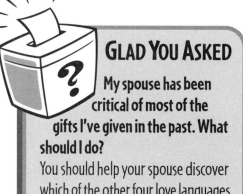

GLAD YOU ASKED

My spouse has been critical of most of the gifts I've given in the past. What should I do?

You should help your spouse discover which of the other four love languages is his or her primary language, because it's almost certainly not "receiving gifts." A person who finds love in the gifts he or she receives is rarely critical of those gifts—unless they're given for the wrong reason, such as to manipulate (get your own way) or out of obligation (which comes with a wrong attitude that your spouse will soon recognize).

4. What kind of importance does your spouse place on his or her wedding ring?

If that seems like an odd question to you, consider this: The wedding ring is presented as *a token of love* at the end of the wedding ceremony. In that sense, your spouse's wedding ring is the ultimate symbol of your love for him or her. If your spouse is someone who places tremendous significance on such symbols, it follows that he or she will treat his or her wedding ring with extraspecial care.

Learning the Language of Gifts

The fact that you weren't born with a giving nature or that you weren't given a lot of presents as a child is no reason to continue that cycle with your own family. Think of it this way: You have a chance to meet your spouse's (or family's) needs in a way that yours weren't met. And you can't plead ignorance as an excuse, since gift giving is one of the easiest love languages to master.

The most important thing you need to remember in learning the language of gift-giving is that your *attitude in giving* is every bit as important as the gift itself. A brand-new Mercedes convertible, given in the wrong spirit, will likely mean less to a person whose love language is receiving gifts than, say, a book that is given in the right spirit. (Of course, those of us who speak one of the other love languages would probably find a whole lot of meaning in a Mercedes, regardless of the spirit in which it's given—but that's beside the point.)

FAMILY TIES

The Good Book says, "Train a child in the way he should go, and when he is old he will not turn from it" (Proverbs 22:6). That concept can have special significance for a spouse whose primary love language is receiving gifts. If you emphasize to your kids from an early age the importance of giving gifts, big and small, to your spouse, you will create a pattern of generosity and expressions of love that may very well continue throughout your spouse's life.

As strange as it may seem, it is possible to be generous and hurtful at the same time. You can send messages of guilt ("We can't afford this, but since you seem to like presents so much, here it is"), anger ("Here, this should shut you up for a while"), condescension ("I'll give you a shiny new present if you'll show me a happy face"), or any number of other emotions in the seemingly charitable act of giving presents—all with just a subtle inflection of your voice or a particular shift in body language.

Wrong Reasons to Give

That's why it's important for you to understand *why* you're giving gifts before you start. In order to understand that, though, you first have to identify and eliminate some of the faulty motivations for giving. Three of the most popular, but flawed, reasons for giving are

➤ to offer a substitute for genuine love and affection.

➤ to compete with other givers.

➤ to earn a reputation as a giver.

Let's take a look at the flaws and dangers in each of these reasons.

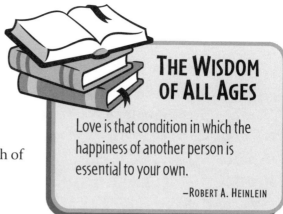

THE WISDOM OF ALL AGES

Love is that condition in which the happiness of another person is essential to your own.

–ROBERT A. HEINLEIN

Gifts are not substitutes for real love.

Many people use gifts as a way of avoiding interaction with their spouses. In the aftermath of an argument or confrontation, they buy presents in order to make the conflict go away as quickly and smoothly as possible. Likewise, when their spouses deserve praise or recognition, they use gifts to communicate their feelings, preferring not to get "personally" involved. The results of such flawed generosity are damaged relationships and spouses who don't know how to open up to each other.

Gifts must always be used *in conjunction* with personal interaction with your spouse, and never *in place* of it. Remember, you're not just throwing bones to your spouse to keep him or her quiet; you're trying to communicate your love for him or her in the most profound way you know.

Gifts are not a means for competing with your friends and acquaintances.

Forget about keeping up with the Joneses. This isn't about matching your neighbors gift for gift in the quest to become the talk of the block. ("Richie just bought his wife a new dishwasher. If I don't give my wife a new washer and dryer, I'm going to look bad.") If your giving is in any way tied to your competitive nature, you're asking for trouble on two different fronts.

First, your spouse will know why you're really giving the gifts. So not only will you not be meeting his or her needs, you will also likely end up alienating him or her. Instead of feeling special or loved, your spouse will feel like a mere excuse for you to upgrade your lifestyle.

Second, keeping up with the Joneses can be an expensive endeavor, especially if the Joneses happen to reside in a tax bracket higher than yours. The worst part about such competition is that it never ends. Unless you come to your senses, you'll be trying to outdo your neighbors all the way to bankruptcy court.

Gifts are not a means for building your reputation.

Many people give in order to feed their ego. Their motivation is that they want to be known as givers. What you need to remind yourself is that the giving process—at least as it relates to love languages and family relationships—isn't about *you*. It's about your spouse—specifically, it's about giving your spouse the love he or she needs. As soon as your spouse begins to suspect that you're looking for as much satisfaction from the presents you give as he or she is, the magic of the gift is gone.

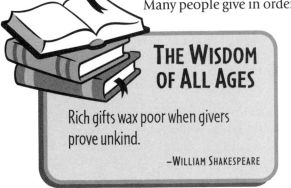

THE WISDOM OF ALL AGES

Rich gifts wax poor when givers prove unkind.

–WILLIAM SHAKESPEARE

Along those same lines, you want to make sure that there are no strings attached to your gifts. In other words, don't give and then expect something in return. Don't complain about being the only generous person in the family. Don't ask, "What have you done for me lately?" Just give.

Right Reasons to Give

If you're going to become a giver, you might as well do it for the right reasons. That means you should give because . . .

> ➤ you know what your spouse likes.

> ➤ you know what your spouse needs.

> ➤ you want to express your love in a way that matters to your spouse.

Why are these motivations better or more honorable than the previous three? Let's take a look.

Give because you know what your spouse likes.

The only way to discover what your spouse likes is to ask. And the very act of giving your spouse a chance to share his or her preferences is an expression of love on your part. What you're doing is demonstrating to your spouse a genuine interest in who he or she is and what makes him or her happy. Doing something to address those desires is the icing on the cake. Your gifts become tangible expressions of your desire and commitment to make your spouse happy.

It's not like there's a lot of work involved. In fact, in many cases, a simple question or two ("Why do you like having flowers around?" "Why is golf so enjoyable to you?") is enough to get the information you need.

Give because you know what your spouse needs.

Even more important than your spouse's desires are his or her needs. If your spouse is struggling in a certain area or facing difficult circumstances or lacking some necessities, you may be able to take care of at least some of those needs with well-timed and well-thought-out gifts.

Some gifts are so practical that they're hardly considered gifts at all. For example, giving your spouse a new Thermos to carry to work or a new pair of sunglasses to use while watching your kids' soccer games may not seem like the kind of act that deserves mention in a chapter like this. The fact is that anything given in the right spirit is a gift. And if a gift just happens to meet a practical need of your spouse, all the better.

> **THE WISDOM OF ALL AGES**
>
> He gives only worthless gold
> Who gives from a sense of duty.
>
> —JAMES RUSSELL LOWELL

Give because you want to express your love in a way that matters to your spouse.

If your spouse's primary love language is receiving gifts, there's nothing you can do to change that. So the decision you're left with is whether to give your spouse what he or she needs. If you decide that your spouse's happiness and fulfillment are worth your time, energy, and money, read on.

Gift Rap

Once you've got your motivation down, it's time to start thinking of the practicalities of gift giving. Here are five tips to get you started in your quest to become the kind of gift giver your spouse needs.

1. Keep your eyes and ears open.

Ideally, most of your gift-giving ideas will come directly from your spouse, whether he or she realizes it or not. If you train yourself to listen to what he or she says, even when your attention is being called elsewhere, you'll find all kinds of valuable clues in your quest to find just the right gift.

That's not to say that every clue will be screamingly obvious ("I wish someone would buy me one of those"). Sometimes you'll need to listen "between the lines." For example, when your spouse talks about his or her childhood, if you listen for the things he or she seems especially nostalgic for, you'll be well on your way to finding a meaningful gift.

That gift doesn't have to be especially awe-inspiring or life-changing. For example, if you hear your spouse complaining about getting hungry on the job, you could take that as a cue to find a snack for him or her to take to work the next day. For the price of a granola bar or two, you can demonstrate your love for your spouse by fulfilling a need—however small or insignificant that need may seem.

2. Get over your self-consciousness.

One of the reasons many people avoid gift-giving is that they're afraid of choosing a present that turns out to be useless or unappreciated. They justify their attitude with reasoning like this: *What's the use in giving a gift that will only be returned or shoved in a drawer or closet somewhere and never used?* They allow their self-consciousness to get in the way of their generosity.

GLAD YOU ASKED

With so many things going on in my life, I'm not sure that I'll be able to remember the things my spouse mentions in conversation long enough to act on them. What should I do?

Invest in a quality notebook and pen and carry them around with you as much as possible. Get yourself in the habit of writing down gift ideas as soon as they occur to you. Once you've compiled a healthy list of ideas, keep track of the ones you use and how well each one is received. You can use the information you collect to continually modify and perfect your gift-giving strategies.

It's important to remember, though, that that type of reasoning carries very little weight when it comes to your spouse. You see, if your spouse's primary love language is receiving gifts, that means he or she is wired to appreciate any sincere gift you give. In other words, if you're really trying to express your love for your spouse in the gifts you give, you can't go wrong.

3. Think "outside the box."

Don't let a limited imagination get in the way of learning your spouse's love language. If you learn to expand your definition of what a gift is, you'll discover just how easy it is to become a gift giver. A box of Cracker Jacks, a homemade card, a pizza, a book from the library, a train ride into the city, and a new pair of workout shoes would all make excellent gifts, if they are presented with the right motivation and in the right spirit.

Let's use pizza as an example. You may never have thought of a pizza as prime gift material. Chances are, you've never swung by your local pizza place on your way to a birthday party and asked for a gift-wrapped pepperoni-and-sausage deep-dish pie and a greeting card to go. And, chances are, you've brought home dozens (or hundreds) of pizzas in your lifetime without ever considering one of them a "gift." But try looking at pizza delivery from another perspective. For a spouse who's planned, prepared, and served twenty other meals during the week, a pizza for Friday night's dinner would likely be a much-appreciated gift. Not only would it be a treat for the taste buds, it would also mean a break from the kitchen.

A word of warning here: Don't carry this concept too far and try to make gifts out of things that clearly aren't intended to be. ("I bought this box of baking soda at the supermarket for you because I know how much you appreciate an odor-free refrigerator.") Remember, there's a fine line between being a creative, thrifty gift giver and being a lazy cheapskate.

4. Think practical.

There's nothing wrong with giving diamond bracelets or bouquets of roses, if your budget can handle it. But, remember, not every gift you give your spouse has to be "romantic" in the traditional sense of the word. For example, new carpeting may never replace silver as the recommended gift for a twenty-fifth anniversary, but that doesn't mean it won't communicate love to a spouse who's been wanting to replace the floor covering in his or her living room for years.

Don't forget, giving gifts to your spouse has less to do with measuring up to society's standards of what is and isn't romantically acceptable and more to do with meeting your spouse's real needs and desires. So don't be afraid to order that new Berber, if that's what you believe will make your spouse happy.

5. Use your talents.

Here's something you'll want to keep in mind. People whose primary love language is receiving gifts *always, always, always* appreciate the personal touch. So anything you design, create, or build yourself will be especially meaningful to your spouse.

If you have an obvious talent, such as carpentry, home repair, or artistic skills, the world of gift giving is wide open to you. If you're capable of . . .

➤ building and installing new kitchen cabinets.

➤ renovating and remodeling a bathroom.

➤ creating a work of art to display.

. . . you have the ability to give your spouse tangible examples of love that he or she will be able to use, appreciate, and draw meaning and inspiration from for years and years.

THE WISDOM OF ALL AGES

The only gift is a portion of thyself.

–RALPH WALDO EMERSON

Any skill can be put to use as a gift. All it takes is a little imagination and effort. If you enjoy writing, you might want to try keeping a journal of your thoughts and feelings about your spouse. If you're musically inclined, you might want to try composing a song or making a mix tape of tunes your spouse would like. If you're an organizational whiz, you might want to try restoring order to your spouse's filing system. The possibilities are endless—or, more specifically, they are limited only by your imagination.

Gift Ideas

If you're struggling to find just the right gift for your spouse, you're not alone. Here are some ideas that worked for other couples. (Only the names have been changed to protect the generous.) With a little imagination, you may be able to use or adapt some of them yourself. Or, better yet, these ideas may inspire you to come up with some of your own.

Andre

Soon after he got married, Andre made a decision to start saving his pocket change so that someday he could buy something nice for his wife. For more than five years, he made a routine of depositing his spare quarters, dimes, nickels, and pennies into a giant glass jug in the back of his closet. He decided that he wouldn't count his money until the jar was full. It took him more than half a decade, but he was finally able to fill it. With the help of a few friends, Andre hauled the jar to the bank, where he learned that he had saved over $900 worth of change. So, without disrupting the family's carefully designed budget, Andre was able to surprise his wife with the beautiful sapphire and diamond necklace she had admired in the window of a local jewelry store on several occasions.

Tina

During a conversation with her mother-in-law, Tina learned that her husband's boyhood idol was Ron Santo, a third baseman who played for her spouse's beloved Chicago Cubs. Tina knew nothing about baseball, but she knew how nostalgic her husband was about his childhood, so she filed the name in her memory.

One Saturday while her husband was listening to a Cubs game on the radio, she heard one of the announcers introduced as "Ron Santo." That gave her an idea. Without her husband's knowledge, she made the trek from her home in the Chicago suburbs to Wrigley Field for the Cubs' next home game. After explaining what she wanted to a couple of stadium personnel, she was ushered into the Cubs' broadcast booth, where she got her husband's boyhood hero to autograph a baseball for him. Imagine her husband's surprise, too, when he heard Ron Santo send him his best wishes during the radio broadcast of that game!

Michael

Michael wanted to give his wife something to decorate the walls of her new office, so he made plaster molds of their kids' hands. With his kids' help, he painted each mold a different color. He

THE WISDOM OF ALL AGES

A gift, with a kind countenance, is a double present.

—THOMAS FULLER

then asked a carpenter friend to make frames for them. The molds are now hanging directly behind his wife's desk, where they have become popular conversation pieces among her clients.

Mackenzie

Mackenzie's idea came to her when she noticed her husband staring at a picture of his father on the fireplace mantel. Her father-in-law had lost his battle with cancer almost a year earlier, and it was apparent that the anniversary of his death had more significance to her husband than Mackenzie had realized. She recalled the scrapbook class she had taken years earlier to make baby albums for her kids, and it occurred to her that she could put those same skills to use for her husband. Mackenzie contacted her mother-in-law and all of her husband's siblings, asking them for photos and other mementos of her father-in-law. Then she arranged those pictures, newspaper clippings, and other documents in a scrapbook she titled "A Life Well Lived." When she gave it to her husband, she saw him cry for only the second time in the fifteen years she had known him.

> ### FAMILY TIES
>
> Most young children love arts and crafts. With a little coordination on your part, you and your kids can work together to create all kinds of cards, knickknacks, refrigerator art, and abstract expressions of love for your spouse. For the sake of posterity, though, make sure that you sign and date everything you make.

Joey

Without telling his wife, Joey called up three of her closest friends and invited them to come over for a movie night with his wife. He rented two "chick movies" he knew his wife would like, filled an enormous bowl with popcorn, loaded the refrigerator with sodas, and set out a few boxes of Junior Mints and Milk Duds to complete the movie-theater effect. When his wife returned home from running errands, Joey loaded up his infant son and took off for the night, leaving his wife and her friends to enjoy the videos and each other's company.

Shelly

Ever since the night Shelly went out with her husband and his friends and watched them play Pop-A-Shot on a miniature basketball hoop for hours, all the while laughing and competing like goofy teenagers, she looked for an exact replica of the game to set up in her garage, as a surprise for her husband. After months of haunting garage sales, flea markets, and sporting goods stores, Shelly finally found what she was looking for in an on-line auction. Her gift earned Shelly not only her husband's gratitude and admiration, but also the title of "World's Coolest Wife" from her husband's friends, who stop by once a week or so to play.

Kayla

When Kayla's husband was transferred from Kansas City to Omaha, he told Kayla that one of the things he would miss most about Kansas City was the rib joint down the street from their house. Kayla's husband, who considered himself an expert on ribs, swore that the secret-recipe barbecue sauce served at the tiny, ramshackle establishment behind Al's Tire and Battery was the best he had ever tasted.

After a year or so in Omaha, Kayla decided that she wanted to do something special for her husband. So she contacted the rib joint back in Kansas City and arranged to have a dozen slabs of ribs delivered overnight to her home in Nebraska.

When her husband got home from work and saw what was waiting for him on the table, his eyes lit up like an eight-year-old's on Christmas morning. He ended up eating those ribs for dinner four nights in a row. And he enjoyed every last bite.

Manny

In the twenty years since she graduated from high school, Manny's wife had lost close to sixty pounds. Since she and her family had moved to another state shortly after graduation, though, she never had a chance to show her old friends—and her old tormentors—how much she had changed.

When the invitation for her class's twenty-year reunion came in the mail, Manny's wife tried to act nonchalant about it. But Manny knew how much it meant to her. The night before the reunion, Manny used the phone book in the hotel directory to schedule a few surprise appointments for his wife. First he arranged for her to have a morning massage to relieve some of her tension and nervousness. Then he scheduled an impromptu shopping trip at a boutique in the city, where his wife found the perfect dress for the reunion. And, finally, he managed to get her an appointment at an upscale salon to have her hair and makeup done by experts.

Needless to say, Manny's wife was the hit of the reunion. She later told Manny that, aside from their wedding day and the births of their two children, it was the best day of her life. "Now I know how Cinderella must have felt at the ball," she told him.

Family Practice

Think you're an expert on giving gifts? Here's a quiz to see how much you know.

1. Which of the following questions is least likely to help you determine whether your spouse's primary love language is receiving gifts?
   a. How does my spouse react to the gifts he or she receives?
   b. How angry does my spouse get when a gift has to be returned?
   c. How often does my spouse talk about gifts that other people receive?
   d. How often does my spouse give me gifts?

2. Why is it common for someone whose primary love language is receiving gifts to place a great deal of importance on his or her wedding ring?
   a. The wedding ring is likely the most expensive gift he or she will ever receive.
   b. The wedding ring is a symbol of his or her spouse's love.
   c. The wedding ring is a reminder of the many gifts that were received on his or her wedding day.
   d. The wedding ring is a good-luck charm that is thought to ward off divorce and marital unhappiness.

3. What is the most important thing to remember as you learn the language of giving gifts?
   a. Your attitude is every bit as important as the gift itself.
   b. If you pay less than fifty dollars for a gift, be sure to cut off the price tag.
   c. If it doesn't have a ribbon or bow on it, it's not really a gift.
   d. It's not the number of gifts you give that's important; it's the total dollar value of all of them.

4. Which of the following should be considered a legitimate reason to give your spouse a gift?
   a. To avoid overly emotional conversations or confrontations
   b. To make your friends and neighbors look bad in comparison

    c. To give your spouse tangible evidence of your love

    d. To make yourself look good in your spouse's eyes

5. Which of the following is *not* a helpful tip to keep in mind when it comes to giving gifts to your spouse?

    a. Always keep your eyes and ears open for ideas.

    b. Get over your self-consciousness.

    c. Use your talents.

    d. Never buy off-brands.

Answers: (1) b, (2) b, (3) a, (4) c, (5) d

Love in Action or Love Inaction?

LOVE LANGUAGE #4: ACTS OF SERVICE

SNAPSHOT

Jan walked in the door and saw her husband, Jimmy, standing in the dining room with a huge smile on his face.

"Ta-da!" Jimmy exclaimed, with a dramatic sweep of his hand.

"Ta-da . . . what?" Jan asked as she set down her briefcase and umbrella.

Jimmy tilted his head toward the kitchen. "Do you notice anything *different* about the house since you left this morning?"

Jan glanced around at the Nike running shoes and sweatpants lying in the middle of the entryway, the dark stain on the living room carpet from Jimmy's spilled Cherry Coke, and the brown smudges all over the sliding glass patio door from his aborted weekend construction project. "No, not really," she replied slowly.

SNEAK PREVIEW

1. Many people find meaningful expressions of love in the simple chores or "acts of service" their spouses do for them.
2. Acts of service may include anything from cooking a meal to cleaning the garage, from walking the dog to raking leaves.
3. All that's really required to learn the acts-of-service love language is a desire to show love to your spouse and a willingness to get your hands dirty.

Jimmy walked into the kitchen and leaned on the sink. "Now do you see anything different?" he persisted.

"You . . . washed the breakfast dishes?" Jan guessed.

"I didn't just *wash* them," Jimmy said with that same huge smile on his face. "I really washed them. It took me about an hour and a half, but I—"

"An hour and a half?!" Jan exclaimed. "Are you serious?"

"Yeah, why?"

"We're talking about the breakfast dishes, right?" Jan pressed. "Nobody broke in, cooked a big Thanksgiving dinner, and then left all of the dishes for you to clean, right?"

Jimmy stared at her for a moment before offering a terse, "No."

"Did someone use all of our pots and pans to melt caramel and then leave them sitting out all day?" Jan asked.

"No, it was *just* the breakfast dishes," Jimmy said through gritted teeth. "I like to do a thorough job, OK?"

"I'll say," Jan agreed. "An hour and a half? What did you do, take before-and-after photos of each piece of silverware?"

"I guess this is the thanks I get for trying to help you out around the house," Jimmy said in a wounded voice.

"I'm sorry," Jan said with a laugh. "I know you were trying to help me, and I appreciate it."

"That's better," Jimmy said, finally satisfied. "You're welcome."

"But, come on," Jan continued with a disbelieving chuckle, *"an hour and a half? What did you do, floss between the prongs of each fork?"*

* * * * * * * * * * * * * *

How are household chores and to-do-list items handled in your home? Are the day-to-day responsibilities divided pretty evenly between you and your spouse?

Have the two of you reached an accord on which responsibilities are yours and which are his or hers? Are both of you satisfied with the way things get done in and around the house?

What if we put the same questions to your spouse? Would we get similar responses—or bemused chuckles? For some couples, household chores and everyday responsibilities are a source of tremendous friction and tension. Arguments abound in their relationship regarding who's supposed to do what and why some things don't get done.

That's a shame, because those couples may never recognize the opportunities they're missing. For many people, simple acts of service— including such common household tasks as mowing the lawn, making the bed, and changing the cat's litter box—are powerful methods of communicating love.

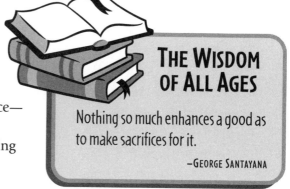

THE WISDOM OF ALL AGES

Nothing so much enhances a good as to make sacrifices for it.

—GEORGE SANTAYANA

So if you treat everyday chores as sources of minor irritation or "necessary evils," there's about a one-in-five chance that you're ignoring your spouse's primary love language.

Acts of service is one of the five primary love languages that people speak, one of the five ways people express and receive emotional love. The other four love languages are as follows:

➤ Words of affirmation

➤ Quality time

➤ Receiving gifts

➤ Physical touch

For better or worse, not everyone speaks the same love language. In fact, many husbands and wives speak love languages that are different from their spouses'. So the things that make you feel cared for and fulfilled may not even get your spouse's attention, and vice versa. It's not hard to see how such differences, if not handled properly, can become a problem in a relationship. That's why you must take it upon yourself to bridge that language barrier and learn to communicate your love for your spouse in ways that he or she understands and appreciates.

If acts of service is your spouse's primary love language, you will need to get a feel for the things you can do in, around, and outside the house that will communicate your love for your spouse and your concern for his or her happiness. You've got to learn how to show him or her the type of service acts that will make a difference in his or her life.

GLAD YOU ASKED

I really hate housework and the kind of acts of service I know my spouse appreciates. I'm just not cut out for that type of work. Are there any alternatives that will mean just as much to my spouse?

Probably not. But there's something you need to keep in mind. Your spouse probably has a pretty good idea of how distasteful most acts of service are to you. So when your spouse sees you doing those things for him or her, the impact will be magnified. The more you're willing to sacrifice–even if it's just your comfort–the more meaningful your acts of service will be. So your best bet is to bite the bullet, do the work, and let your spouse reap the benefits.

What About Your Spouse?

First, you'll need to make sure that your spouse's primary love language really *is* acts of service. You could clean bathrooms and trim hedges from now until your grandchildren are senior citizens, but if your spouse doesn't understand the acts-of-service love language, your efforts aren't going to do a thing—at least, not emotionally—for him or her.

Fortunately, with a minimum of effort on your part, you can avoid making such a long-term mistake. If you want to determine whether or not your spouse's primary love language is acts of service, all you really have to do is answer three simple questions.

1. How often does your spouse ask you to help with things around the house?

We might as well start with the most obvious clue. If the personal favors your spouse asks of you include things like dusting the entertainment center, replacing the tile on the bathtub walls, or taking care of any other household chores or responsibilities, there's a good chance that you're married to someone whose primary love language is acts of service.

In extreme cases, your spouse's repeated requests may seem like nagging to you. If, however, you understand that those requests are motivated by his or her love language, and not by a dissatisfaction with you or a perverse desire to fill your schedule with busywork, you can avoid conflicts that might otherwise put a crimp in your relationship.

You can then start planning a strategy for demonstrating your love through acts of service. Rather than making your spouse come to you with requests to get things done, you can take the initiative and do those things yourself—before your spouse has a chance to ask.

2. How much appreciation does your spouse show when you do work around the house?

Maybe your spouse is prone to giving you standing ovations every time you change a lightbulb. Maybe your spouse weeps uncontrollably at the sight of a clean toilet bowl. Or maybe your spouse just seems especially grateful or pleased when you take out the garbage. It doesn't matter *how* your spouse chooses to show his or her satisfaction; what matters is that your spouse makes it a point to let you know, verbally or nonverbally, that he or she appreciates your work.

If that's true of your spouse, it's likely that he or she places a high priority on acts of service. The expressions of appreciation that you may have chalked up to common courtesy or overexcitement may actually be subtle efforts on your spouse's part to get you to repeat certain acts of service again and again.

THE WISDOM OF ALL AGES

The applause of a single human being is of great consequence.

—SAMUEL JOHNSON

3. How diligent is your spouse in taking care of household chores?

Many people whose primary love language is acts of service are extremely conscientious about performing such acts for their spouses. You might say they make a habit of modeling the type of behavior they would like to see (and receive) from their spouses.

If your spouse makes Martha Stewart or Bob Villa look like a lazy couch potato—if he or she runs a tight ship, where household chores and everyday responsibilities are concerned—there's a very good chance that he or she will respond well to acts of service from you.

Obviously, the best way to discover your spouse's primary love language is to talk to him or her about it. Until you have an opportunity to do that, you may be able to get the information you need simply by paying attention to the things your spouse says and does.

Three Poor Excuses

Unlike words of affirmation or physical touch, there's nothing inherently romantic or obviously caring about the acts-of-service love language. Compared to the other love languages, acts of service may seem a little nondescript and, to be perfectly frank, *boring.* You won't find a lot of anniversary cards or Valentines with pictures of people folding laundry or deodorizing wastebaskets on them. In fact, because of its seemingly nonromantic nature, acts of service can be easily overlooked as a legitimate love language.

> ## THE WISDOM OF ALL AGES
>
> A thought which does not result in an action is nothing much, and an action which does not proceed from a thought is nothing at all.
>
> —GEORGE BERNANOS

Here are three of the most popular reasons people offer for neglecting or overlooking acts of service.

1. "I don't have the time."
It's a busy world we live in. Between your job and your social responsibilities, between your community/church duties and your kids' sports commitments, if you don't have something demanding your immediate attention right now, you probably will in an hour or so. A quick glance at your schedule would probably confirm that you just don't have time to do something as menial and unimportant as, say, clearing the leaves from your gutters.

Of course, you may not phrase your excuse in exactly those terms. With a little effort, you might even be able to convince your spouse that you wish you had the time to take care of things around the house or that you would really enjoy a chance to work with your hands and feel like you're really accomplishing something. If you're sincere enough, you might even be able to convince yourself of it . . . before you turn your attention to more "important" things—things that are more deserving of your valuable time.

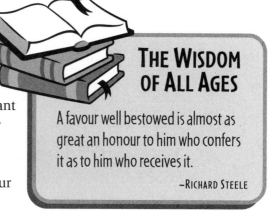

THE WISDOM OF ALL AGES

A favour well bestowed is almost as great an honour to him who confers it as to him who receives it.

—RICHARD STEELE

Regardless of how crowded your schedule is, there's one inescapable truth that you have to face: You *make* time for the things that are important to you. Priorities aren't things you *talk* about; they are things you *live*. You can't just *say* something is important to you and leave it at that. You demonstrate how important it is by dedicating your time to it.

For the sake of this chapter, we'll assume that your spouse places fairly high on your list of priorities. If that's the case, it follows that you will make time for your spouse. And if your spouse is the type of person who receives love primarily through acts of service, you know what that means for you. It means you have to find the time to do the menial and unimportant tasks that mean so much to your spouse.

2. "It's not my job."

This is the old division-of-responsibilities ploy. The excuse can best be summed up this way: "The reason I don't _____ is because it's not my responsibility." You can then fill in the blank with anything you're asked to do, from "wash dishes" to "feed the goldfish."

Sometimes the divisions are based on gender stereotypes ("That's a woman's job" or "That's no job for a woman"); sometimes they're based on family roles ("My job is to make enough money to support the family; my spouse's job is to keep the house clean and take care of the kids and pets").

The more "traditional" your own family was when you were growing up, the more likely it is that you will fall back on this excuse in your own marital relationship. If your father was the stereotypical "breadwinner" of the family and your mother was responsible for taking care of the house and kids all day, you may consider that type of arrangement to be the "right" way for a family to operate.

In our fast-changing society, the problem is that the models and patterns of the past have little or no relevance to the families of today. Do you remember watching reruns (or even the original run) of that popular 1950s TV show *Leave It to Beaver*? If the Cleavers were raising kids today, it's likely that Ward would be putting in eighty-hour weeks at the office, trying to recover from the massive financial hit he took when his Internet stocks went south. And June would be so busy hauling Wally and the Beaver back and forth between soccer tryouts, track meets, band practice, and Boy Scout bake sales that she'd barely have time to microwave burritos and open a bag of chips for dinner.

The point, at least as far as love languages are concerned, is not whether something is your "job"; the point is whether you care to demonstrate your love for your spouse in a way that is meaningful to him or her. If that's something that's really important to you, you're going to have to face the prospect of blurring the lines of responsibility in your home and doing things that aren't "your" job.

3. "I can't do it as well as my spouse does."
Some people try to excuse themselves from acts of service based on their inexperience. Their reasoning goes something like this: "What sense does it make for me to try to do a job when there's a good chance I'll only make things worse. Besides, my spouse can do the job ten times faster and ten times better than I can."

Other people may try to take things one step further and lay the blame on their parents. The justification usually goes something like this: "My mom and dad always did everything for me when I was a kid, so I never learned how to cook or do laundry or even make simple home repairs."

The good news is that when it comes to household chores and to-do-list items, an old dog can always

GLAD YOU ASKED

You warn about stereotypes. Are you suggesting that it's wrong to have specific jobs that I do and specific jobs that my spouse does?

Absolutely not. Every person on earth is uniquely gifted. The fact is, there are certain things that you can do better or more efficiently than your spouse can. Conversely, there are certain things your spouse can do better and more efficiently than you can. In order for your household to run smoothly, you and your spouse have to figure out how to put your unique gifts, strengths, skills, and abilities to use in ways that will ultimately benefit the entire family. What we are suggesting is that you don't allow stereotypes or personal preferences to dictate what you will or won't do in, around, or outside the house.

learn new tricks. It may take some time for you to become adept at certain tasks, and there may be some casualties along the way (like when white and red fabrics inevitably meet in the wrong laundry cycle), but eventually, with enough persistence and determination, you'll be able to provide the kind of acts of service that will make a difference in your spouse's life.

These are three of the most popular excuses for neglecting or overlooking acts of service. You may be able to come up with a couple more of your own, but it's unlikely that any of them will hold much water—especially when you compare them to the benefits of being able to communicate with your spouse in his or her primary love language.

Why Acts of Service Matter

Demonstrating your love through acts of service involves doing things you know your spouse would like you to do. In order to do those things effectively, you need to have at least some understanding of what makes your spouse tick and what the acts of service mean to him or her.

The first thing you need to understand is that this isn't about your spouse's "clean freak" tendencies—if, indeed, he or she has any. Until you have a grasp of the acts-of-service love language, you may suspect your spouse of using emotional blackmail to get you to clean out the attic or to walk the dog. After all, if your spouse receives feelings of love through acts of service, it only stands to reason that he or she receives feelings of rejection when those acts *aren't* done. And who wants to make his or her spouse feel rejected?

With a little time and experience under your belt, you will come to understand that it's not simply the acts themselves that are important to your spouse. You see, acts of service require . . .

> ➤ thought

> ➤ planning

> ➤ time

> ➤ effort.

And it's your willingness to sacrifice those things that make acts of service so meaningful to your spouse. When you understand that, it's not hard to see how acts of service, when done with a positive spirit, can indeed be expressions of love.

FAMILY TIES

Here's a way to give your kids a chance to demonstrate their love for your spouse through acts of service. If, like many families, you have an allowance system set up in your household, make sure you identify specifically which jobs each child is responsible for. In other words, you want to make sure your kids know exactly what they're being paid for. Once those jobs have been identified, encourage each of your kids to choose one more job to do each week for free—as an act of love for your spouse.

At Your Service

If you happen to be a novice when it comes to this particular love language, don't sweat it. Learning to express your love through acts of service doesn't require a lot of mental preparation on your part. In fact, all that's really required is a willingness to "get your hands dirty."

If you're serious about wanting to perform acts of service for your spouse, your options are practically endless. There's probably no shortage of jobs and responsibilities to be taken care of in, around, and outside your home. To get you started on the right foot, here are ten tips for performing *quality* acts of service.

1. Remember the three most important elements of a genuine act of service: attitude, attitude, and attitude.

The spirit in which you approach and undertake your acts of service will make all the difference in the world in the way your spouse receives and reacts to them. So it's important that you get the right attitude down before beginning.

No one is suggesting that you have to whistle while you work or wear a happy grin in order to make an act of service meaningful. But there are some things you'll want to keep in mind—some mistakes you'll want to avoid—for the sake of your spouse.

For one thing, you don't want to remind your spouse of other things you could be doing with your time. It's one thing to spend a Saturday afternoon pulling out a tree stump from your backyard. It's another thing to keep saying things like, "I can't believe I gave up my tee time this morning" or "I really should be working on my sales presentation for Monday's meeting" while you're doing it. The point is not to make your spouse beholden to you, but to make him or her happy. And the only way you're going to do that is if your attitude matches your actions.

And then, you don't want to tackle a project with a this-is-how-it's-done attitude. This is especially important to remember if you're treading on your spouse's territory—that is, tackling a job that he or she normally handles. Even if you believe that your way of doing things is better than your spouse's, keep your thoughts to yourself. Go about your business with modesty and respect for the work your spouse does.

THE WISDOM OF ALL AGES

To serve is beautiful, but only if it is done with joy and a whole heart and a free mind.

—PEARL S. BUCK

2. Express your admiration.

If your spouse typically does most of the work around the house, your attempts to show your love through acts of service may be eye-opening experiences for you. It's easy to take household chores and everyday responsibilities for granted, especially if your spouse is efficient in getting things done. You may have no idea how much time, energy, and effort are required to maintain the status quo of your household.

With some firsthand experience of your own, you will start to get a sense of the amount of work involved. And when you do, it would be a great gift to your spouse if you would share your discoveries with him or her.

Be sure to express your admiration for the many different jobs your spouse does day in and day out ("How in the world do you find time to get everything done around the house and still get the kids where they need to be every day?"). Show some empathy regarding the difficulties of various jobs ("I don't know where you find the energy or patience to fold and put away clothes every single day"). Apologize if you are guilty of having taken your spouse for granted on occasion ("I had no idea how hard it is to run a household and, because of that, I underestimated what you're really capable of").

3. Don't be afraid to ask, "What can I do for you?"

After making the decision to perform acts of service for your spouse, the question you need to ask yourself is, "What do I do first?" Nine times out of ten, the idea you come up with will place a distant sixteenth or seventeenth on your spouse's actual list of priorities. That's why it's important to occasionally let your spouse be your guide in choosing an act of service to tackle.

A word of warning: If your spouse is accustomed to doing household chores and related jobs himself or herself, he or she may be tempted to dismiss your offer for help out of courtesy or convenience. If that happens, it doesn't mean you're off the hook. You can't just shrug your shoulders, shake your head, and say, "Well, I tried" as you walk away. Be persistent. Let your spouse know that you're serious about wanting to demonstrate your love through acts of service. Find out what he or she would really like to have done, then do it.

Asking for your spouse's input may ruin the element of surprise, but at least you'll ensure that you and your spouse are on the same wavelength. And that's what's really important.

4. Don't shy away from distasteful tasks.

Your willingness to perform acts of service that aren't easy or pleasant will likely make a *big* impression on your spouse. After all, it's one thing to volunteer to place knives and forks on a table; it's quite another thing to volunteer to scrub couch cushions and Berber carpeting after your child is unable to hold down the Spaghetti-O's and fruit punch he had for lunch.

What it comes down to is this: Someone has to scrub the toilets. Someone has to clean the bugs from the windshield of your car. Someone has to empty the cat's litter box or scoop up after the dog. Unless you have a live-in maid, the two most

GLAD YOU ASKED

I feel like I'm being taken for granted because my spouse never acknowledges my acts of service. Is there anything I can do to change that?

It's important for you and your spouse that you not allow yourself to become a "doormat" in your marital relationship. If you feel like you're being taken for granted, share your objections with your spouse as soon as possible. Ask if he or she is satisfied with the work you do around the house. Explain how frustrating it is never to receive any acknowledgment for your work. Give your spouse a chance to explain why he or she seems to overlook your acts of service.

likely candidates for each of these jobs are you and your spouse. That means if you don't do it, your spouse will have to. And which option do you suppose would best demonstrate your love for your mate?

5. Don't overlook the small stuff.

Of course, not all acts of service are of the disgusting variety. In fact, not all acts of service require a lot of effort on your part. There are hundreds of minor, yet important, things that you can do in just a few minutes to make life a little easier for your spouse. Most of them may not even be worth writing down on a to-do list, but that doesn't mean they won't be appreciated.

For example, when you know that your spouse will be driving your car after you, adjust the seat to his or her desired position and tune the radio to his or her favorite station. (Better yet, put one of your spouse's favorite tapes in the cassette deck.) Or when you see your spouse scrambling to get to work on time, round up your partner's keys, sunglasses, jacket, and any other necessary paraphernalia and have them sitting by the door, ready to go.

Such acts may not require a lot of your time, but they go a long way toward communicating the fact that you're constantly thinking of your spouse's well-being.

6. Don't look for glory or credit.

Do you remember, as a kid, doing a job so well and being so pleased with the results that you just *had* to show your parents? If you're a newcomer to acts of service, you may find yourself experiencing similar urges. When, after twenty minutes of hard scrubbing, you see a sparkling white toilet bowl staring back at you, your first instinct may be to find your spouse, take him or her by the hand, and say, "Come look at what I did!"

THE WISDOM OF ALL AGES

The charity that is trifle to us can be precious to others.

—HOMER

Resist that urge. For one thing, acts of service aren't about you. If you're looking to have your ego stroked, find another venue. Acts of service are about demonstrating love to your spouse.

For another thing, there's probably a good chance that your spouse has done that same job, just as well, hundreds of times without once looking for critical adoration from you. So you'll only be embarrassing yourself when you call attention to something that's actually pretty unremarkable in the whole scheme of things.

Do your job with pride—and with as little fanfare and self-satisfaction as possible.

7. Let your spouse occasionally "catch" you in an act of service.

On the other hand, you don't want to do your acts of service in complete anonymity. After all, if your spouse doesn't recognize what you're doing, it's unlikely that he or she will receive much love from your acts.

So occasionally—repeat, *occasionally*—you may want to perform an act of service in a way that your spouse notices. For example, you might make it a point to cancel a weekend outing in order to complete a project that your spouse wants done. Or you might say to your spouse, "I have four hours free this evening. What would you like me to do with them?"

Spare your spouse any theatrics or histrionics. Don't try to get his or her attention through heavy sighs and groaning. Remember, your goal is not to make your spouse feel guilty or to feel sorry for you. It's to help your spouse recognize what you're willing to do in order to demonstrate your love in a way that he or she can appreciate.

8. Do the job right.

If your acts of service are something new, as far as your spouse is concerned, there's a good chance that he or she will be impressed with even a 75 percent effort on your part. The very idea of your doing something to help him or her may be enough to excuse a less-than-stellar actual effort on your part.

But that's no reason to give a 75 percent effort. If you're going to do acts of service for your spouse, you need to make sure that your efforts match the stakes. In other words, go the extra mile.

For example, instead of just cleaning out the garage, give your spouse a deluxe "garage overhaul." Depending on the condition of your garage, that might involve going through all of the stuff that has accumulated in boxes and on shelves over the years, throwing out what you don't need and organizing what you do need. It might involve scouring and scrubbing the oil stains from the floor. It might involve installing new storage shelves, replacing your old automatic garage door opener, and putting hooks in the ceiling to hang bicycles from. In other words, it will involve more than sliding a few boxes around and running a broom over whatever floor is visible.

If that seems a bit extreme, ask yourself two questions:

➤ How much is "too much" when it comes to demonstrating my love for my spouse?

➤ Why settle for a "Thank you" from my spouse when I can get a "Wow"?

9. Practice preventive maintenance.

Maybe you've heard the old saying, "An ounce of prevention is worth a pound of cure." That principle certainly applies to household chores and everyday responsibilities. In fact, doing what you can to prevent messes and extra work for your spouse can be an act of service in itself.

Preventive household maintenance may require a hefty dose of discipline, and perhaps some lifestyle changes, on your part. But if you can get in the habit of picking up after yourself, putting your clothes away, clearing your dishes from the table, and doing what you can to keep things presentable and functional in your house, your spouse will likely take note of your efforts. And that's the whole point, isn't it?

THE WISDOM OF ALL AGES

The greatest pleasure I know is to do a good action by stealth, and to have it found out by accident.

–CHARLES LAMB

10. Don't limit your possibilities for acts of service.

There are more chores and responsibilities that need to be taken care of in, around, and outside your house than you can possibly imagine. Why not try your hand at as many of them as possible? As we wrap up this chapter, we offer this incomplete list of possible acts of service for you to consider (all of which have varying degrees of difficulty and distastefulness).

FAMILY TIES

If you're not the primary caretaker of your kids—that is, if you're not the one who spends most of the day with them—you may not fully appreciate the time and energy that is required for the job. If your spouse is the one who spends most of the day with your kids, probably the most helpful act of service you can provide is to assume responsibility for your children for a while. That may involve taking them out to a park or a movie or staying at home with them while your spouse goes out. Whatever you choose to do, your goal should be to give your spouse a much-needed break.

➤ Prepare a meal.
➤ Set the table before the meal.
➤ Clear and wash the dishes after the meal.
➤ Vacuum the carpet and rugs throughout your house.
➤ Clean the toilet.
➤ Scrub the mildew from the bathroom tub and sink.
➤ Unclog the shower drain.
➤ Clean the mirrors throughout your house.
➤ Remove and clean window screens.
➤ Rub the "bug juice" from your car's bumper and windshield.
➤ Change the baby's diaper.
➤ Dust your bedroom furniture.
➤ Fix the hinges on a closet door.
➤ Stack wood for your fireplace.
➤ Replace the medicine cabinet in your bathroom.
➤ Go through your storage boxes and throw out all of the junk you find in them.
➤ Change the cat's litter box.
➤ Trim and shape the shrubs and bushes in your yard.
➤ Edge your lawn.
➤ Vacuum and clean your car's interior.

Remember, the key to successful acts of service is *genuine effort.* Even if you're a novice housekeeper at best, the fact that you even make an effort to do things to make your spouse's life easier or more pleasant will not go unnoticed or unappreciated by him or her.

Family Practice

Think you're an expert on demonstrating love to your spouse through acts of service? Here's a quiz to see how much you know.

1. Which of the following questions is least likely to help you determine whether your spouse's primary love language is acts of service?
   a. How often does my spouse ask me to help with things around the house?
   b. How much appreciation does my spouse show when I do work around the house?
   c. How diligent is my spouse in taking care of household chores?
   d. How many breaks does my spouse take when he or she cleans the house?

2. Which of the following is not a popular excuse for avoiding or neglecting acts of service?
   a. "I don't have the time."
   b. "It's not my job."
   c. "I can't do it as well as my spouse does."
   d. "There's nothing that needs to be done."

3. What is important to understand about people whose primary love language is acts of service?
   a. What really matters to them is the thought, planning, time, and effort their spouses put into the acts of service.
   b. They are all just a bunch of clean freaks.
   c. They like to use emotional blackmail to get their spouses to do their bidding.
   d. They really need to find another love language.

4. Which of the following is *not* a helpful tip to keep in mind when it comes to performing acts of service for your spouse?
   a. Be willing to do the distasteful tasks.
   b. Give a little less than 100 percent effort when your spouse isn't looking.
   c. Don't look for glory or credit.
   d. On occasion, ask your spouse, "What can I do for you?"

5. Which of the following is not true of acts of service?
   a. Preventive maintenance is just as important as any cleaning or repairing jobs.
   b. Minor ones can mean just as much as major ones.
   c. It's by far the most difficult love language to learn.
   d. It's every bit as valid a love language as words of affirmation or physical touch are.

Answers: (1) d, (2) d, (3) a, (4) b, (5) c

CHAPTER 7

Making Contact

LOVE LANGUAGE #5: PHYSICAL TOUCH

SNAPSHOT

Leon stumbled into the kitchen, shielding his eyes from the bright morning sun.

"Good morning, sleepyhead," Wanda greeted him. "The coffee's on and the bagels are in the refrigerator."

"Thanks, Hon," Leon mumbled as he threw his arms around her.

Wanda stiffened a little, then gave him a quick pat on the back before twisting out of his embrace.

Leon looked at an imaginary stopwatch on his wrist. "You lasted 2.8 seconds that time," he announced. "I believe that's a personal best for you."

"Don't start with me this morning," Wanda said, as she grabbed a utensil from the counter. "I've got a spatula and I'm not afraid to use it."

"What's the problem this time?" Leon asked. "Is my deodorant not working overtime? Is it my morning

SNEAK PREVIEW

1. Initiating physical contact with your spouse, through playful pats, kisses, hugs, and caresses can be a powerful expression of your love for him or her.

2. People whose primary love language is physical touch have an emotional need for contact with their spouses; however, this love language should not be equated with a strong physical desire for sexual intercourse.

3. The key to giving your spouse the kind of love he or she needs through physical touch is communication—that is, talking to him or her about what does and doesn't feel good.

breath? Or is your 'sensitive skin' acting up again?"

"There's no *problem*," Wanda snapped. "I just don't feel the need to touch people twenty-four hours a day."

"Are you saying that I do?" Leon asked.

Wanda took a deep breath. "All I know is that every time I turn around you're either rubbing my shoulders, putting your arm around me, tickling me, or giving me bear hugs," she said.

"You're right," Leon replied with mock solemnity. "Those things have no place in a marital relationship. People will start thinking that we actually love each other or something."

"That's not what I mean!" Wanda objected. "I'm just saying, isn't it possible to show love without always hugging or kissing or caressing or doing some other kind of touching?"

"My wife, the incurable romantic," Leon muttered as he gave Wanda an exaggerated roll of his eyes. He pretended to think for a moment, then said, "I suppose we could draft a formal resolution and hammer out the specific details of our love."

"Don't get smart with me," Wanda warned.

"We could even shake hands formally after signing the agreement," Leon continued. "That is, if you're comfortable with it."

"Are you finished yet?" Wanda asked.

"Almost," Leon replied. "Hey, we could also set up some kind of penalty system in our relationship—like in football, with 'illegal hands to the body' and that kind of stuff. How does that sound?"

Wanda shook her head. "It sounds to me like you don't need physical contact with anyone else, because you're already a little 'touched,' in the head, if you know what I mean."

* * * * * * * * * * * * * *

There's nothing particularly radical or ground-breaking about the concept of communicating love through physical touch. Child development experts have long known that babies who are held, hugged, rocked, and kissed develop healthier emotional lives than babies who are left untouched for long periods of time.

What we tend to forget is that for many people that need for tactile love never goes away. Physical touch does for them what words of affirmation, quality time, receiving gifts, and acts of service do for others; it meets their deepest love needs. Without physical touch, they feel unloved and unwanted.

If such a person marries someone who doesn't understand the physical touch love language, it can present some interesting challenges to their relationship.

Doug's Story

Doug grew up in a home in which physical affection was very nearly absent. His father, a distant man by nature, was not prone to displays of emotion or expressions of any kind. On one or two occasions—his college graduation and maybe his wedding day—Doug remembered his father offering his congratulations with a handshake. Beyond that, Doug could recall little or no physical contact with his father. To say his father wasn't a "hands-on" type of guy would be a laughable understatement.

However, Doug's mother made his father seem like Leo Buscaglia or Richard Simmons in comparison. She seemed to regard physical contact of any kind as distasteful. When he was in college, Doug learned from a cousin that his mother may have been sexually abused as a young girl. Doug never had a chance to ask her about it before she died. But looking back, he realized that could very well have been the case. His mother's actions and demeanor seemed to be consistent with what he knew about victims of abuse. Obviously, Doug had no clue about his mother's past when he was growing up. He just knew that his mom didn't care for hugs and kisses the way other moms did.

Not surprisingly, based on his upbringing, Doug himself isn't very comfortable with physical interaction or visible expressions of love and affection. That's not to say he's weird about it or anything. He doesn't wear surgical gloves or wash his hands ten times after coming into contact with someone. He's just naturally reserved. He keeps his hands to himself and expects others to do the same.

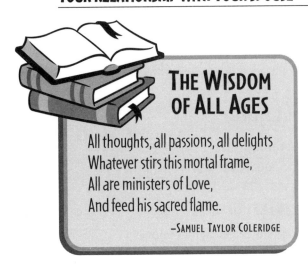

THE WISDOM OF ALL AGES

All thoughts, all passions, all delights
Whatever stirs this mortal frame,
All are ministers of Love,
And feed his sacred flame.

–SAMUEL TAYLOR COLERIDGE

Carrie's Story

Carrie grew up in a home in which physical affection was a constant. Her father was the type of man who at Christmastime would occasionally hug complete strangers in the mall when the spirit of the season overtook him. (This was back before people talked about things like *sexual harassment.*) At the time, his behavior was considered odd and a little forward, but never inappropriate. People usually walked away from his embraces with big smiles on their faces.

Carrie's mother was no shrinking violet, either. All of the kids in the neighborhood called her "Mom." Depending on her mood, she would greet kids and adults alike with bear hugs, pats on the back, hair touslings, and sometimes even playful kicks to the "fanny" (as she called it).

As you might imagine, Carrie's parents' attitude toward physical expressions of love *rubbed off* on her (sorry, we couldn't resist). As a result, Carrie is a very tactile person. In conversation, she makes a habit of grabbing people's arms or touching their legs when she wants to make a point. In church and other social settings, she's quick to offer hugs and encouraging pats. Her friends joke about putting on football equipment when they see her coming, because of her physical nature.

When Doug and Carrie Got Together

Never let it be said that Cupid doesn't have a mischievous sense of humor—and a finely honed sense of irony. Improbable as it may seem, Doug and Carrie fell in love at college. A year after graduation, they got married.

Within six months, they began noticing some problems in their relationship. Care to guess what the root of their problems was? Here are a couple of hints. Doug told Carrie that he felt "smothered" by her constant need for affection. Carrie told Doug that she felt isolated from him and that she couldn't stand his "coldness" toward her.

If you guessed that Doug and Carrie's problems were the result of speaking two different love languages, give yourself a round of applause. If you guessed that

Carrie's love language is physical touch and Doug's isn't, give yourself a standing ovation. And if this situation seems at all familiar to you, keep reading.

What You Should Know About Love Languages

Before we delve into the topic of physical touch, let's take a quick look at the topic of love languages in general. There are five major love languages that people speak, five methods by which they demonstrate and understand emotional love from their spouses. Physical touch is one of those love languages. The other four are . . .

➤ Words of affirmation

➤ Quality time

➤ Receiving gifts

➤ Acts of service

You need to understand that not everyone speaks and responds to the same love language. In fact, there's a good chance that you and your spouse don't speak the same love language. For the sake of your relationship, then, what you have to do is figure out your spouse's primary love language and become fluent in it.

This chapter is for people whose spouses respond to physical touch. If your spouse falls into that category (or if you suspect that he or she might fall into it), read on. You'll find the information you need to begin speaking his or her language.

FAMILY TIES

You can tell a lot about your spouse's primary love language from the way he or she interacts with your kids. If your spouse does a lot of chasing, wrestling, tickling, hugging, and high-fiving with your kids, it may be a way of expressing love through his or her primary love language. You should also know that, for better or worse, your spouse's interaction with your kids will go a long way toward shaping the way they express and understand love with their own future spouses.

Are You Married to a Physical Toucher?

Of course, the first thing you need to do is to confirm that physical touch is your spouse's primary love language. That probably won't be a very difficult thing to do.

Physical touch is probably the most obvious of all the love languages. If your spouse's primary love language is physical touch, you probably already have a pretty good idea of it. If you don't, however, there are three questions you can ask yourself to help you reach a conclusion.

1. How physically demonstrative is your spouse?

When your spouse is happy, does he or she show it by hugging or high-fiving? When your spouse is talking to you, does he or she make a point of touching you? Is your spouse prone to giving impromptu back rubs? Does he or she like to wrestle or tickle?

If you answered yes to one or more of these questions, it's likely that physical touch is your spouse's primary love language.

2. How often does your spouse complain about not feeling close to you?

People whose primary love language is physical touch equate contact, tactile interaction, with closeness. So, if your spouse often says he or she feels distant from you or as though the two of you aren't connecting, he or she may be referring to physical contact. You may be able to safely assume that your spouse receives love through physical touch.

3. How does your spouse respond in the absence of physical touch?

If you notice your spouse withdrawing from you or becoming more irritable and distant in the absence of regular contact with you, that's a pretty good sign that physical touch is his or her primary love language. These absences of touch are most obvious after long business trips or in the aftermath of heated arguments, when the two of you aren't communicating.

Remember, if physical touch energizes your spouse—as it does with most people for whom it is the primary love language—it follows that the absence of physical touch will have a draining effect on him or her.

Physical Touch: What It Is and What It Isn't

Many spouses, particularly wives, look at the list of the five primary love languages, see the words *physical touch*, and say, "Aha! My spouse seems to have a constant need for sex, so that must be his primary love language!" However, you should not necessarily jump to that conclusion.

In order to make an informed identification of your spouse's love language, you first have to separate his or her physical needs from his or her emotional needs. For men, the strong desire for sexual intercourse has a physical root. Males were created with a *biological* need for sexual release. In other words, men are wired in such a way that sex feels necessary for them.

That doesn't mean sex—or the physical touch that goes with it—is an emotional need. If that's a sticking point for you—if you're not sure whether or not physical touch is your spouse's primary love language—try answering these questions:

➤ Does your spouse seem to enjoy holding hands with you?

➤ Does your spouse like to be patted, stroked, and caressed in a loving, but nonsexual, way?

➤ Does your spouse like to be hugged?

➤ Does your spouse enjoy kissing as an expression of affection, as opposed to a prelude for sex?

If you answered no to one or more of these questions, physical touch may not be your spouse's primary love language—regardless of what his biological urges may be toward you.

I Married a Physical Toucher

If your spouse's primary love language is physical touch, there are some things you need to understand about the way he or she perceives physical contact. Whether he or she verbalizes it or not, your spouse's mind-set can probably be summed up this way: *Whatever there is of me resides in my body; so to treat my body with love, through purposeful, caring contact, is to show me love.*

Just as important to understand is the flip side of that sentiment, the mind-set that can be summed up this way: *To resist, ignore, or avoid contact with my body is to resist, ignore, and avoid me.*

It's not overstating the matter to say that physical contact can make or break a relationship for the person whose primary love language is physical touch. For

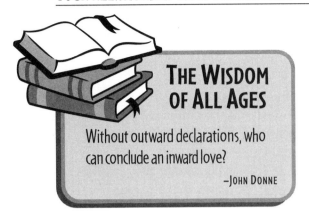

this person, the feelings that are communicated through a hug— or the refusal to hug—register much more vividly than the words "I love you" or "I hate you." Likewise, a physical expression of anger, such as a push or a slap in the face, will register much more starkly with a person whose primary love language is physical touch.

To take that one step further, a sexual infidelity, which would damage any relationship, would be especially devastating to a spouse whose primary love language is physical touch. Not only must he or she work through the betrayal and dishonesty inherent in all extramarital relationships, he or she must also deal with the fact that his or her spouse demonstrated love physically to someone else while withholding the same physical love from him or her.

What it comes down to is this: Providing your spouse with financial security, material possessions, stimulating conversation, and constant praise and encouragement is fine, but if physical touch is what your spouse craves and you don't offer it, none of those other things will ultimately matter. All your spouse will experience is the rejection that comes from not receiving tactile love.

Physical Education

For those of you who skipped Biology 101 in school, we're going to offer a quick refresher course on the "tactile functions" of the human body. (And, yes, you will be quizzed on this material, so stay awake.) Our skin contains millions of tiny receptors that, when touched or pressed, send impulses (via the nervous system) to the brain. The brain then processes and interprets those impulses, allowing us to perceive the object that touched us as being hot or cold, smooth or sharp, hard or soft. Depending on the nature of the touch, we will experience it as pain or pleasure. We will also interpret it as being loving or hostile in nature.

Got that? OK, let's move on.

These receptors aren't scattered evenly over the body. Instead, they are grouped in clusters. The result is that certain areas of the body are more sensitive than others. The more sensors in a cluster, the more sensitive that area of the body will be. The tip of the tongue, the tips of the fingers, and the tip of the nose are among the most sensitive areas of the body. The back of the shoulders is generally the least sensitive area.

What does all this scientific mumbo jumbo mean for you? Well, with millions of your spouse's tactile sensors to work with, it means you can express your love for your spouse just about anywhere on his or her body. That opens up the playing field quite a bit, doesn't it? It means you don't have to stick with the same two or three "touching zones" all of the time. It means you can be creative and try different kinds of touches on different parts of your spouse's body.

The Right Touch– and the Wrong Ones

That's not to say that all touches will bring about the same results. Some forms of physical contact are bound to bring your spouse more pleasure than others. Of course, the only way to learn for sure what works for your spouse and what doesn't is to ask him or her. After all, your spouse is the one to whom you're trying to show love.

GLAD YOU ASKED

When we first got married, it seemed like my spouse and I couldn't keep our hands off each other. Now it seems we barely have any contact at all. What causes couples to drift apart, physically speaking?

Busyness and indifference, for the most part. If you're like most people, your schedule is so packed and your mind is so occupied by other commitments that you don't have time to shower your spouse with affection, the way he or she (or you) would like. The other culprit is indifference, a lack of interest in what your spouse is thinking or doing. If you're not particularly concerned about what your spouse needs, you're probably not going to

Let your spouse guide you in understanding what he or she perceives as a loving touch and what he or she perceives as an irritating or uncomfortable touch. If you want to put a name to it, call it learning his or her "love dialect." You already know that physical touch is his or her love language; now it's time to get more specific in your communication.

If your spouse indicates that certain kinds of physical contact are uncomfortable or irritating, stop using them. You may not understand why your spouse finds them irritating, but that doesn't matter. All that matters is that you respect your spouse's wishes.

GLAD YOU ASKED

I suffered some physical abuse as a child and, as a result, I have problems with being touched and with touching others. How can I get comfortable with showing love to my spouse, whose primary love language is physical touch?

You really need to talk to a professional counselor to work through the pain and damage caused by your abuse. Until you do that, you will not be able to give your spouse the kind of love he or she craves–at least, not in a way that's comfortable to you. And if you're not comfortable, your spouse probably won't be comfortable, either.

If you think we're being a little uptight, look at it this way. If you insist on using touches that your spouse dislikes, not only are you throwing the whole concept of love languages out the window, you're actually communicating the *opposite* of love to him or her. What you're saying to your spouse in those circumstances is that you aren't terribly concerned about his or her needs. Worse yet, you're communicating the fact that you don't necessarily mind bringing displeasure to your spouse. And if you have any desire whatsoever for a healthy relationship, that's the last thing you want to convey.

Know When to Say When

Vince learned that lesson the hard way. He had grown up with a father who expressed his love through tickling. Every night when Vince's dad would come home from work, he would chase each of his three sons around the house until he caught them. He would hold each one down and tickle him until the boy was gasping for air. Between fits of ticklish laughter, the boys would scream, "No!" and "Help!" but their father never let up until he was good and ready.

Because that kind of behavior was normal to them, Vince and his brothers never thought much about the ticklings. They didn't exactly look forward to them, but they never minded them much, either.

When Vince married Angela, he brought those same notions of how love is expressed into his marriage. Whenever Angela looked especially vulnerable, Vince would grab her and tickle her until she was out of breath. He thought it was a cute way of showing his love for her.

Angela, on the other hand, dreaded what she called Vince's "tickling attacks." She tried yelling at him to leave her alone, screaming for help, staying silent, and anything else she could think of to get him to stop. But nothing seemed to work. Vince couldn't understand why Angela would get upset with him over something that seemed so natural.

One afternoon, the tickling came to a halt in a way that Vince has regretted ever since. Vince had grabbed Angela from behind, the way he usually did when he tickled her. This time, instead of falling to the ground in a defensive pose the way she usually did, Angela tried to squirm from his grasp. As she did, she twisted her arm in a way that wrenched her shoulder from its socket with a loud, sickening "pop."

Vince tried to apologize all the way to the hospital, but Angela wouldn't listen to him. She just stared out the car window and sobbed. As he explained what happened to Angela, the emergency room nurse gave Vince a suspicious stare—the kind she probably gave most of the wife beaters she encountered in her job. Vince half-expected to be questioned by the police before the day was over, but Angela managed to convince the attending physician that Vince's account of how the injury occurred was the truth.

Vince doesn't tickle Angela anymore, but the two of them haven't been able to fully reconcile since the incident. Embarrassment and remorse have put a little emotional distance between them. Vince is embarrassed and remorseful about taking his tickling fetish too far. Angela, on the other hand, is embarrassed and remorseful about the fact that she never sat Vince down and explained to him exactly how she felt about his tickling before it came to such a dramatic ending.

Sharing a Love Language

It probably won't come as much of a surprise to learn that Vince's primary love language is physical touch. But would it surprise you to learn that Angela's primary love language is also physical touch?

We're not suggesting that all "bad touch" incidents will end like Vince and Angela's did. But their experience raises a possibility that you must consider. If you and your spouse share the same primary love language—physical touch—you need to make sure that you keep your assumptions in check.

GLAD YOU ASKED

How can I let my spouse know that I can't stand certain kinds of touch without hurting his or her feelings?

Depending on how urgent the situation is, you can try one of two strategies. The first is immediate feedback. If your spouse touches you too hard, say, "Ouch!" or "That hurts!" right away. If your spouse touches you in a way that makes you uncomfortable, say, "I really don't like that." It may seem a little harsh at first, but if you're specific enough, you'll be doing your spouse a favor by letting him or her know exactly what you don't like. The second option is to suggest an alternative kind of touching that you do like. When your spouse touches you in a way (or place) that hurts or irritates you, place his or her hands somewhere you like to be touched and say something like, "You know what I'd really like from you? One of your world-famous back rubs."

Specifically, you'll need to avoid the assumption that the kind of physical contact that brings you pleasure will do the same for your spouse. The fact is, there's a good chance that it won't. The two of you probably don't share the same taste in friends, clothes, movies, or music, so why would you assume that you share the same touch preferences?

The way to learn precisely what your spouse prefers is also the way your spouse will learn precisely what you prefer: communication. Pay attention to your spouse's reactions and body language when you touch him or her. What kinds of contact does he seem to enjoy, and what kinds does he seem to shy away from or simply "endure"? Answer those questions enough times and in enough situations, and you'll get a good sense of how to communicate love to your spouse in a way that he appreciates.

When Touch Is a Must

Learning to provide your spouse with the kind of physical touch he or she needs may take some time, especially if you don't come from a family that places a high priority on physical expressions of emotion. There are certain times, however, when you absolutely *must* forget about your own comfort level and give your spouse the physical love he or she needs.

We are referring specifically to crisis situations. If you're married, you and your spouse will face crisis times together, including . . .

➤ the declining health and eventual death of your parents.
➤ accidents that injure, maim, or cripple loved ones.
➤ disease and other health problems.
➤ firings and layoffs.
➤ emotional breakdowns.
➤ fears about the future.
➤ threats to your or your family's safety.

The most important thing you can do for your spouse during times of crisis is to show your love. If your spouse's primary love language is physical touch, your job during trying circumstances is to hold your spouse and to give him or her an actual shoulder to cry on.

Any words of comfort or encouragement you have to offer may be *tolerated,* but any act of physical compassion you have to offer will likely be *appreciated.* There's a big difference between being a person who's merely tolerated and being someone who's genuinely appreciated.

Crises offer a unique opportunity for expressing your love. Your tender touches will likely be remembered by your spouse long after the crises are over. Your failure to provide tender touches may never be forgotten.

Getting Ideas

There are two ways you can show love to your spouse through physical touch. The first method we'll call *explicit contact,* and the second method we'll call *implicit contact.*

Explicit touches are those that demand your full attention and often involve some advance planning on your part. Back rubs and sexual foreplay as a prelude to intercourse are two examples of explicit touches.

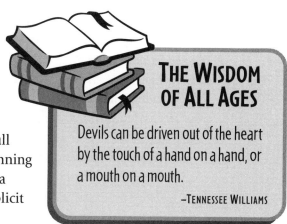

THE WISDOM OF ALL AGES

Devils can be driven out of the heart by the touch of a hand on a hand, or a mouth on a mouth.

–Tennessee Williams

Explicit touches may also require you to develop an understanding of *how* to communicate love to your spouse in a certain way for maximum effectiveness. For example, if a back rub communicates love to your spouse, you may want to invest some time and energy—and perhaps a little coinage—in learning the art of massage and relaxation therapy. (You can probably find a whole shelf full of titles at your local video store, if you're so inclined.)

THE WISDOM OF ALL AGES

kisses are a better fate than wisdom

—E E CUMMINGS

If sexual intercourse is your spouse's primary dialect, you may want to invest some time and energy in learning how to please and satisfy your mate sexually. You can get the information you need through frank, detailed discussions together. Beyond that, you can read books and articles on the art of lovemaking.

Implicit touches are those that require little time or planning, but which still convey a boatload of meaning and emotion to your spouse. Because implicit touches require less involvement than explicit ones, the opportunities for implicit touch are much more plentiful.

Here are a few specific examples of how you can use implicit touch to communicate your love for your spouse.

➤ Put your hand on your spouse's arm as you look over his or her shoulder to read a newspaper article.
➤ As you pass in the hallway, instead of trying to make a wide berth around your spouse, make as much contact as possible as you slide your way past him or her.
➤ Instead of anchoring the opposite side of the couch when you watch a video with your spouse, plop yourself down right next to him or her.
➤ Give your spouse frequent high fives when you play, compete, or exercise together.
➤ Give your spouse a quick pat on the rear end when no one is looking.
➤ Flag your spouse down in the driveway as he or she is pulling away in the car. When your spouse rolls down thE window to see what you want, plant a kiss on his or her cheek.

➤ Rub your spouse's knee under the table the next time you eat at a restaurant.

➤ Grab your spouse's hand as you walk through the mall, just like you did when you were teenagers.

➤ Put your arm around your spouse while you share a tub of popcorn in a movie theater.

Chances are, you looked at this list of implicit touch ideas and were underwhelmed. Your first reaction may have been, *Is that all it takes to give my spouse pleasure or a sense of my love?* And the answer is, quite likely, *yes.* Obviously, you can and should learn to touch your spouse in a way he or she desires. But that doesn't mean that your touching has to be any more complicated or involved than the ideas on this list.

What More Do You Want?

If you're still not sure about this physical touch stuff—or if perhaps your spirit is willing but your body is, well, less than willing—here are three tips to get you started on your way toward fluency in your spouse's primary love language.

FAMILY TIES

Few things in this world communicate genuine love and affection as quickly or as effectively as a child's hug or kiss. If your spouse's primary love language is physical touch, you can do him or her a lifelong favor by training your children to demonstrate their love for your spouse through physical gestures such as hugs and kisses. Call it the gift that keeps on giving.

1. Share your feelings with your spouse.

If physical touch isn't something that comes naturally to you, you need to let your spouse know it. The news may be a little disappointing or upsetting to him or her at first, but ultimately your spouse will likely appreciate your openness and honesty.

That's not to say you should use your discomfort as an excuse for not providing your spouse with physical touch. What we're suggesting is that you lay your cards on the table and say, "I don't have a lot of experience in expressing myself physically, but I'm going to do my best to give you what you need. Just please be patient with me as I learn."

Chances are, nothing will be more meaningful to your spouse than your willingness to explore uncharted emotional territory for his or her sake.

Remember, you want to maintain your own comfort zone, too. Honesty is one of the best ways to do that. If you're self-conscious or uncomfortable with a certain area of physical contact, let your spouse know. Talk about your feelings and try to reach some compromise. Later, if you become comfortable with providing that kind of physical contact, it will mean all the more to your spouse because of your willingness to overcome your initial reluctance.

2. Keep track of how often you touch your spouse.

If you don't share your spouse's primary love language, you may not think about physical touch more than, say, two or three times a month. And that's not good news for your spouse. That's why it's important for you to know how often you're actually providing your spouse with physical expressions of love.

Don't allow obliviousness or inadvertent neglect to damage your relationship. Stay on top of your "physical touch schedule" in the same way you stay on top of your social schedule. If that means you have to keep a journal with entries like "Touched his shoulder at 6:52 A.M." or "Held hands for fourteen minutes at Kmart," do it.

3. Take it easy.

Earlier in the chapter we told you what happened to Vince and Angela when Vince carried his physical touching a little too far. Before we wrap up this chapter, we want to give you one final warning about keeping a rein on your physical impulses when it comes to your spouse. Keep in mind that there's a fine line between *playful* aggressiveness and *scary* aggressiveness. Your goal should be to stay as far away from that line as possible.

Obviously you can't learn *exactly* how to touch your spouse from a book like this. That's something the two of you are going to have to work out through a process of trial and error. If, however, you

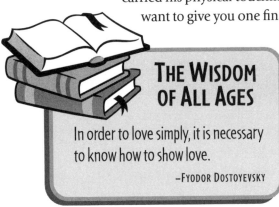

THE WISDOM OF ALL AGES

In order to love simply, it is necessary to know how to show love.

–FYODOR DOSTOYEVSKY

demonstrate a *willingness* to provide physical expressions of love for your spouse, following the guidelines we've presented in this book, you'll be well on your way to creating a healthy, loving, mutually satisfying, and lifelong relationship.

Family Practice

Think you're an expert on showing love to your spouse through physical touch? Here's a quiz to see how much you know.

1. What have child development experts found to be true of babies who experience significant physical touch, as compared to babies who are left for long periods of time without physical contact?
   a. They need to be bathed more often.
   b. They bruise less easily.
   c. They are more likely to develop healthy emotional lives.
   d. They learn to walk much sooner.

2. Which of the following questions is least likely to help you determine whether your spouse's primary love language is physical touch?
   a. How does my spouse respond in the absence of physical touch?
   b. How sensitive is my spouse's skin?
   c. How often does my spouse complain about not feeling close to me?
   d. How physically demonstrative is my spouse?

3. What is a "wrong" physical touch?
   a. One that irritates your spouse
   b. One that you learn in a sex manual
   c. One that your spouse has to tell you he or she likes
   d. One that is not listed in this book

4. When is physical touch an absolute necessity?
   a. After a big argument
   b. When dinner gets burned
   c. The first thing in the morning
   d. In times of crisis

5. Which of the following is *not* a helpful tip to keep in mind when it comes to giving your spouse physical touch?

   a. Always check with your friends before trying a new kind of touch on your spouse.

   b. Share your feelings with your spouse.

   c. Take it easy.

   d. Keep track of how often you touch your spouse.

Answers: (1) c, (2) b, (3) a, (4) d, (5) a

"THE WORLD'S EASIEST GUIDE"

Your Relationship
With Your Kids

8

An Old Family Recipe, Part 1

FIVE INGREDIENTS OF A HEALTHY FAMILY

SNAPSHOT

Martin looked around the dinner table at his wife and three kids. "Now *this* is the way a family is supposed to eat: everyone at the table together, enjoying each other's compan—"

"Stop elbowing me, Sam!" Hannah cried as she gave her brother a shove.

"If you don't like it, scoot your chair over!" Sam barked back.

"Stop it, both of you," Pamela warned. "Your father is trying to talk!"

"Sorry, Mom," Hannah and Sam replied in unison.

Martin sighed and continued. "What I was going to say is that there are some things I'd like to see us start doing to grow closer as a family."

"Does that mean I don't have to move my chair?" Hannah asked.

"That's *not* the kind of closeness I'm talking about!"

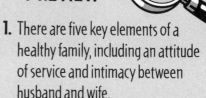

SNEAK PREVIEW

1. There are five key elements of a healthy family, including an attitude of service and intimacy between husband and wife.

2. An attitude of service fosters a sense of interdependence among family members and encourages them to recognize and meet each other's needs.

3. Intimacy between husband and wife is necessary because their relationship is the bedrock on which the entire family is built.

155

Martin snapped. Then he regained his composure and continued. "I've been reading a book on family relationships and—"

Hannah dropped her fork. "Book!" she gasped. "Oh, no! I left my history book at school, and we've got a big test tomorrow!" She stood up and threw her napkin on the table. "I've got to call Maggie to see if I can study with her tonight."

"You have to do that *now*?" Martin asked. "I was just getting ready to talk about what we can do to make sure that our family is healthy."

"Dad, come on," Hannah said. "I'm talking about something *important* here."

Martin dismissed her with a wave of his hand. "OK, I'll fill you in on the details later," he said. Then he turned back to the table and continued. "As I was saying, there are some suggestions and exercises in the book that I'd like to put into practice in our fam—"

"Practice!" Sam shouted as he jumped from his chair. "Oh, no! I forgot that Coach changed soccer practice from Wednesday to today! I've got to be at Woodland Park by 6:15!"

Pamela tossed her napkin on the table and stood. "Get your bag from your room," she instructed. "I'll be in the car waiting for you."

"What about our family dinner and discussion?" Martin asked.

"I'm sorry, Honey," Pamela said as she fished around in her purse for her car keys. "It looks like the real world is intruding on your big plans."

"No, no, that's fine," Martin sighed. He pointed to his remaining son at the table. "David and I will continue the conversation ourselves. So, tell me, Dave, what do *you* think is the key to a happy family?"

"A great big hug and a kiss from me to you," David replied with a big smile.

"Pamela, did you hear that?" Martin gasped. "David just told me that our family needs more one-on-one displays of affection!"

"Honey," Pamela replied with a sympathetic pat on the back, "he's only eighteen months old. He was singing the *Barney* theme song."

* * * * * * * * * * * * * * *

You've probably heard the old saying, "Everyone talks about the weather, but no one ever does anything about it." The same thing might be said of the family. It seems you can't pick up a newspaper or magazine or turn on a news program without reading or hearing about a growing problem facing families today. If it's not divorce, it's mothers and fathers who both work outside the home. If it's not child abuse, it's emotional neglect. If it's not alcoholism among parents, it's drug use among kids. If it's not a lack of values in the older generation, it's a lack of ambition in the younger one. And on and on it goes.

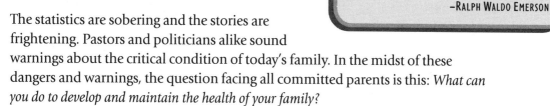

THE WISDOM OF ALL AGES

We put our love where we have put our labor.

–RALPH WALDO EMERSON

The statistics are sobering and the stories are frightening. Pastors and politicians alike sound warnings about the critical condition of today's family. In the midst of these dangers and warnings, the question facing all committed parents is this: *What can you do to develop and maintain the health of your family?*

Gimme Five

If you're looking for suggestions, here's one. Your first step should be to decide what a healthy family looks like. We've identified five ingredients that are a recipe for a healthy family. As you examine your own family, you can use these ingredients, or characteristics, as a checklist to help you determine which areas you need to focus on.

The five ingredients of a healthy family are

> ➤ An attitude of service

> ➤ Intimacy between husband and wife

> ➤ Parents who teach and train

> ➤ Children who obey and honor parents

> ➤ Husbands who are loving leaders

In this chapter, we will focus on the first two ingredients of a healthy family: an attitude of service and intimacy between husband and wife. The other three ingredients are explored in detail in chapter 9.

Ingredient #1: An Attitude of Service

Many people enter into marriage with misguided expectations—that is, they expect to be serviced by their spouses. In the throes of romantic love, they assume that their spouses will do everything in their power to make them happy for the rest of their lives. For better or worse, if those expectations somehow manage to survive the wedding day, they will likely die a quick death on the honeymoon. And when premarital expectations run into marital reality, the result is seldom pretty. It won't take long for those people with high expectations to realize that (1) *their* happiness is not the sole reason for their spouses' existence, and (2) their spouses are entering the marriage with expectations and agendas of their own.

You'd think that those two realizations would put an end to self-serving expectations, but you'd be wrong. The hopefulness that existed before the wedding may turn into resentment, but the expectations will still be there. And when kids come along, those expectations will be passed on to them, adding to the family fun.

It Is Better to Give . . .

Unless those expectations and views are corrected, the family will miss out on one of life's great mysteries: True fulfillment and happiness come not from being served, but from serving. To put it in more recognizable terms, it is better to give than to receive.

Of course, that promise of fulfillment and happiness assumes that the serving or giving is being done in the right spirit. If it's not, it's not really service—at least, not the kind of loving service we're talking about in this chapter. For example, true service is not given in a spirit of fear. If your spouse and kids are serving you because they're afraid of your reaction if they don't, they are not serving you in love.

Loving service is given freely. It is given out of a desire to make another person happy. And it is all the more meaningful because of it.

In a healthy, functional family, loving service should be the order of the day. Between folding laundry and feeding pets, making beds and mopping floors, preparing meals and washing cars, there's certainly enough opportunities for service to go around. What you, your spouse, and your kids must understand is that if one of you chooses not to take advantage of those service opportunities, the end result is more work for everyone else in the family.

Working with an Attitude

Unfortunately, a spirit of service isn't something you can dictate. You can't announce, "Starting tomorrow, everyone in this family is going to have a serving spirit." It doesn't work that way. A serving spirit is something that must be instilled over time. And the earlier you start instilling it in your kids, the quicker they will adopt it.

The way to start is to teach your kids to work. You'll note that we didn't say "teach your kids the *value* of work." This isn't a place for homilies or stories about your grandfather who worked in a coal mine twenty-two hours a day, seven days a week. We're talking about *physically* training your children to do particular jobs around the house. We're talking about letting them work with you as you load dishes in the dishwasher, vacuum the floor, clean the bathtub, and change the oil in your car. We're talking about showing your kids what to do and then letting them do it themselves. We're talking about on-the-job training.

GLAD YOU ASKED

How can I correct a poor job by one of my children without making him or her feel discouraged or unappreciated? Use good timing. Don't start criticizing or correcting immediately after a job is finished. Instead, acknowledge and praise your child's effort. Then, the next time your child prepares to do the same job, offer some pointers to help him or her avoid making the same mistakes.

By giving your kids the knowledge and the confidence to do various jobs, you are removing one of the biggest obstacles to loving service. No longer will your kids be able to plead ignorance or inexperience when jobs need to be done.

Of course, teaching your kids *how* to do household chores is only one step in

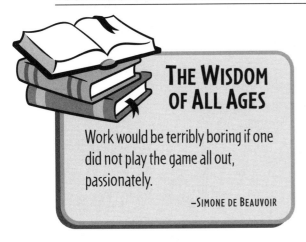

developing an attitude of service in your family. There's also the little matter of helping them understand the *purpose* of learning those chores, the reason for doing the work.

An attitude of service is much more than a willingness to get work done. In a healthy family, members have the sense that doing something good for the benefit of other family members—even if it's washing their dishes or folding their clothes—is, well, noble. They believe that in completing mundane and often thankless tasks, they are doing something genuinely worthwhile. And they get an emotional sense of satisfaction from doing them.

Making an Attitude of Service a Reality in Your Family

If you're having a hard time picturing your kids, your spouse, or even yourself committing that fully to the concept of loving service, keep your mind open. You may be surprised at how capable you and your family are.

To get you started, here are three practical tips designed to introduce and foster an attitude of service in your family.

1. Identify current examples of service going on in your home.

Chances are, there are already more than a few regular acts of service going on in your home. The problem is, the rest of the family may not be aware of them.

When your family is together for a meal or a long car ride, make a point of throwing a spotlight on those acts of service.

If possible, find an example of service on the part of every person in your family. When you reveal each act of service, let that person know how much his or her service is appreciated and how, exactly, that service benefits the family. For example . . .

➤ Taking out the trash allows your family to live in a presentable, clean-smelling home, and it keeps away would-be fly and ant invaders.

➤ Washing dishes kills the germs that come from food residue and avoids embarrassment when you have dinner guests.

➤ Walking the dog keeps your family's beloved companion fit and happy.

Once your family recognizes that a spirit of service already exists to some degree in your home, they may be more inclined to take that spirit to the next level and become more obvious in their service.

2. Find out what kind of service your family members would like.

As a follow-up to the first step, give each member of your family a chance to share one thing he or she would like done by another member of the family. This service request may involve anything (within reason) that can be done by another family member. For example . . .

➤ Barry may ask his sister to organize his closet in the same way she organized her own.

➤ Lita may ask her mother to make homemade pizza for her sleepover on Friday night.

➤ Joan may ask her husband to serve her breakfast in bed on Saturday morning.

➤ Melvin may ask his son to edge the lawn before houseguests arrive on Monday.

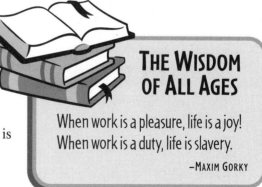

THE WISDOM OF ALL AGES

When work is a pleasure, life is a joy!
When work is a duty, life is slavery.

—MAXIM GORKY

That doesn't mean the person who's asked a favor is automatically obliged to do it. Remember, an attitude of service is all about freedom—and that includes the freedom to say no. If a family member chooses to deny a request, don't argue or complain about it. Let it go. What you'll probably find is that other family members will step in and offer to fulfill the request. That, in turn, may be powerful motivation for the person who originally denied the request to reconsider his or her decision.

GLAD YOU ASKED

What can I do if my spouse absolutely refuses to participate in family-building exercises?

Go ahead and do them with your kids. What it comes down to is this: Someone has to take the first step in introducing the characteristics of a loving family in your home. If your spouse won't do it, it's up to you. What may happen when you focus your attention on your kids, though, is that their enthusiasm about and commitment to "the program" will rub off on your spouse in a way that your "preaching" and guilt trips never could.

The point of this exercise isn't to make the people in your family feel so guilty that they will do whatever you ask. The point is to help them understand the opportunities for service that exist in your family and to help them experience the satisfaction of serving others. If you can maintain a nonjudgmental and nondemanding attitude throughout the exercise, you will go a long way toward building an attitude of service in your family.

3. Don't tie expressions of love or self-worth to acts of service.

The last thing you want to do is teach your children that your love is something that must be earned through good deeds. Don't say, "You can sit on Mommy's lap only after you pick up your blocks" or "Daddy won't give you a hug until your bike is in the garage." Expressions of love should never become a "bargaining tool" with your kids.

Your children must know that you love them unconditionally. Once they are secure in that knowledge, you can introduce the topic of developing an attitude of service. Children who grow up believing that they have to "earn" love usually become workaholics who believe that acceptance and reward are based on performance, instead of personal characteristics and qualities.

Likewise, if you attack your kids' self-worth based on their work performance ("You can't even wash a load of laundry without ruining something!"), you will set them up for a life filled with guilt and feelings of inadequacy. When it comes to acts of service, your kids' efforts alone should be enough to earn your praise and support. If extra training is needed in order for them to learn how to do something right, take care of it later. But don't punish or demean them if their work doesn't meet your standards.

Taking Your Attitude of Service on the Road

Once the concept of loving service has been learned and practiced in your home, you can start expanding your service boundaries to include your neighborhood, your community, and beyond. What higher compliment could your family be paid than to have it said that you—collectively and individually—made a difference in other people's lives?

If you don't come from a background in which community service was a priority, you may be wondering how to pass on to your kids the importance of maintaining a serving spirit outside the home. Here are three steps you might want to consider.

1. Set an example.

"Do as I say, not as I do" doesn't apply when it comes to serving outside your home. If you want to introduce your kids to the satisfaction and joy that comes from serving others, personal experience is your most potent ally.

If you are currently involved in a service ministry or organization, invite your kids to join you on special projects. Give them some "field experience," whether it involves . . .

➤ baking cookies and delivering them to a new neighbor,

➤ chauffeuring nursing home residents to and from church,

➤ mowing the lawn of an elderly neighbor,

➤ going out for coffee with a lonely acquaintance from work,

➤ searching for a lost pet in the neighborhood, or

➤ collecting clothes and supplies for missionaries.

Talk with your kids about why you choose to serve people and how your efforts have been repaid, whether through lifelong friendships or simple peace of mind. Give your kids a taste of what serving others is like.

GLAD YOU ASKED

My children don't seem to have the right attitude toward service; they sure don't do it cheerfully. What can I do?

No matter how hard you push an attitude of service, you shouldn't expect your kids to get to the point where they're whistling Disney tunes as they skip merrily from chore to chore. For all of the highfalutin talk about family service, taking out the trash is still taking out the trash. What you can work toward, though, is developing an attitude in your family that you are all working toward a common purpose, as part of a unit.

2. Find a family project.

If your kids' first step in developing an attitude of service toward people outside the home is observation, the second step should be hands-on experience. And what better atmosphere is there for kids to learn how to serve than being surrounded by the people who mean the most to them—their family?

Once a month or so, set up a service project that your entire family can do together. Chances are, you can find dozens of possibilities by talking to your pastor or representatives from any number of service organizations.

You'll discover that a family service project is a two-for-one deal. Not only do you get the satisfaction of having given of yourselves to help others, you also get shared experiences together. And those shared experiences will serve as building blocks for your future interaction as a family. If those experiences involve service, it will continue the spirit of service in your home.

3. Encourage solo flights.

After your kids have had some experience in serving others with your family, encourage them to seek out individual opportunities for service, whether at school, through your church, or on the job. Help them identify their talents and strengths—characteristics that they can put to good use in their service.

Ingredient #2: Intimacy Between Husband and Wife

Intimacy is vital to a marriage—and the second ingredient of a healthy family. But the word intimacy means different things to different people. For the purposes of this chapter, we'll say that intimacy involves two people opening their inner selves to each other—not just physically and not just emotionally, but in every area of their lives.

Most couples experience intimacy early in their relationship—back in the days when they think nothing of staying up until all hours of the night, walking hand in hand or talking on the phone, sharing their deepest thoughts, fears, hopes, and dreams. That willingness to share lies at the heart of intimacy. Ultimately, marital intimacy is the result of two elements of communication: revealing yourself and receiving your spouse's self-revelation.

Revealing Yourself

If you want your spouse to love you for who you are, you have to open yourself up to him or her. That opening-up process involves sharing your thoughts, dreams, hopes, fears, experiences, shortcomings, regrets, and feelings.

With apologies to Kreskin, the Amazing Randi, and their ilk, the fact is, there is no such thing as mind reading. Your spouse can't telepathically pick up the unvoiced signals you send. And if, through your silence, you force your spouse to guess at what's going on inside you, you may be surprised at the misperceptions that result. Many noncommunicative spouses would probably be shocked to learn what their spouses believe about them. The only way to prevent misperceptions—and foster intimacy—is through communication, talking to your spouse about what's going on "below your surface."

Revealing yourself isn't a one-time process. You could spend days sharing your past history, present feelings, and future dreams to your spouse and still not reveal 10 percent of what goes on inside you. Every one of us changes every day. Those changes affect the way we think, the way we feel, the people we trust, the priorities we favor, and so on. That's why self-revelation must be a constant process. If you neglect it for a month at a time, there's a good chance your spouse may lose track of who you really are.

Receiving Your Spouse's Self-Revelation

The second half of building intimacy requires your best listening skills. As your spouse opens up and shares his or her thoughts, dreams, hopes, fears, and feelings with you, you have to receive that communication in a way that will encourage him or her to open up more and more.

That will require a nonjudgmental, noncritical attitude on your part. Your primary reaction should be open-ended interest to your spouse's self-revelation.

Whether the revelations are good or bad, they are part of what makes up your spouse and, as such, deserve your highest attention.

The Big Picture of Marital Intimacy

Those of you keeping score at home should know that there are five components of marital intimacy: the intellectual, the emotional, the social, the spiritual, and the physical. And, lest you get tempted to take a baseball approach to these statistics and conclude that "four out of five ain't bad" or that 60 percent is an acceptable score, keep this in mind: Unless all five components are being addressed in your relationship, marital intimacy may be beyond your reach.

Let's take a quick look at each of the five elements of intimacy.

The Least You Should Know About Intellectual Intimacy

Don't let the word *intellectual* throw you. This isn't about sitting around with your spouse, second-guessing Einstein's theory of relativity or critiquing the second movement of Beethoven's Fifth Symphony or dissecting the films of Sergei Eisenstein. Intellectual intimacy is about sharing and discussing thoughts with your spouse.

Look at it this way: The majority of our lives is spent processing our thoughts. From the moment we get up in the morning, our brains are at work. (OK, maybe five minutes after we get up in the morning.) The decisions we make, the priorities we set, and the things we choose to do are all the result of our intellectual processes. To leave your spouse in the dark about those processes is to cut him or her off from a large part of who you are.

Whether the topic is favorite breakfast cereals, the cost of natural gas, or people who laugh at their own jokes, every thought you have reveals something about you. When you make your spouse privy to those thoughts—and when you become privy to his or her thoughts—you start to get a sense of what makes each other tick. And that is the essence of intellectual intimacy.

The Least You Should Know About Emotional Intimacy

Feelings are our spontaneous, emotional responses to the events of our lives. They reveal as much about us as our thoughts do. On the surface, all that's visible—all your spouse can see—are the *results* of your emotions. Your spouse can see you cry over a setback at work, but may not be aware of the conflicting emotions that produced those tears. Your spouse can see you get angry when you hear of your child being bullied at school, but may not be aware of the memories that brought on the anger. Your spouse may see you laugh like a hyena, but may not be aware of all that's causing joy in your life.

Intimacy comes when you and your spouse discuss your emotions and the reasons behind them. It's a risky proposition, to be sure. It requires a heaping helping of vulnerability to let your spouse inside your emotional world. You have to trust that your spouse will not be repulsed by or condemning of what he or she discovers in there.

It will take some work—and more than a little trial and error—to achieve emotional intimacy. There will be times when you or your spouse will inadvertently ruin an intimacy-building opportunity by saying the wrong thing at the wrong time ("What are you mad about? I'm the one who should be feeling angry!").

If you're committed to building intimacy, eventually you will learn to respond in ways that encourage further sharing and discussion ("I understand why you feel nervous about facing your boss tomorrow. Would you like to talk about ways to handle the situation?").

Discussing feelings—the highs and lows—can be one of the most satisfying aspects of marriage. Sharing your deepest emotions with your spouse is one of the most powerful examples of love you can demonstrate. What's more, sharing positive emotions seems to intensify the pleasure of them, while sharing negative emotions tends to bring comfort and support.

The Least You Should Know About Social Intimacy

Life is made up of routine and unexpected events. Sharing both with your spouse is a necessary part of building social intimacy. The events of your day—the good, the bad, the ugly, and the dull—should, and will, matter to your spouse. Anything that gives him or her a glimpse into the areas of your life that he or she can't witness will eventually bring the two of you closer together.

That's not to say that a simple summary will do the trick. Your social interaction with your spouse should not read like a police blotter: "9:46 A.M.—learned of employer's plan to downsize the company; 9:49A.M.—confronted boss near men's restroom." You must also learn to share your thoughts and feelings *about* your social encounters ("When I first heard about the downsizing, I got scared. But then I started thinking about what my boss said about job security during my last performance review, and I got a little angry").

The other, more obvious, aspect of social intimacy is doing things together with your spouse. Whether you're with a group of friends or on your own, the two of you must spend time in each other's company. In short, you've got to continue (or resume) your dating life.

Every "date" you go on, whether it's an afternoon spent pulling weeds in the garden or two weeks on a Caribbean cruise, will further your social intimacy. What's more, the memories you create together socially will foster future intimacy when you and your spouse recall and relive them together years from now.

The Least You Should Know About Spiritual Intimacy

You can't achieve intimacy with your spouse without exploring the spiritual aspects of your lives. Reasoning like, "You keep your religious views to yourself and I'll do the same with mine," just doesn't cut it when you're life partners.

That's not to say you and your spouse should *agree* on every theological point. Spiritual intimacy isn't about trying to win over your spouse to a certain way of thinking; it's about feeling comfortable enough with your beliefs to share them with your spouse. It's about discovering the experiences, philosophies, and interpretations that affect your spouse's beliefs about spiritual things. The purpose is not agreement, but understanding.

Spiritual intimacy should involve more than just talking. Shared experiences, whether it's participating in church services or ministry work or even praying together, can draw you closer to your spouse, spiritually speaking, than almost anything else.

The Least You Should Know About Physical Intimacy

Physical or sexual intimacy first requires an understanding of the differences between men and women when it comes to physical expressions of love. Men, as you know, prefer tender expressions of love and concern, a romantic note here, a flower there—

(Relax, we're just testing you to see if you're paying attention.)

Actually, for most men, physical intimacy involves touching and feeling—specifically, the kind that occurs between foreplay and climax. The physical sensations that are created during the sexual act are what bring them closer to their spouses.

For women, the emotional aspect of sex is usually what's important. Feeling loved, cared for, admired, and appreciated is what encourages intimacy in them.

Because of the differences between the sexes, you and your spouse may have to work to achieve physical intimacy. You're going to have to put some effort into learning, understanding, and fulfilling each other's sexual necessities. The key to finding physical intimacy is taking the time to fully comprehend what it means to give pleasure to one another.

Intimacy Lost

Unfortunately, intimacy is much easier to lose than it is to create. Many couples destroy intimacy a little piece at a time without even realizing it. What happens is that they place block after block between them until their closeness disappears behind a giant wall or barrier. Sometimes those blocks are put up knowingly; other times, they're put up unwittingly. Either way, the "wall" that's ultimately created between the spouses prevents the flow of information and shared experiences that are necessary for intimacy to occur.

For example, one block in the wall may be set in place when a husband chooses to play softball on his wife's birthday. Another block may be stacked next to it when the wife bounces three checks. Given enough time—and blocks—a couple can erect a fairly sizable barrier between themselves. And until they recognize that barrier and commit to removing it, they have little hope for intimacy.

Constructive Destruction

If intimacy is lost when a wall is erected between spouses, it follows that the best way to restore intimacy is to tear down the wall. The bad news is that the dismantling won't be easy. The good news is that you can get started on it right away.

The first thing you need to do is figure out what happened. With your spouse, go back to the point in your marriage in which you believe your intimacy began to decline. Ask yourselves, "What happened at that time that interrupted our closeness?" After you've identified the cause, discuss exactly how it interrupted your intimacy.

For example, one of the most likely answers you'll come up with is the birth of your children. You need to ask yourself, "How did our parenting style detract from our intimacy? Knowing what we know now, could we have done anything differently? What changes can we make now?"

That's not to say that children are always the culprit. A new job, a move to a new area, a betrayal, or the death of a loved one could all be blocks in the wall that separates you and your spouse. Regardless of what the causes are, you need to review the situations, talk about what you could have done differently, and find lessons to learn from them.

THE WISDOM OF ALL AGES

Neither sex, without some fertilization of the complementary characters of the other, is capable of the highest reaches of human endeavor.

–H. L. MENCKEN

List as many of those blocks as you can remember, in as much detail as you can remember. Encourage your spouse to do the same. Then compare lists. Remember, your purpose is not to start up long-dormant arguments or to kick off a "reblaming" process. Your purpose is to remove and examine the blocks in the wall that stand between you and your spouse.

Your purpose is not to present a defense for past failures. In fact, as hard as it may be, the best response you can offer to your spouse's memories of past "intimacy robbers" is something like this: "I can understand now how that hurt you, and I am sorry. Will you forgive me?"

If the thought of saying something like that to your spouse sends chills up your spine, you need to figure out why. What can you gain by holding on to past hurts and refusing to resolve them? Pride? A sense of justice? If so, are those things worth a weakened relationship with your spouse—and a weakened family dynamic?

This process of acknowledging and forgiving past failures is what will bring down the wall between you and your spouse. Once that wall is down, you can begin to build new bridges of intimacy in its place.

Intimacy Regained

Of course, you can't just say to your spouse, "Let's be intimate again." It's not that easy. You will have to make regular, conscious efforts to build that unity. The best way to do that is to devote yourselves to reestablishing unity in one area of your relationship at a time.

What follows is a program designed to help you and your spouse tackle one area of intimacy a week. The program will require a minimum of an hour a week, for five weeks. (You and your spouse should feel free to exceed that hour any time, and every time, you so desire.) If it's absolutely impossible for you and your spouse to find a whole hour to spend together, by yourselves, each week, you'll need to . . . find a way to do the impossible. Intimacy is *that* important.

Remember, this isn't just your marital relationship we're talking about here; it's your family relationship. If you want your family to be all that it can be, you must find a way to restore intimacy with your spouse. The following program will not be easy; it will require not only time, but considerable effort, as well.

Let's take a look at how you can go about reestablishing intimacy with your spouse, beginning with the intellectual element of your relationship.

Developing Intellectual Intimacy
Your first week of the intimacy program will focus on intellectual intimacy. Reconnecting with your spouse on an intellectual level requires sharing and discussing your thoughts. Your goal is to answer for each other the question, "What have you been thinking today?" As we mentioned earlier, this involves sharing not only your experiences of the day, but also your thoughts about those experiences. It means sharing with your spouse the thoughts that have been vying for your attention all day.

If you need some ideas for developing intellectual intimacy—things to talk about during your hour with your spouse—try these.

➤ Divide your day into three-hour segments, starting at 6:00 A.M. (or whatever time you finally haul your carcass out of bed). Make a point of writing down in a journal some of the thoughts you have during each of those three-hour periods. When you get together with your spouse, you can use the journal to refresh your memory and share your thoughts from the day. (In the process, you'll be able to give your spouse a more complete representation of your thoughts.)

➤ Discuss with your spouse your answer to these two questions: "Which thought of mine today am I most proud of?" "Which thought of mine today am I least proud of?" Becoming intellectually intimate requires you to share the good *and* the bad with your spouse. Unless he or she is aware of both, you can't claim to be truly intimate.

➤ Choose a newspaper or magazine article that you will each read and then later discuss together. Give each other a chance to share your thoughts and feelings about the article. In the process, you may discover some deeply held beliefs of your spouse of which you weren't aware.

➤ Watch a movie or TV show together and then discuss it afterward, using questions like these: "What was the message of the movie or the show?" "What did you find objectionable about the movie or show and why?" "What did you find entertaining about the movie or show and why?"

If it seems odd or uncomfortable to hold such intentionally structured conversations with your spouse, go with it anyhow. You'll find that these conversations will eventually stimulate intellectual intimacy. The one thing you want to make sure of is that you and your spouse respect each other's right to think—even if you don't necessarily agree with each other's opinions. This isn't a forum for "arguing your case" or helping your spouse "see the light." It's a forum for exchanging ideas and appreciating what you learn from and about each other.

That means you need to keep a tight rein on critical comments or facial gestures during these conversations with your spouse. You'll also need to prevent inappropriate humor or sarcasm from ruining the party. Take off your judge's robe, accept your spouse's ideas for what they are, and then leave it at that.

Developing Emotional Intimacy

Your second week of the intimacy program will focus on emotional intimacy. Your goal here will be for you and your spouse to learn to share your feelings with each other. The key question you want to address is, "What emotions have you experienced today?" That will involve discussing not only the emotions themselves, but the events that triggered them.

One of the processes for establishing emotional intimacy is similar to the first suggestion for establishing intellectual intimacy. Again, you'll probably want to use a journal as a memory refresher. And again you'll probably want to divide your day into three-hour segments, starting at 6:00 A.M. (or whatever time you wake up).

During each of those periods, write down some of the feelings you experience. When you get together with your spouse, you can refer to your journal and share feelings such as these:

> ➤ "On the way to work, I felt ashamed when I got angry and honked at a guy whose car had died."

> ➤ "Between nine and twelve, I felt nervous because I realized I was unprepared for my lunch meeting with my boss."

> ➤ "Just before lunch, I felt extremely relieved when my boss had to cancel our lunch meeting."

> ➤ "Around three o'clock, we had Fred's retirement party, and I felt a little sad because I realized that this was probably the last time I'd ever see him, since he's moving to Arizona."

FAMILY TIES

If you want clues as to your intimacy level with your spouse, pay attention to your kids. Many children have almost a sixth sense when it comes to marital discord or distance. If your kids sense a lack of meaningful interaction between you and your spouse, they may try to "help" by urging the two of you to go out together or by inventing reasons for the entire family to be together. The other possibility is that they will vent their frustrations and fears about your relationship by acting out and getting in trouble. That's not to say you can expect such actions from them–but it's still a good idea to watch for telltale signs.

Notice how the previous examples included not just the feelings themselves, but the circumstances and events that trigger them. That's what you want to give your spouse—the "big picture." Also make it a point to include an equal representation of positive and negative emotions. Don't give your spouse a one-sided view of yourself.

Members of a loving family allow one another to experience and express emotions. Living in harmony is fine, but living authentically and intimately is a lot better. And the way to live authentically and intimately is to give each other the freedom to describe thoughts, feelings, struggles, experiences, and reactions openly and without fear of repercussions.

Developing Social Intimacy

Your third week of the intimacy program will focus on social intimacy. If you need some help in creating social intimacy with your spouse, here are some ideas to consider.

➤ Make a point of discussing with your spouse one social encounter you have each day. It could be anything from an exchange with the person behind the counter of a fast-food restaurant to an unexpected conversation with an old friend you hadn't seen in years. The point is not to create spellbinding theater for your spouse—or even to have an exciting story to tell—but to make him or her a part of your life outside the home, to give him or her a glimpse of what your life is like when he or she isn't around. (You'll note that we set the bar relatively low here. Discussing one social encounter is the required minimum; discussing three social encounters would be even more beneficial.)

➤ Evaluate with your spouse the time the two of you have spent together during the past six months. Refer to your calendars and Day-Timers, if necessary. Come up with a list of sporting events, movies, plays, concerts, school programs, church events, banquets, and other activities you have attended together. When you're finished with that, make a list of the activities and projects the two of you have worked on together. This list might include everything from making scenery for your child's school play to working together to prepare a meal to washing your car. After you've completed both lists, go back over all of the activities one at a time. Talk about the ones you enjoyed the most and why they hold such pleasant memories for you. Encourage your spouse to do the same. Identify the activities that you would like to repeat.

➤ On a scale of 0–10, rate your level of satisfaction regarding your social involvement with your spouse over the past six months. Ask your spouse to do the same. Compare your scores and explain why you feel the way you do. Using that conversation as a springboard, plan a social activity that you and your spouse can enjoy within the next two weeks. When that one's done, make plans for another activity in the following two weeks. If you have different social preferences, take turns planning activities. Just make sure that you maintain the two-week (or less) cycle for seeing your spouse on a social basis.

GLAD YOU ASKED

What qualifies an activity as a "social event" with my spouse?

The key is interaction. You don't necessarily have to be in a "social setting" such as a restaurant or party. In fact, you don't even have to leave your house for a social event with your spouse. All that's required is quality time being spent together for a common purpose, whether it's planting a tree or talking for hours at a time.

In this final activity, you'll find that as you make it a point to experience and learn to enjoy each other's social preferences, you'll begin to have more and more in common with each other. And establishing commonality is a big step toward developing intimacy.

Developing Spiritual Intimacy

Your fourth week of the intimacy program will focus on spiritual intimacy. Even if you don't consider yourselves to be "religious" people, you will need to build a spiritual element into your relationship.

Depending on where you're at spiritually, you might try one of the following ideas.

➤ If you or your spouse are spiritual novices, you might want to start your quest for spiritual intimacy by focusing on the basics. For example, you might share your past experiences with churches and organized religion. Or you might share your thoughts on key questions such as these: What is the origin of humankind? What is our purpose in life? What happens after we die?

➤ If you and your spouse are a little beyond the novice category, you might want to explore the possibility of finding a church in which you are both comfortable. Visit several churches in your area to see if you can find one that feels right. Commit yourselves to attending services together each week. Make a point of talking about what you learn each week. Talk to the pastor about where the two of you are at in your spiritual journey.

➤ If you and your spouse are active churchgoers, you might want to take your involvement a step further. Find a ministry in your church that the two of you can do together. Chances are, your church will have dozens of opportunities, one of which is likely to be a good fit for you—anything from taking care of toddlers in the nursery to visiting elderly members in nursing homes.

Developing Physical Intimacy

Your fifth week of the intimacy program will focus on physical intimacy. The question you want to address is this: "How can we develop a deeper sense of sexual fulfillment?" It doesn't take a relationship expert to figure out that if the sexual aspect of your relationship is deepened, your overall sense of intimacy will be increased.

Standing in the way of your efforts to deepen your sexual relationship is the fact that you and your spouse likely have different thoughts, desires, expectations, likes, and dislikes when it comes to physical intimacy. That's why your first order of business should be to share your desires in detail with your spouse and then encourage your spouse to share his or her desires with you.

After you've "laid your cards on the table," you can begin looking for common ground or a place to meet each other halfway in your physical preferences. What you should not do is try to convince your spouse to change his or her desires or to see the logic in yours. You can't demand sexual intimacy.

If you're unused to or uncomfortable with the idea of talking about sexual matters with your spouse, you may not know where to begin. Here are a few questions to help you get started:

➤ What do you like about our present sexual patterns?

➤ What do you find uncomfortable about our present sexual patterns?

➤ What could we do for each other to make the sexual aspect of our marriage better?

➤ What causes you to become sexually excited?

➤ What hinders or lessens your sexual excitement?

Beyond your discussion, you and your spouse may want to commit to reading a book on sexual intimacy together. (If you're looking for suggested reading, try *The Gift of Sex* by Clifford and Joyce Penner.) After you each finish a chapter, talk about what, if anything, you would like to incorporate into your own sexual patterns.

No Five-Week Cure

We're not suggesting that at the end of the five-week intimacy program, you and your spouse will be as close as you need to be. These suggestions are intended as a starting point in a lifelong quest for intimacy.

Perfection shouldn't be your goal. You will never reach a state of complete intimacy with your spouse. That's what's so exciting about becoming intimate: there's always more to look forward to. So be content to simply grow with your spouse. Intimacy is a process, and if you are moving in the right direction, you will reap the benefits from it.

Family Practice

Think you're an expert on developing an attitude of service and intimacy in your family? Here's a quiz to see how much you know.

1. Which of the following is not a characteristic of a healthy family?
   a. An attitude of service
   b. In-laws who are intimately involved in the decision-making process

    c. Intimacy between husband and wife

    d. Parents who teach and train

2. Which of the following is true of an attitude of service?

    a. If it's not given freely by family members, it should be compelled by the head of the household.

    b. It's often more destructive than helpful to family dynamics.

    c. It's an open invitation for family members to take advantage of each other.

    d. It instills a sense of emotional satisfaction in completing mundane tasks.

3. Which of the following is *not* a helpful tip for introducing and fostering an attitude of service in your family?

    a. Remove the things in your kids' lives that you believe are higher priorities than serving the family.

    b. Identify current examples of service going on in your home.

    c. Find out what kind of service your family members would like.

    d. Don't tie expressions of love or self-worth to acts of service.

4. What is the key to developing intimacy with your spouse?

    a. Weekly sexual encounters

    b. Self-revealing conversations

    c. An open schedule

    d. Nagging guilt

5. Which of the following is *not* one of the five areas of intimacy that must be achieved between spouses?

    a. Intellectual intimacy

    b. Social intimacy

    c. Career intimacy

    d. Physical intimacy

Answers: (1) b, (2) d, (3) a, (4) b, (5) c

CHAPTER 9

An Old Family Recipe, Part 2

FIVE INGREDIENTS OF A HEALTHY FAMILY

SNAPSHOT

"Hey, Mom, catch." Mark tossed the car keys at his mother on his way through the kitchen. "I filled it up on the way home. Oh, hi, Aunt Donna!"

Sharon grabbed the keys in midair. "Thanks, Sweetie."

"Hi, Mark," Donna replied. Then, when he was out of earshot, she turned to her sister and asked, "What are you holding over *his* head?"

"What do you mean?" Sharon asked.

"I mean, that whole filling-up-the-gas-tank business," Donna said. "What brought that on? He must really be trying to get in good with you. So, tell me, is he trying to make up for something he did or is he trying to get something he wants?"

"Neither, as far as I know," Sharon said with a shrug. "We have a rule in our family about the kids filling up the car after they use it."

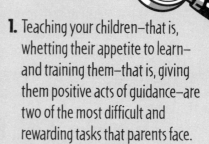

SNEAK PREVIEW

1. Teaching your children—that is, whetting their appetite to learn—and training them—that is, giving them positive acts of guidance—are two of the most difficult and rewarding tasks that parents face.
2. One of the most obvious signs of a loving family is obedient children, sons and daughters who recognize and respect their parents' authority.
3. A husband who is a "loving leader" will demonstrate responsibility, dependability, and deep commitment to his family.

"Yeah, I know," Donna said. "We have the same rule in our family. It's right there next to the rules about being home in time for dinner every night and not watching more than five hours of TV a day. It's just kind of a shock to see somebody . . . well, actually pay attention to it."

"Well, Mark did learn the hard way," Sharon acknowledged.

"What does that mean?"

"Oh, he forgot to fill up the tank about a month ago and lost his driving privileges for a week," Sharon explained. "So if he needed to go anywhere, he had to ask me or George to take him."

"Then it sounds like you and George learned the hard way," Donna said.

"Yeah, it was tough," Sharon concurred. "But I think Mark really learned something from it."

* * * * * * * * * * * * * * *

What elements are necessary in the family environment in order to foster growth and closeness? In chapter 8, we looked at two of the five ingredients for a loving family. To complete the quintet, let's take a look at the final three ingredients: parents who train and teach, children who obey and honor parents, and husbands who are loving leaders.

Ingredient #3: Parents Who Train and Teach

No, that title is not a redundancy. Teaching and training are two different, yet equally important, forms of instruction. In order to provide your kids with the education and "street smarts" they need to survive and thrive in this society, you need to offer them a combination of teaching and training.

For many people, the word *teaching* prompts unpleasant flashbacks to long hours in a classroom, sitting behind a desk several inches too small for them, listening to terminally dull instructors drone on and on about things they forgot before they even heard them. Fortunately, we aren't talking about that kind of teaching.

For the purposes of this chapter, we'll define creative teaching as whetting your children's appetites for knowledge. You'll note that the definition doesn't assume any special expertise on your part. In fact, all that's required of you is time, effort, and a desire to see your children succeed.

Characteristics of Creative Teaching

There are four aspects of creative teaching that we need to look at: instruction, encouragement, correction, and affirmation.

Creative Instruction

Creative instruction involves communicating to your children things that you believe to be important. That could include everything from family history and traditions to social dos and don'ts, from spiritual values to movie trivia.

John's father made a game of quizzing his son on the spelling of words whenever they were together. Evie's mother helped her daughter understand what the president and the United States Congress do so that Evie could write an extra-credit report about them. When Anthony was in third grade, his father taught him to recite, in order, every winner of the Indianapolis 500. Sandy's mother taught her daughter the value of prayer by periodically sharing requests that she'd had answered. All of these are examples of creative instruction.

You'll find that the most effective form of creative instruction is a dialogue between you and your children. A question ("How do caterpillars change into butterflies?"), an observation ("A boy in my class talks funny"), or a request ("I want to see cows and pigs on a farm") is all that's needed to trigger an "instruction" session. You can talk for minutes or hours about a topic, depending on the feedback and interest level of the child. And the best part of all is that your

FAMILY TIES

One thing you need to be aware of is that your kids will likely take whatever you say to be the absolute truth on a matter (until they reach their teen years, that is, at which point they will go to the opposite extreme and start questioning *everything* you have to say). So when you give instruction, it's important that you know what you're talking about. If you don't know the answer to a question, don't try to bluff an answer in order to save face. Instead, admit that you don't know and offer to help your child find the answer.

instruction often sinks in before your kids even realize they're being taught!

Creative Encouragement

Creative encouragement is the process of instilling in your kids the courage to take risks and to move beyond failure. How does it make you feel to know that you have the power to spur a child on to explore possibilities, overcome setbacks, and accomplish what others find impossible? It should excite and humble you, because with that power comes responsibility.

You have the responsibility to provide encouragement to your kids, not only when they get things right, but also when they turn in less-than-perfect efforts. For some parents (and you've probably seen them at peewee soccer games or Little League baseball games) that's a problem. They're afraid that encouraging mediocre performance will only inspire mediocrity in the future. Actually, the opposite is true. If you withhold praise and encouragement from your children until they reach an "acceptable" level of achievement, they will never rise to their potential.

The key to successful encouragement is to focus on your child's efforts, and not so much on the results of those efforts. Encouragement based on effort inspires kids to try again when they fail. It doesn't trap them in performance-based limbo, where they can be encouraged only when they duplicate or better their previous performance.

Creative Correction

The purpose of creative correction is to stimulate your children to positive behavior. Toward that end, there are three things you need to keep in mind when it comes to creative correction.

First, don't correct behavior that doesn't need correcting. If that sounds like an obvious principle to you, you may be surprised at the number of times you've violated it. Too often, ill-timed and ill-considered "correction" only serves to stifle creativity in kids. For example, to say something like, "That's not the way we make our beds in this house," is to give correction that's not necessary. All you're doing is suppressing your children's creativity and individuality. The best way to avoid this mistake is to ask yourself, "Is the behavior I'm about to correct really detrimental to my child?" If the answer is no, keep the correction to yourself.

Second, make sure that you explain as you correct. Remember, your goal is to enhance the well-being of your children, not to vent your anger over some wrong. So detailed explanations of the behavior you'd like to see changed will go a lot further than a tongue-lashing will. More specifically, "I've got an idea about how you can avoid making that mistake again" is a much more effective approach than "I can't believe you just did that!"

Third, make sure that you address only the matter at hand. In some situations, you may be tempted to dredge up your children's past offenses to make a point. Resist that urge. Leave the past in the past. Help your children feel secure in the fact that their past failures won't be trotted out and thrown in their faces every time they have a conflict with you. You don't want your kids to feel defeated by past failures. You want them to understand that failure is never final; in fact, it's just the first step toward success.

Creative Affirmation

Creative affirmation is different from creative encouragement in that it focuses on the kids themselves, and not on their actions. Creative affirmation would include statements such as . . .

- ➤ "I love you."

- ➤ "You have a great sense of humor."

- ➤ "Your younger brother really looks up to you."

- ➤ "I really enjoy spending time with you."

In loving families, parents seek to build their children's self-esteem through creative affirmation. Let's face it, they are going to have their negative characteristics brought into the open and examined under a microscope time and time again by their peers, by a media fixated on physical perfection, and by themselves. Why not let your voice combat that negativity and point out the many positive things you see?

The Challenge of Consistent Training

Consistent training involves giving children positive acts of guidance—literally, *showing* them what to do. One aspect of consistent training is acquainting the

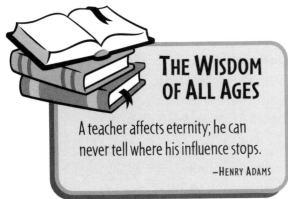

child with necessary skills, such as getting dressed, reading, writing, riding a bike, and dialing 911. Another aspect of consistent training is encouraging character growth by demonstrating the importance of values such as honesty, hard work, and courage. A third aspect of consistent training is equipping him or her to respond to emotions such as fear, anger, and disappointment.

If consistent training seems like a lot of work to you, you don't know the half of it. But you'll never do anything more rewarding or more important in your entire life.

There are three primary methods for giving children consistent training. They are modeling behavior, showing them how, and weaving actions with words.

Let's take a look at how you can incorporate each of them.

Training by Modeling Behavior

This type of training occurs whether you realize it or not—and whether you like it or not. For better or worse, your kids are watching you for clues on how to live their own lives. The first thing they are looking for is confirmation that your actions match your words. If and when he or she finds inconsistencies between the two, you can bet that you will hear about it.

At some point, your children are going to stop listening to what you say and start emulating what you do. If that thought sends a shiver up your spine, you're not alone. Many parents cringe at the thought of their kids falling into the same traps that they fell into or repeating the same patterns of destructive behavior.

But where there is potential for danger, there is also cause for celebration. The fact is, you don't have to be a family relationship expert to make a difference in your child's life. All you have to do is live a life worth emulating.

If you come from a dysfunctional family background, that's easier said than done. But one of the wonders of the human condition is the ability to change. There is no law of nature that says you can't break the chain of dysfunction for the sake of your own family. If you need a little more incentive, keep this in mind: Your decision to change—to refuse to continue a destructive pattern or to adopt a more positive approach—will not go unnoticed by your kids. There's a good chance that they will file away that bit of recognition in the area of their brains reserved for positive examples to follow.

Training by Showing How

You could teach your child to ride a bike by showing him or her an instructional video. You could teach your child to wash dishes by explaining how much liquid soap to pour into the sink and then describing the proper technique for getting rid of ketchup stains, crusty pasta, and greasy residue. And you could teach your child to do laundry by having him or her read the back of a detergent box.

> ### THE WISDOM OF ALL AGES
>
> The whole art of teaching is only the art of awakening the natural curiosity of young minds for the purpose of satisfying afterwards.
>
> —ANATOLE FRANCE

But how much better would it be to . . .

> ➤ put your child on a bike and then start running up and down the street, with your hand steadying the frame, until your child was able to stay up under his or her own power?

> ➤ hand your child a dishrag, put him or her on a chair next to you, and take turns washing the pots, pans, plates, bowls, and silverware in the sink?

> ➤ bring your child into the laundry room to help you sort clothes, measure detergent, set the dials on the washer and dryer, and clean out the lint trap?

Taking the time to provide hands-on instruction for your children may mean the difference between confident, eager-to-help kids and nervous, uncertain ones—at least, where life skills are involved.

Training by Weaving Actions with Words

Whatever you are trying to teach, it's helpful to ask the question, "What can I do to make this lesson more effective for my child?" The answers you come up with will probably be experiential in nature. After all, experts tell us that children learn by doing or by gaining firsthand knowledge or experience.

That means if you're trying to teach your children about the nature of war, you can simply regurgitate lessons (or what you remember of them) from your high school or college world history class or you can regurgitate those lessons while walking with your child through a World War II exhibit at a history museum. The combination of sight and sound will likely provide an experience your child will never forget.

Use your creativity to make your "together times" with your family "learning times" as well. It will take some effort on your part, but that effort will be quickly repaid when you see your kids latch on to a concept or nugget of knowledge that they may not have been exposed to otherwise.

In a loving family, parents provide guidance for their children by consistently training them from the time they are infants to the time they are young adults—and beyond.

Professionals Need Not Apply

The one overriding concern that may be standing in the way could probably be voiced this way: "I'm not a teacher! I wouldn't know where to begin training my kids! In fact, if you want to know the truth, I could use a little training myself. Wouldn't my kids be better off learning from professional instructors?"

That's an excellent point and a matter that deserves serious consideration. The fact is, there are quality schools, programs, and teachers that are geared to reach children at the most effective level possible, focusing specifically on their individual learning styles and

Glad You Asked

My parents never offered me or my siblings much teaching or training, and we turned out all right. Why can't I take the same approach with my kids?

The simple reason is that society has changed since you were a kid. If you choose not to provide your child with teaching or training in "life skills," there will be scads of people, companies, and organizations willing to do it for you. Everyone from overhyped professional athletes to violence-spewing rappers will be thrust at your kids to fill the void left by your refusal to get involved in their development. And what are the odds that those people will do the kind of teaching and training you want your kids to have?

using scientifically tested techniques for enhancing later recall.

Big deal. None of that changes the fact that you and your spouse are the most effective teachers your children will ever have. No one has more vested interest in your children's ultimate success and happiness than you do. No one will be willing to go to greater lengths to ensure their future viability. And, most importantly, no one knows better what your child is really like—and really capable of being and doing.

That's not to say you should rest on your laurels (whatever they may be), content with the fact that what you know now is sufficient for your child. In fact, there are things you can and should do to improve yourself as an instructor. Here are four suggestions for you to consider.

1. Bring it home.

Chances are, you've experienced your share of teaching and training in your educational and vocational career. You've learned necessary skills to function in your job and in society in general. You've developed communication skills to guide you through all kinds of personal interaction. But how many of those skills have you brought home?

The first thing you need to do is identify the skills you've learned that will make a difference. For example, you've probably used charts (or had charts used on you) to communicate sales figures or some other complicated concept. But when was the last time you used a chart to explain something to your kids? Likewise, you've probably mastered the art of reflective listening, demonstrating your attentiveness by repeating back to someone what you heard them say ("If I understand you correctly, you're saying that . . ."). But when was the last time you showed that same courtesy to your children?

With your spouse, make a list of all the skills you've acquired over the years concerning how to relate to people, how to communicate information, how to lead people in decision making, how to train people, and so forth. Then decide which of those skills you might be able to use with your children to become a more effective teacher or trainer.

2. Go get it.

If you don't believe you have the necessary skills to train and teach a child—if you really believe that you're not up to the task—you may need to acquire those skills through higher education. Many community colleges offer courses on child development, learning patterns of toddlers and adolescents, and parenting teenagers. Depending on the curriculum and the instructor, those classes may provide the information and skills you need to become a good teacher.

If college classes are out of the question, you might also consult local churches and libraries, which often schedule speakers to talk about parenting and child education issues. A few phone calls may hook you up with programs that will make a difference in your parenting skills.

What it comes down to is this: If there's an area of parenting in which you feel lacking, there's a good chance that you can find a class or seminar addressing that area—if you look hard enough.

3. Observe others.

You can discover a lot about which methods of instruction work and which ones don't simply by paying attention to what other parents do. Keep your eyes and ears open in public settings—parks, restaurants, grocery stores, and such—when you see parents interacting with their kids. You'll see both positive and negative examples of instruction and training. Make sure that you learn from both.

For a more "formal" education, schedule an appointment to visit a classroom at school. Pay attention to the strategies the teacher uses to get kids' attention and to communicate at their level. Observe the way he or she weaves words, actions, and visuals together to make his or her point.

If your children are not of school age, ask to sit in on a preschool session or a children's Sunday school

FAMILY TIES

One of the best ways to learn about your child's preferred learning methods is to ask him or her about a favorite teacher at school. Find out what your child likes about the teacher, what techniques the teacher uses to get information across, how the teacher speaks to your child, and any other information you get about what makes that teacher so special. You can then use the information you receive to craft your own teaching and training style.

class at your church. Chances are, you'll come away with some extremely helpful observations.

One other option is to watch children's educational programming on TV. Many of the shows were created by or are overseen by professional educators. The methods the shows employ to teach children are generally the result of a great deal of research, which means that they're generally very sound and on-target. (A word of warning: If you've not spent time watching children's programming before, you should be aware of the "repeat effect." That's when an annoyingly catchy song for children lodges itself in your brain and repeats itself over and over and over again. In extreme cases, the repeat effect has been known to last for months. And there is currently no known cure for it. "Teletubbies, Teletubbies, say hel-lo!")

4. Read a book.

You knew this one was coming, didn't you? The fact that you're reading this sentence suggests that you recognize the importance of books in the parenting process. What you also need to recognize is that regardless of how old your kids are, you can find books on-line, in a well-stocked bookstore, or in your local library that will equip you to teach and train them. Keep in mind that *reading* about good parenting should not interfere with your actual parenting responsibilities. Ready or not, there comes a time when you have to put what you learn into practice.

Ingredient #4: Children Who Obey and Honor Parents

Don't let the words *obey* and *honor* mislead you. This isn't a preparation for the Marine Corps. We're not talking about demanding a "Sir, yes, sir!" relationship with your child. We're not suggesting that your child salute you every time the two of you pass in the hall.

Learning obedience is really just a matter of learning to live by the rules. Like it or not, rules are a necessary part of life in our society. Imagine what life would be like if there were no rules about . . .

➤ driving on the right side of the road.

➤ selling alcohol to minors.

➤ paying taxes.

OK, forget that last one.

The point is, without rules, there is no structure. Without structure, life is chaos. And very little flourishes in the midst of chaos. There must be rules—and consequences for violating rules. It's true in society, and it's true in the family.

THE WISDOM OF ALL AGES

Lawful and settled authority is very seldom resisted when it is well employed.

—Samuel Johnson

In the functional family, it's not just the fear of consequences that inspires obedience. The love for family members and the concern for their well-being are also powerful motivators.

Obedience isn't a trait we have at birth. If you've ever watched a two-year-old pushing the boundaries of his or her parents, you know what we're saying. Obedience is something that's *learned.* What's more, obedience is *best* learned when kids feel loved by their parents—when they believe their parents care about their well-being. If kids are convinced that the demand for obedience is simply an effort to spoil fun, that obedience will be much harder to come by.

The key to encouraging a spirit of obedience in your kids is to help them understand that all actions have consequences. Obedient actions bring about positive consequences; disobedient actions bring about negative consequences.

So your two-part focus in introducing obedience should be . . .

➤ making your child feel loved.

➤ making sure your child experiences the consequences of his or her actions.

This process involves three elements: setting rules, setting consequences (good and bad), and administering discipline. Let's take a closer look at each one of them.

Setting Rules

Rules are the dos ("Make your bed before you go to school," "Take out the garbage Thursday morning") and don'ts ("Don't stay out after 10 P.M. on a school night," "Don't give out personal information when you're on-line") that guide life in your household. But the fact that rules are a necessity doesn't mean that all rules are healthy or beneficial. (Was that a shout of "I told you so!" coming from your child's room?)

Good rules have four things in common:

➤ *Good rules are intentional.* Before you carve a rule into your "family stone," make sure you've thought about it. Don't allow yourself or your family to be held captive by a rule that exists only because that's the way things were done in your house when you were a kid. Instead, put some thought into why the rule is needed, what its purpose is, and how it benefits your family. Know why you do or don't want something done.

➤ *Good rules are mutual.* Neither you nor your spouse should be the rule setter in your house. The guidelines that dictate behavior in your household should be the result of a joint agreement between you and your spouse (and, when they're old enough, your kids). Chances are, you and your spouse will bring differing opinions about and attitudes toward rules into your family dynamic. Both points of view must be considered before rules are established. In some cases, you may find easy agreement. In others, you may need to reach some sort of compromise. For example, if your spouse feels that 10 P.M. is a good curfew for a school night and you feel that 11 P.M. is more reasonable, you may want to compromise and set a curfew of 10:30. In order for rules to be effective, both you and your spouse must have a sense of ownership in them.

➤ *Good rules are reasonable.* Healthy rules must serve some positive function. To help you determine whether a rule fits that criteria, here are a few questions to ask yourself:

1. Does this rule have some positive effect in my child's life? (If so, what?)

2. Does this rule keep my child from danger or destruction?

3. Does this rule teach my child some positive character trait, such as honesty, hard work, kindness, or the importance of sharing?

4. Does this rule teach my child the importance of caring for possessions?

5. Does this rule teach my child to respect and protect property?

6. Does this rule teach my child responsibility and/or good manners?

➤ *Good rules are discussed with the entire family.* As children get older, they should be brought into the decision-making process regarding rules. (We'll give you a moment to regain composure after that suggestion.) The fact is, if a rule applies to your kids, and they are old enough to have an opinion about it, they should be allowed to have a say in establishing or abolishing the rule.

A caution about this final principle about rules: Letting children have input doesn't mean they will have the final word when it comes to rules. It does mean, however, that you should consider their feelings before setting a rule. In letting them have input, you will not only be teaching responsibility, you'll also be giving valuable experience in setting rules themselves.

Setting Consequences

Obedience is developed as a result of suffering the consequences of disobedience. It's a tough way to learn. But it's also effective. To deny your kids the opportunity to experience such consequences — regardless of how well intentioned your motives may be—is to do them a great disservice. Breaking rules *should* cause discomfort or inconvenience to the rule breaker.

GLAD YOU ASKED

Is spanking an acceptable consequence for disobedience?

In certain circumstances, perhaps. For example, if your child physically hits his or her brother or sister, you could tie in the physical consequence of spanking. What you should not do is use spanking as a standard action for all disobedience. Consequences delivered in the heat of the moment won't mean as much as one that has been explained and for which the child is prepared.

As parents, it's up to you and your spouse to determine the consequences for various infractions. And, unless you choose to set an automatic two-week grounding for every offense, that's going to take some thought on your part.

One of the first things you'll want to consider is setting consequences that are as closely associated to their corresponding rules as possible. For example, if you have a rule about returning library books on time, you might set a consequence of no bedtime story for one night for breaking that rule. Or if you have a rule about putting gas in the car after using it, you might set a consequence of a loss of driving privileges for two days for breaking that law.

It's important to establish consequences at a time of peace in your family, with the input and involvement of each member. That way you won't be tempted to act in the heat of the moment when a rule is broken, establishing a consequence that you later regret. Establishing consequences before a rule is broken will also give your kids vital information for when they are considering the pros and cons of obeying that rule.

You should know that in some cases, the consequence of disobedience on the part of your kids will make life more difficult for you. For example, if your teenage son loses his driving privileges for coming home after curfew, that means you and your spouse will have to act as chauffeurs for him. But you can use that inconvenience to make a point to your teenager. One of the fundamental realities of life is that one's behavior has an effect on others. If your teenager believes that you and your spouse love and care for him and want only the best for him, he is going to be further motivated to obedience by seeing you suffer the consequences of his actions.

Administering Discipline

Once the rules of your household have been defined and the consequences of disobedience have been spelled out, your responsibility becomes making sure that your child *experiences* those consequences in the face of disobedience. This is going to require a great deal of consistency and dedication on your part.

If you choose to be a stickler for rules one day and lenient the next, the end result will be a disobedient,

GLAD YOU ASKED

What if my spouse and I determine that a long-standing rule in our home doesn't meet the criteria of a good rule?

Get rid of it, and let your kids know why. You may be nervous about setting some kind of precedent that your kids will use later to get other, positive rules abolished. But that's probably not the response you'll get. When your kids see your willingness to reevaluate rules and make the hard decision to get rid of them, they will likely come to appreciate you and your family's rules a little more.

disrespectful child. Inconsistent discipline is the most common pitfall of parents who are trying to raise responsible children.

Such inconsistency is understandable. The fact is, discipline takes a lot of time and energy. On many occasions parents are just too tired to deal with their kids' disobedience. But don't let your tiredness get the best of you. Pull yourself together long enough to make sure your child experiences the consequences of his actions.

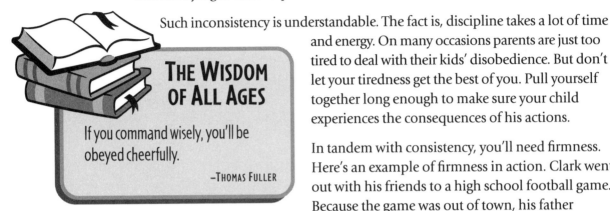

THE WISDOM OF ALL AGES

If you command wisely, you'll be obeyed cheerfully.

—THOMAS FULLER

In tandem with consistency, you'll need firmness. Here's an example of firmness in action. Clark went out with his friends to a high school football game. Because the game was out of town, his father extended Clark's curfew till midnight, but warned that if he came home late, the consequence would be a weeklong grounding. For reasons too complicated to explain, Clark didn't get home until 12:45. When his father reminded him of the consequence, Clark nodded his head in agreement, but made one request.

"I know I deserve that punishment," he admitted. "But next Friday is the youth group's trip to Cedar Point. Would it be possible to divide the grounding into two sections—the five days before the trip and the two days after it? It would still be seven days; it just wouldn't be seven days in a row."

"I'm sorry, Son," his father replied, "but the rules were clear."

"I know, Dad," Clark said. "But we've been collecting money for this trip all year. Everyone is going. This is going to be the best thing our group's ever done."

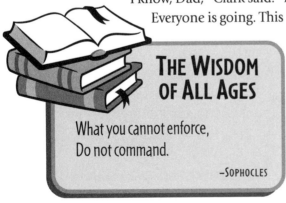

THE WISDOM OF ALL AGES

What you cannot enforce, Do not command.

—SOPHOCLES

"I'm sorry, Clark," his father repeated. "But you have to face the consequences for your actions."

It's not that Clark's dad didn't want his son to have a good time with his youth group. It's just that he considered it more important for Clark to experience the consequences of his actions. So Clark's dad remained firm. As a result, he gave his son a lesson he won't soon forget.

As we wrap up this section, we will give you three steps to administering discipline that you need to keep in mind.

1. *Express your love for your kids.* Don't preface your discipline with yelling and accusing. Instead, let them know that you care deeply and want only the best for them. Before (and after) the discipline process, you might give a hug, talk about the events of their day, or give them a cookie.

2. *Clearly explain the "why" of the discipline.* Tell your kids exactly what rule was broken and remind them of the consequences of that disobedience. That may not make the discipline seem any fairer to your kids in the heat of the moment, but at least they will know that you're not acting out of anger.

3. *Make certain that your kids experience the consequences of disobedience.* Resist the urge to shield from pain or loss. Unless he or she experiences the full force of consequences, they may not learn the lessons they need to learn. As painful as it may be for them—and you—the downside of giving in to your sentiments is too severe.

Ingredient #5: Husbands Who Are Loving Leaders

Imagine stumbling across the following personal ad in your newspaper:

Looking for a man who is in touch with his feelings, equally comfortable with expressing pain and joy, sympathy and encouragement. Should value partnership and be able to relate to those close to him on an emotional level. Experience in caring for the well-being of others a plus. Ideal candidate will be strong, responsible, dependable, and willing to accept leadership role. Dictators and weaklings need not apply.

If you're a woman, would you be happy with a spouse who fit the criteria of the ad? If you're a man, would you feel qualified to answer such an ad?

The final ingredient in our recipe for a healthy family puts the spotlight on husbands. If your goal is a loving, functional family, the person described in the ad is the kind of husband you need at the helm.

Look at the last two words of ingredient #5 again: *loving leaders.* That's a unique combo—one that requires married men to walk a narrow line. Lay on the authority too thick, and you're no longer loving. Back off of the authority too far, and you're no longer a leader.

What Makes a Husband Healthy?

Becoming a loving leader is a tall order, to be sure. If the concept is new to you, you may not even know what a loving leader is like. For the purposes of this chapter, we've broken down the male's leadership role in the family into two positions: the healthy husband and the healthy father.

Let's take a look first at six characteristics of a loving husband.

1. *A loving husband views his wife as a partner.* It's one thing to say that your wife is your partner. It's quite another to treat her like one. In a healthy family, a husband invites his wife to share equally in decision making, finances, vacation planning, discipline, and every other area of family life.

2. *A loving husband will communicate with his wife.* Here's that C word again: *communication*—the secret to *everything* (or so it seems). As we pointed out in chapter 8, the average couple spends several hours a day apart. Only through verbal communication can you share your experiences, feelings, and desires with your spouse. In order to make sure that communication takes place, the husband must make time for a daily discussion with his wife, in which they open their lives to each other.

3. *A loving husband will put his wife at the top of his priority list.* This is another one of those areas in which lip service is meaningless. You can't just say that your spouse is your top priority; you have to demonstrate it in the way you live, the way you spend your time, money, and energy.

4. *A loving husband will love his wife unconditionally.* Unconditional love on the part of a husband involves looking out for his wife's best interests and seeking only what's best for her, regardless of whether she's doing the same for him. Conditional love is based on performance; it must be earned. Unconditional love is given without reservation—and without cause.

5. *A loving husband is committed to discovering and meeting his wife's needs.* Among the most common needs met by healthy husbands are affection,

tenderness, kindness, and encouragement. The best way for a husband to discover his wife's needs is through—you guessed it—communication.

6. *A loving husband will seek to model his moral and spiritual values.* You can file this one alongside the first and third characteristics above. "Talk is cheap," and the only valid way for a husband to communicate his values is by living them, demonstrating them in his daily life. Moral values are beliefs about what is right and wrong. Spiritual values are beliefs about what exists beyond the material world. Together they should form the bedrock of the husband's life.

What Makes a Father Healthy?

Now that you know what a healthy husband is like, let's take a look at characteristics of a healthy father. If you're a guy reading this, it will help to give you a sense of where you are.

Here are the seven characteristics of a loving father:

1. *A loving father will be active in his fathering.* This is a matter of taking the initiative in his relationship with his kids, instead of passively waiting for his kids to approach him with requests. The goal of a loving father is to be personally involved in his kids' lives in a hands-on way.

2. *A loving father will make time to be with his children.* That's not to say that loving fathers are any less busy than other dads. The fact is, time is scarce for most people. The difference between a healthy father and a not-so-healthy one is in the scheduling. A healthy, loving father puts his kids on his schedule and then protects that appointment more jealously than any other in his appointment book. A loving father is not content to give them the "leftovers" of his time.

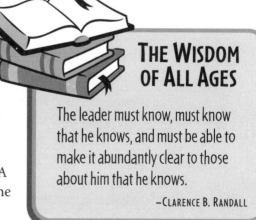

THE WISDOM OF ALL AGES

The leader must know, must know that he knows, and must be able to make it abundantly clear to those about him that he knows.

−CLARENCE B. RANDALL

3. *A loving father provides for and protects his children.* This is Parenting 101 stuff, the basic level of fathering. This is about providing food, clothing, shelter, and protection for kids. The loving father's first priority is to take care of his family's necessities.

4. *A loving father engages his children in conversation.* It's easy to talk *to* kids— you just tell them what to do and why they should do it. Talking *with* them, however, takes a little more effort—but is infinitely more rewarding. Two-way conversation is a vehicle whereby a loving father gets to know his kids and lets his kids get to know him. Asking questions about thoughts, feelings, and desires is the way to get to know them. Sharing his own thoughts, feelings, and desires with them is the way he builds intimate relationships.

5. *A loving father plays with his children.* Fun—that's what this characteristic is all about. If fun means playing computer games with his teenager, the loving father plays computer games. If it means holding a tea party for four of his daughter's closest doll friends, the loving father holds a tea party. If it means bouncing his infant son on his knee for an hour, the loving father bounces. The loving father seeks to evoke laughter and enjoyment. And he does it on *their* terms; he does not impose his own ideas of fun on his kids and expect them to get enjoyment from them.

6. *A loving father teaches his values.* Values are the strongly held beliefs we use to create order in our lives. A loving father who values honesty, kindness, and hard work will take the time to explain why those values mean so much to him and how they play out in his daily life.

7. *A loving father loves his children unconditionally.* The loving father doesn't bestow and withhold his affection based on performance or "worthiness." He doesn't wait until his kids bring home a good report card, make the all-star team, or complete their household chores to show his love for them. The loving father makes a point of saying, "I love you no matter what."

A Little Help for the Loving Father-in-Training

Perhaps as a father you realize you don't measure up in some of these areas. Here are some things you can do to become a more loving leader as a father. Let's consider the final four characteristics. (For suggestions on developing your skills as a loving husband, see pages 203–213 in my book, *Five Signs of a Loving Family*.)

If engaging your kids in conversation is difficult for you, you might try these ideas:

1. Practice asking questions that invite and inspire conversation—questions like "What was going through your mind at the end of the game today?" or "What did you think of that video we watched last night?" or "If you could change one thing about our family, what would it be?"

2. With younger children, read a book together and ask them questions about it. The questions should focus on how your kids interpret the story, how it makes them feel, and why they like it (or dislike it).

3. With older children, start a two-person "book club." Let your child choose a book that you can read together. Set up a schedule of reading a chapter (or so) a night and discussing it together the next day.

If your struggle is with playing with your child, here are three things you can do to address the problem:

1. Once a month or so, declare a "No Screen Night" in your family, when everything with a screen or monitor in your home must be kept off all night. Without the usual distractions, you and your child may be more open to the idea of having fun together.

2. Set up a board game "tournament" in which family members compete at Parcheesi, Trivial Pursuit, Monopoly, Scrabble, Clue, or any other favorite board game. You can make your tournament as simple or as elaborate as you choose. (For example, you might award a certain number of points for each win, each second-place finish, and so on.)

3. Make a list of the games you played when you were a child. One at a time, try each game out with your kids to see whether they like it or not. If they

do, incorporate it into your family "routine." If they don't, explain to them what you liked about it as a boy, then move on to the next game.

If teaching values is difficult for you, consider the following ideas:

1. Identify the values that you consider to be most important in your life. Make a list of them and keep the list handy so that you can refer to it often. After all, if you're going to share your values, you're going to have to know those values pretty well first.

2. Ask yourself this question: "If my kids turn out to be exactly like me when they are adults, will I be happy?" If your answer is "no" (or even if it's a qualified "yes"), identify the areas in which you would like your kids to be different from you. Then make a list of the changes you need to make in your own life in order to be able to answer the question with an unqualified "yes."

3. Make arrangements to have some alone time with each of your kids. During your time together, share with each child one value that you believe to be extremely important. Then share some examples of how that value has made a difference in your life.

If you have problems giving unconditional love, here are three things you can do:

1. Schedule some time to spend alone with each of your children. Open up to them about occasions in the past in which you demonstrated conditional love to them—that is, times when you "turned your love on and off," based on the way they acted or the way they treated you. Ask your kids to forgive you for those instances of conditional love.

2. Ask your children to share situations in which they felt conditional love from you. Then ask them how they would have preferred that you respond in each of those situations. Take notes on their suggestions so that you can use them in the future. Make a commitment to correct those mistakes.

3. About a month or six weeks later, schedule another appointment to talk about any progress you might have made in showing them unconditional love. Encourage them to give you honest feedback.

Family Practice

Think you're an expert on coaxing obedience from your children, providing them with valuable teaching and training, and promoting the model of husband-as-loving-leader in your family? Here's a quiz to see how much you know.

1. Which of the following is *not* an element of creative teaching?
   a. Creative interpretation
   b. Creative encouragement
   c. Creative correction
   d. Creative affirmation

2. Which of the following suggestions would be least helpful in improving your training skills?
   a. Apply some of the things you've learned in your career to your relationship with your children.
   b. Take a class on parenting at your local community college.
   c. Ask your kids what you should be doing before every step of the training process.
   d. Schedule appointments to watch elementary, preschool, or Sunday school teachers in action.

3. Which of the following is *not* one of the steps in encouraging obedience?
   a. Calling in reinforcements
   b. Setting rules
   c. Setting consequences
   d. Administering discipline

4. Which of the following is *not* true of a healthy husband?
   a. He views his wife as a partner.
   b. He is careful not to show too much affection to his wife and kids, lest they lose respect for him.
   c. He communicates with his wife.
   d. He puts his wife at the top of his priority list.

5. Which of the following is *not* true of a healthy father?
    a. He is active in his fathering.
    b. He loves his children unconditionally.
    c. He teaches his values.
    d. He uses playtime to train and condition his kids for the grueling sports-centered future that lies ahead of them.

Answers: (1) a, (2) c, (3) a, (4) b, (5) d

CHAPTER 10

Big Talk for Little Ones

(THE FIVE LOVE LANGUAGES FOR CHILDREN)

SNAPSHOT

Arlene was on her way home from a relaxing day of shopping when the car phone rang. "Hello?" she answered.

"Honey, I think we need to have Jimmy checked out."

Though there was static on the line, Arlene recognized her husband's voice and could hear their son crying in the background. "Ronnie, what's the matter?" she asked. "What's wrong with Jimmy?"

"I don't think he has a love language," Ronnie replied.

"What?" Arlene asked.

"You remember," Ronnie said. "That book we read about the different love languages. It said we could find out our child's primary love language by seeing which one he responds to."

"And?"

SNEAK PREVIEW

1. Unconditional love must be present before any love language can be communicated effectively to children.
2. The five love languages of children are the same as for adults: words of affirmation, quality time, gifts, acts of service, and physical touch.
3. You can discover your child's primary love language by observing the way he or she expresses love, personal requests, and complaints.

"Well, I've been trying to communicate with Jimmy for the past two hours using different love languages, and he hasn't responded to any of them."

"Did you try physical touch?"

"Yeah, I tried hugging him, but it was like trying to squeeze a greased pig. He just kept twisting away. And when I tried to wrestle with him, he just went limp and refused to budge. Finally, he sicced his dinosaur on me to get me to leave him alone."

"You forced our son to use a stuffed tyrannosaurus as a weapon?" Arlene asked.

"Come on, I'm being serious," Ronnie replied. "It was the same with *all* of the love languages. When I tried to do an act of service by picking up the goldfish crackers he dumped on the floor, he poured his juice box on my head. When I tried to give him words of affirmation by telling him how well he did eating his lunch, he just kept shouting, 'No, Daddy, no!' Anyone walking past the window would have thought I was beating the kid. And then when I gave him a pinecone that we found together as a gift, he tried to eat it."

"Did you try quality time?" Arlene asked.

"Oh, yeah."

"And how did that go?"

Ronnie sighed. "He just kept repeating, 'Barney, Barney, Barney,' until I finally put in a *Barney* video for him."

"I'm sorry things didn't go the way you wanted," Arlene said.

"Do you think this is something serious?" Ronnie asked. "Is it possible that Jimmy's built a wall of resentment between him and us?"

"Honey, Jimmy's only eighteen months old," Arlene reminded him. "He can't even build a wall of Legos yet."

* * * * * * * * * * * * * *

Learning to speak your child's love language will be an adventure. We can give you the information you need to familiarize yourself with the five different love languages. We can give you examples of how love languages have manifested themselves in the lives of other kids and parents. We can give you clues to look for as you search for your own child's love language.

We can't, however, make the "translation" process run smoothly. We can't change the fact that becoming fluent in your child's love language is largely a matter of trial and error—discovering what works by discovering what doesn't work. We can't change the fact that your young child (we'll talk about teenage children in the next chapter) may not be able to make the requests like your spouse can. Like we said, learning to speak your child's love language will be an adventure. But it's an adventure you and your child will grow to love.

In the Beginning . . . Love

First comes love. Before physical touch is expressed, before words of affirmation are spoken, before gifts are given, there is love. Love is not only what's communicated through the five languages covered in this chapter, it's the motivation for learning those languages.

And this isn't just any old love we're talking about. It's not the kind of love that's been prettied up by screenwriters so that Disney Channel audiences can have a feel-good moment or two. This is a warts-and-all kind of love.

This is unconditional love.

Unconditional love compels you to accept and affirm your children for who they are and not for what they do. That means if your son decides to use your best china for skeet-shooting practice with his BB gun, your love for him will not waver. It means if your daughter forgets to tell you that she's spending the night with a friend after a concert, leaving you wide awake and panicked all night, your love for her will be the same when she gets home as it was before she left.

That's not to say your son and daughter shouldn't suffer the consequences for their actions. They most certainly should. But those consequences should never include the loss or diminishing (even temporarily) of your love.

Unconditional love is a constant, like death, taxes, and unfunny sitcoms on TV; it's *always* present. Unconditional love is the foundation on which your entire relationship must be based. Only kids who feel genuinely loved—only those who have the security and hope of unconditional love—can reach their full potential.

But, But . . .

A common fear regarding unconditional love is that it produces "spoiled" children. The reasoning goes something like this: If kids know that they have their parents' love, no matter what they do, they will take advantage of it by living wild, debauched lives, and then crawling home to Mommy and Daddy whenever they need a little TLC.

But that's not the case at all. Kids are spoiled by a lack of training from their parents or by an inappropriate, reward-based kind of love. Real, unconditional love, on the other hand, will never spoil children because there's no such thing as getting *too much* of it.

> **THE WISDOM OF ALL AGES**
>
> All love is sweet,
> Given or returned.
> Common as light is love,
> And its familiar voice wearies not ever.
>
> –PERCY BYSSHE SHELLEY

If that's hard for you to swallow, or if it goes against your current parenting style, all we ask is that you give unconditional love a try. You'll find that the more you practice it, the more results you'll see. Some of the results may be dramatic and some may be barely recognizable, but you *will* see results. Your unconditional love will change your kids' lives.

Express Yourself

The next question is obvious. *How* do you demonstrate your unconditional love for your children? The fact that you're reading this chapter suggests that you deeply love them. Unfortunately, your feelings of love will do no good unless you learn to express them in a way that can be recognized and understood.

You can't assume that they automatically know you love them. And you can't assume that simply saying, "I love you" will convince them of your feelings, either. Kids are *behaviorally motivated*. That means they respond to actions —the things you do with them. So if you're going to reach them with your unconditional love, you're going to have to do it on *their* terms, through your actions.

That brings us to the five love languages: words of affirmation, quality time, receiving gifts, acts of service, and physical touch. One of these five languages will communicate love to your child more sincerely and more completely than anything else you could do. Discovering what that language is and then learning to speak it are the most meaningful actions you can demonstrate to your child.

We've already covered the five love languages in depth in chapters 3–7. If you'd like specific details about any of the languages, you should probably check there. The purpose of this chapter is not to rehash the basics of each love language, but to identify how each one is communicated by and to each child.

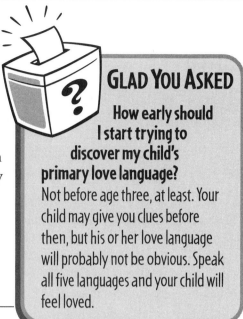

GLAD YOU ASKED

How early should I start trying to discover my child's primary love language?

Not before age three, at least. Your child may give you clues before then, but his or her love language will probably not be obvious. Speak all five languages and your child will feel loved.

Your Child and Physical Touch

The first love language we want to look at is physical touch. OK, it's not the first language on our list for husbands and wives, but there's a reason for putting physical touch at the top of a list for showing love to children: Physical touch is probably the easiest love language to learn, because it doesn't require any "excuse" or preparation on your part. Anytime you're in the same room with your kids, you have an opportunity to make physical contact with them. You can hug them, kiss them, squeeze their hands, run your fingers through their hair, rub their shoulders, pat them on the back, give them high fives, or wrestle them to the floor. The more you experiment with physical touch and work it into your daily routine, the better idea you'll have of what kind of touch works best with your kids.

Just keep in mind that most kids love frequent touches from their parents. They know it means they're loved.

That's not to say physical touch comes naturally or easily to all people. Parents who never experienced much physical affection when they were kids may have a hard time reaching out to their own kids with tactile expressions of love. Other people may draw back from giving healthy, loving touches out of fear that their touches will be seen as "unhealthy." The high profile of child sexual abuse

THE WISDOM OF ALL AGES

There are one hundred and fifty-two distinctly different ways of holding a baby—and all are right.

—HEYWOOD BROUN

allegations has left them wary and uncertain about how to physically communicate with their kids. And that's a shame. The fear of accusation should never keep anyone from expressing appropriate affection.

Growing Strong with Physical Touch

As far as physical contact is concerned, the first few years of a child's life are critical. Babies and infants aren't cuddly for nothing! They're *meant* to be held, stroked, caressed, kissed, hugged, and tickled. Would it surprise you to learn that babies who are given such "hands-on treatment" develop healthier emotional lives than those who are left for long periods of time without physical touch?

As your baby grows, so does his or her need for physical interaction with you. Hugs and kisses, piggyback rides, and other playful loving touches are essential to your infant's emotional development.

When your child begins school, the need for physical contact intensifies. Facing new experiences at school each day and trying to sort through positive and negative emotions he or she feels toward teachers and students are bound to make your child feel vulnerable and uncertain. A hug given before your child leaves for school in the morning may give him or her the emotional security to face another day in juvenile academia. A hug given when your child gets home from school may be enough to keep him or her content and satisfied for the rest of the evening. What you want to do is make your home a haven, a place where unconditional love flows freely—a place where your kids feel comfortable and fulfilled.

Touch for Boys . . . and for Girls

In your quest to provide necessary physical touch to your child, you may hit a bumpy stretch between the seventh and ninth birthdays—especially if your child happens to be male. Many boys at that age go through a stage in which they are resistant to affectionate touch. Attempts to hug or kiss your son during this period may be met with uncomfortable squirming or other defensive strategies.

The key to reaching your son at this age is to "rough up" your contact a little. Seven- to nine-year-old boys tend to respond well to more vigorous forms of contact, such as wrestling, jostling, playful hitting, and bear hugs. The best way to provide this kind of contact naturally is through games or competition. Basketball, football, and soccer are all contact sports. By competing with your son in those and other sports, you will be giving him two love languages—physical touch and quality time—for the price of one.

For girls, changes in touching behavior occur a few years later, as they approach adolescence, around the time they're in sixth grade. The need for assurances of unconditional love seems to reach its peak for girls around the age of eleven. During this time, girls have a particular need for physical expressions of love from their fathers.

Here's the way it works. Girls who have a strong and healthy sense of self-esteem and sexual identity in their adolescence are comfortable with themselves. They are also comfortable around their female peers as well as members of the opposite sex. As a result, their behavior patterns are consistent and stable. They are held in high esteem by boys and are able to form supportive, meaningful friendships with girls. As an added bonus, they are better able to resist negative peer pressure and think for themselves.

Care to guess what makes the difference in the lives of these girls, as opposed to girls who are shy, withdrawn, uncomfortable, alienated, and likely to conform to the whims of their adolescent peers? If you guessed the emotional love and physical affection they receive from their father as a preadolescent (and continuing in their teen years, as we'll see in chapter 11), well, you chose the obvious answer. And you're right.

GLAD YOU ASKED

If physical touch is important for all children, why should I try to determine if it's my child's primary love language?

A tender hug communicates love to most kids. But for a child whose primary love language is physical touch, a tender hug practically screams, "I love you!" By the same token, a negative use of contact, whether it's a stiff-armed refusal to hug or a slap in the face, will be devastating to a child whose primary love language is physical contact. So it's especially important to recognize this primary love language in your child and then respond accordingly.

Your Child and Words of Affirmation

The second love language we want to focus on is words of affirmation. For many kids, words of affection, endearment, praise, encouragement, and guidance are powerful expressions of love. When the kids receive words of affirmation, they feel fulfilled and special. When those words are absent, the kids feel insecure and neglected. Let's take a look at how different types of affirmation can impact your child's life.

Words of Affection and Endearment

Long before children learn to interpret the meanings of words, they are able to receive emotional messages. Your verbalized expressions of endearment may sound like gibberish to your young children, but they can understand what's being communicated by looking at your face, recognizing the affection in your voice, and sensing your physical closeness. All of those factors add up to love, as far as young children are concerned.

When your children are old enough to understand the words "I love you," you can use those same nonverbal tactics to imbue your words with special meaning. For example, you may make a point of drawing your children close, perhaps even nose to nose with you, when you say, "I love you." Or you may connect those words to regular events in their lives, such as bathtime, storytime, or bedtime. Anything you can do to make your words of affection stand out or resonate beyond the time it takes to say them will go a long way toward meeting your children's love needs.

Words of Praise

Don't confuse words of praise with words of affection. Words of affection express appreciation for who your child is. Words of praise express appreciation for what your child does. It may seem like a minor distinction, but it's an important one.

Praise involves recognition of your child's achievements, behavior, and conscious attitude—all things he or she can control, to a certain degree. For many kids, praise is more meaningful than affirmation for that very reason. They get a sense of having "earned" praise.

In order to maintain your praise's status as a valuable commodity to your child, you'll need to make sure that you don't give it away too freely ("That was a great catch! And so was that one! And that one! And that one!"). Otherwise, before long, it will have little positive effect on your child.

You'll also need to guard against praising too broadly and relying on generalities. Two of the most common examples of broad praise are "You're a good boy (or girl)" and "You're so nice." It's more effective to offer specifics in your praise, such as, "You are such a good listener! You picked up your crayons the first time I told you to!" and "I'm so proud of the way you shared your popsicle with Alison."

> ## THE WISDOM OF ALL AGES
>
> Children are remarkable for their intelligence and ardor, for their curiosity, their intolerance of shams, the clarity and ruthlessness of their vision.
>
> –ALDOUS HUXLEY

Make sure, too, that the praise you offer is justified. Don't say, "Great report card!" when it's just an average report card. Don't say, "You're the best shooter on the team," when your child is clearly not the best shooter. This is important, because you can bet your child will know whether your praise is justified or not. If your child believes you're just blowing smoke, he or she will likely regard your praise as flattery, which is the same as lying, as far as he or she is concerned.

Words of Encouragement

Encouragement is what empowers kids to stretch their boundaries and explore the outer reaches of their ability. The right words spoken at the right time can inspire most kids to dust themselves off after failure, overcome their wariness, and try again. But for a child whose primary love language is words of affirmation, encouragement can do even more than that; it can actually make him or her feel loved.

There's one thing you need to keep in mind when it comes to encouraging your children, especially young ones. Almost everything they do—from learning to ride a bike to ordering a meal at a restaurant—is a new experience for them. They don't have past successes to recall to help build their confidence. All they have is the knowledgeable, caring, and encouraging voice of a parent who loves and believes in them.

That voice—your voice—may ultimately determine not only whether they succeed or fail, but also how they approach new challenges in the future.

If you find it hard to offer encouraging words to your child, it may be because you're encouragement-deficient yourself. When you feel encouraged, you are better able to encourage your child. What that means for two-parent households is that mothers and fathers should provide frequent encouragement to each other. Single parents, on the other hand, should find trusted friends or family members to keep their encouragement levels high.

Words of Guidance

Loving guidance *always* has a child's best interests at heart. It's not about making you, as a parent, look good; it's about helping your child (1) develop qualities that will serve him or her well in the future and (2) avoid people, problems, and situations that will hurt him or her in the future.

You'll note that guidance is a two-part procedure. There's a positive aspect and a negative aspect to it. Remember that! At some point in your parenting career, you're going to be tempted to do what many other parents do when it comes to guidance. You're going to be tempted to become the Great Prohibitor, the Duke or Duchess of Don't. When you do that, your spotlight is only on the negative aspect.

Prohibition should not be the major element in your words of guidance. Sure, it's important for kids to know that they shouldn't drink, smoke, experiment with drugs, exceed the speed limit, give out personal information on-line, or accept rides from strangers. But warnings like these are just the secondary aspect of guidance.

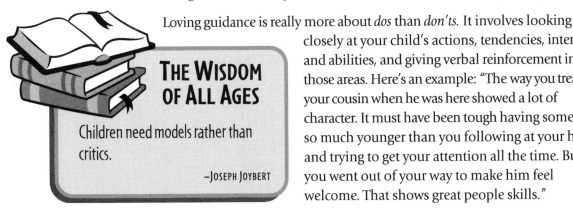

THE WISDOM OF ALL AGES

Children need models rather than critics.

–JOSEPH JOYBERT

Loving guidance is really more about *dos* than *don'ts.* It involves looking closely at your child's actions, tendencies, interests, and abilities, and giving verbal reinforcement in those areas. Here's an example: "The way you treated your cousin when he was here showed a lot of character. It must have been tough having someone so much younger than you following at your heels and trying to get your attention all the time. But you went out of your way to make him feel welcome. That shows great people skills."

Look closely behind the affirmation and you'll find guidance in those words. The unspoken lesson to your child is that patience, attentiveness, and concern for others are positive qualities and necessary ingredients for healthy social interaction. Recognizing the child's people skills will likely cause him or her to further develop and refine those skills in the future.

A Final Thought on Words of Affirmation

For kids whose primary love language is words of affirmation, nothing is more important to their sense of well-being than to hear expressions of affection, endearment, praise, encouragement, and guidance from the people who love them. But the reverse is also true—negative expressions and words of condemnation will hurt them very deeply. Harsh, ill-considered words are unpleasant for any child to hear, but they can be devastating to someone whose primary love language is affirmation. In fact, those words may affect that child for the rest of his or her life.

FAMILY TIES

If your spouse seems unaware of his or her negative communication patterns with your kids, try recording a day's worth of his or her conversations with and without comments to your kids. When you and your spouse have a block of time to talk to each other alone, play back the recording and let your spouse listen to the results. What he or she hears will probably be surprising and sobering, to say the least. It might also be life-changing.

No one expects perfection in your communication with your kids. We all have moments of weakness when we say things we don't mean or later regret. For the sake of your child, you must follow up those moments of weakness with an apology right away. You may not be able to erase your negative words, but you can minimize their effect.

Your Child and Quality Time

Quality time is focused attention. Sitting in the same room as your child is not necessarily quality time. Spending the day alone with your child isn't even necessarily quality time. Giving your child your undivided attention when the two of you are together is quality time.

Most kids begin life with a surplus of quality time from their parents. The feeding, changing, burping, and rocking of newborns and infants practically demand your undivided attention. (Heaven help the parent whose mind drifts in the middle of a diaper change.)

As your child grows, the natural opportunities for quality time diminish. You'll find that most kids of school age are resistant to being fed, changed, and rocked by their parents. And they're more than capable of burping themselves, thank you. So if you're going to spend quality time with your child, you're going to have to figure out new ways to do it.

Compared to physical touch and words of affirmation, quality time requires some significant effort on your part. For most people, there aren't enough hours in the day to do the things they need or want to do. Throw time with a child into the mix, and something's got to give. For better or worse, that *something* will probably be a high priority in your life (relatively speaking, of course—when it comes to expressing your love for your child, few things measure as high in importance).

Further complicating matters is the fact that as kids grow toward adolescence, they often require quality time just when we parents are exhausted, occupied with other matters, or emotionally spent. Enter sacrifice.

GLAD YOU ASKED

Is there anything I can do for my child that will enhance our quality time together?

While you're together, make sure you give your child plenty of pleasant, loving eye contact. Not only does it demonstrate the fact that your focus is solely on your child, it's also a powerful way of conveying love from your heart to his or her heart.

Quality time is a gift that parents give to a child. It is an act of sacrifice that says to the child, "Everything else that is vying for my attention right now pales in importance to you. I am choosing to spend my time with you because I like being with you." Imagine what that sentiment, spoken or unspoken, will do for the self-esteem of a child whose primary love language is quality time!

Getting Together

We've got some good news and some bad news about spending quality time with your child. The good news is that you can do it anywhere. Remember, it's not *what* you do that's important, it's the fact that you're doing it with your child and doing it purposefully together. So you don't have to go anyplace special for quality time. You can offer focused attention practically anywhere (except perhaps in front of the TV). The fact is, most of your nurturing quality times will probably take place in your home.

The bad news is that you can't give quality time at your own level. Instead, you need to go to your child's level of physical and emotional development. That means if your child is learning to crawl, you sit on the floor with him or her. When your child graduates to swimming pools and sandboxes, you get wet and sandy, too. When school and organized sports enter the picture, you find academic and athletic ways to spend quality time together. If that sounds like a lot of work, just think of it as an investment of your time and energy. The dividend will be an emotionally happy and healthy child.

Opening Up

Quality time is not just a matter of doing things with your child; it's also a matter of getting to know your child better—and letting him or her get to know you better. A natural result of spending quality time with your child is good conversation about the things that are going on in your lives.

Here's what a quality-time conversation starter between a father and son might sound like from the father's perspective: "Remember when I told you about that project I finished last week—the one I'd been working on for a year and a half? Well, today my boss called me into his office to tell me what a great job I did on it and how pleased he is with my work. And my boss is not the type of guy who hands out a lot of compliments. That's why I'm in such a good mood today. How about you? You seem awful happy yourself. Is it because you aced that English test this morning or because you finally worked up the nerve to talk to Lori?"

You can also use conversation to reveal a little of your personal history to your child. ("That swimming pool is where your father and I first met. He was showing off with his friends, trying to impress me and my friends, when he hit his head on the diving board. He tried to act cool about it, even though he had a knot the size of a golf ball above his eye.") What child wouldn't want to hear interesting details of his or her parents' lives?

This kind of "real" conversation communicates deeply to a child on an emotional level. The thought of being a "confidant" to parents is extremely exciting and satisfying. Your conversations will provide valuable models as he or she begins to develop other relationships, including friendships, romances, and business associations. Your child will learn to process thoughts and communicate in a thoughtful, caring way that respects the ideas of others.

Your Child and Gifts

The fourth love language we want to look at is receiving gifts. This is probably the least understood of the five love languages. Parents who have run the hideous gauntlet known as Toys R Us with their kids in tow will likely raise a skeptical eyebrow at the suggestion that buying a toy (or anything else) for their child will somehow demonstrate their deep love.

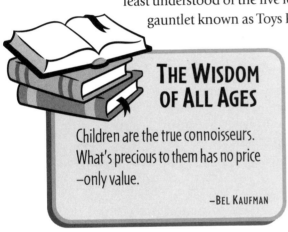

THE WISDOM OF ALL AGES

Children are the true connoisseurs. What's precious to them has no price —only value.

—BEL KAUFMAN

But the truth is, giving and receiving gifts *can* be a powerful expression of love. Meaningful gifts become symbols of love for your child and will continue to convey that love long after they are given.

Giving and receiving gifts is unique among the love languages. In order for it to be truly effective, the other four love languages must be spoken as well.

Your child must recognize that you truly care before he or she can accept a gift in the spirit you intend it. What that means is that you need to use a combination of physical touch, words of affirmation, quality time, and acts of service in order to become fluent in the child's love language of gifts.

The "Don't Bother" Kind of Giving

At first glance, it would seem that gift giving is as simple as love languages get. In fact, it's one of the most complex of the five languages. It's not the gift itself that ultimately matters; it's the way the gift is given. And you'd be surprised at how many ways there are to give a gift in the wrong spirit.

The first thing you need to understand is that true gifts are not given as payment for "services rendered." Offering to buy your child a new CD if he or she will help you rake leaves is not a true gift; it's a payment. Promising a trip to McDonald's if your child will let you get your work done is not a true gift. It's a bribe. You know it, and your child will know it.

The second thing you need to understand is that true gifts are not substitutes for emotional involvement in your kids' lives. You can't shower your children with toys and clothes because you're uncomfortable with communicating on a deep level and then expect their love needs to be fulfilled. If you insist on doing so, what will eventually happen is that your children will become materialistic and manipulative, and will learn to use people to get the things they want.

The third thing you need to understand is that true gifts are given in moderation. When children are inundated with toys and gadgets to the extent that the local Toys R Us store calls *your* house during the holidays to see if you have certain items in stock, those gifts lose their "specialness" and meaning. Eventually your children will become emotionally dead to receiving gifts. (And you don't have to be an experienced family counselor to know that the words *emotionally* and *dead* should never be used together when describing a child.)

Good Gifts

Rather than concentrating on the quantity of gifts you give, try focusing on quality. Give gifts that you know will be *meaningful* to your child (perhaps a set of favorite books or a leather-bound diary to record his or her innermost thoughts), as opposed to those that are simply impressive (say, a six-foot-tall stuffed gorilla).

As your child gets older, let him or her help you choose gifts. There will come a time of definite and specific opinions on clothes, shoes, backpacks, music, and practically everything else. Being aware of your child's tastes will help you when it comes time to select a gift.

Remember that your gifts don't necessarily have to come from a store. A paper-clip structure, created by you during your downtime at the office, may be just as meaningful as an expensive stuffed animal. If your present stimulates creativity, and if he or she recognizes the love that went into it, it can bind the two of you together.

Your Child and Acts of Service

The fifth and final love language we want to look at is acts of service. Even if it doesn't apply to your child, you're probably familiar with the dynamics of this love language. After all, parenting is a service-oriented vocation. From the time your first child was born, you've been "on the clock" as a server. And you're not going to be able to "punch out" until you've put in a good eighteen years (at least) of work.

Having said that, we need to point out that for some kids acts of service are genuine expressions of love. When your child asks you to fix his bicycle chain or sew the tear in her Barbie doll's dress, he or she is not just asking for a task to be done, but for an expression of emotional love as well. That's why it's important for you to be able to recognize requests like that (whether they're spoken or unspoken) for what they are and respond to them properly.

As you consider acts of service, keep in mind that your primary motivation is not to please, but to do what's best. Pleasing your child would be easy. All you'd have to do is serve donuts for breakfast, candy bars for lunch, and ice cream for dinner. Doing what's best, on the other hand, requires a little (OK, a lot) of thought.

FAMILY TIES

You've heard of the expression "Like father, like son"? That's the result you're looking for from your acts of service. Your ultimate purpose is to help your child emerge as a mature adult who is able to give love to others through acts of service–the very kind of acts that you modeled for him or her.

From Act-or to Teacher

In order to be effective, your acts of service must be age appropriate. That means doing things that a child cannot do for himself or herself. Helping your three-year-old get dressed in the morning is an act of service. Helping your twelve-year-old get dressed in the morning is ridiculous—and damaging—in the long run.

As you serve your child, you need to be aware of skill development. When you believe he or she is ready, you can incorporate teaching into your acts of service, so that your child can learn to perform those acts for himself or herself—and for others.

If you've ever tried to teach your child a skill—like

making a grilled cheese sandwich—you know that it's not a quick and easy process. In fact, it's quite time-consuming. You could probably finish a dozen sandwiches yourself in the time it takes your child to butter the bread. But speed isn't the issue— at least, it shouldn't be. The issue is your child's best interests, and where they are concerned, the cost of time should be irrelevant. Your child needs to learn to cook. And if you're committed to serving, you will do whatever it takes to teach that art.

It's All About the Attitude

Because service is such a constant thing for parents, it's easy to forget that your child may be viewing your actions in a different way. The acts that seem like drudgery to you may have a lifelong impact. That's why you need to make sure that your attitude toward your work demonstrates love. If you serve with a spirit of bitterness and resentment, you miss the point of the love language. You may be fulfilling the physical needs, but you're devastating the emotional needs.

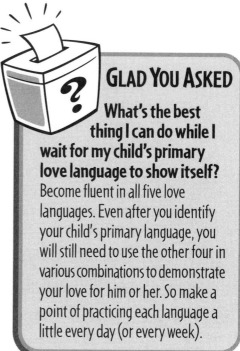

GLAD YOU ASKED

What's the best thing I can do while I wait for my child's primary love language to show itself? Become fluent in all five love languages. Even after you identify your child's primary language, you will still need to use the other four in various combinations to demonstrate your love for him or her. So make a point of practicing each language a little every day (or every week).

If your child's primary love language is acts of service, it doesn't mean you have to rush to fulfill every request. It does mean that you have to give each request serious consideration. Consider your child's motivation for the request, what is actually needed from you. Most importantly, whether you perform the act of service or not, make sure that you give a loving, thoughtful response to his or her request.

Which One Is It?

Now that we've introduced you to the five major players, let's take a quick look at how to figure out which one is your child's primary love language. We've broken down the discovery process into five steps. We should point out that not all of the steps will be equally helpful to you in your search. Some may reveal no clues at all; others may have you shouting, "Eureka! I found it!"

Step #1: Observe how your child expresses love to you.

Your child may very well be speaking his or her own love language without your realizing it. For example, if you notice that your son playfully hits you a lot or instinctively reaches for your hand when you're together or tries to initiate wrestling matches with you, it may be an indication that his primary love language is physical touch. In other words, he may be giving you what he wants to receive from you.

Step #2: Observe how your child expresses love to others.

A child whose primary love language is receiving gifts receives tremendous pleasure from getting presents and will likely want to share that pleasure with others. Consequently, he or she will be motivated to buy, make, or find gifts for people as often as possible. If your daughter insists on drawing or coloring a picture to give to Grandma every time you go to her house, it may be an indication that her primary love language is giving and receiving gifts.

Step #3: Listen to what your child requests most often.

Most kids aren't shy about voicing their requests, preferences, and desires. If you learn to listen "between the lines" to the things your child is requesting, you may hear his or her primary love language. For example, if your daughter frequently looks to you for evaluation, asking questions like "Did you like the way I sang my song in Sunday school?" or "Did you see how hard I hit the ball?" it may be an indication that her primary love language is words of affirmation.

GLAD YOU ASKED

Should I ask my child to help me discover his or her primary love language?

No, it's probably best not to discuss your search with your child, especially if he or she is older than six or seven. Kids are self-centered by nature. Your child may see your search for his or her love language as an opportunity to manipulate you into satisfying his or her momentary desires.

Obviously, you shouldn't jump to conclusions here. *All* kids need and will seek affirmation. But if your child's desire for it seems especially intense, it may be the love language is making itself known.

Step #4: Listen to your child's most frequent complaints.

When you consider the amount of whining and grumbling you probably hear each day, categorizing your child's complaints may seem like a daunting (and thoroughly unpleasant) task. But the results may surprise you. You may find that more than half of the complaints fall into a category corresponding with one of the love languages. Complaints like "You always play with the baby!" and "Why do you always have to work on Saturdays?" may actually be requests for quality time.

That's not to say that each complaint has merit and should be carefully considered. (After all, how are you going to categorize something like "Mom, he's breathing on me again!"?) Frequency is the key to determining whether complaints are related to love language. The more frequently your child complains about something, the more likely it is that a love language is involved.

Step #5: Give your child a choice between two options.

Try introducing your child to situations where there are choices between two love languages. For example, you might say, "I've got the whole afternoon free. Would you prefer that I get out the bikes so we can take a ride together or put up your new basketball hoop on the garage?" In that situation, you're asking your child to choose between quality time and an act of service.

As you present choices like that, pay close attention to the decisions made. Find out which love languages "beat" others in head-to-head competition. The one left standing —the love language your child chooses most often—may very well be the primary love language.

Family Practice

Think you're an expert on the five love languages of children? Here's a quiz to see how much you know.

1. Which of the following is *not* one of the love languages of children?
   a. Receiving gifts
   b. Acts of service
   c. Pretending
   d. Physical touch

2. Which of the following is good advice when it comes to sharing words of affirmation with your child?
   a. Never give affirmation after your child fails at something.
   b. Don't give praise away too freely.
   c. Encouragement should be reserved for older kids.
   d. Unless your words of guidance contain strong warnings, your child will ignore them.

3. Which of the following is true of your child's primary love language?
   a. It can be changed pretty easily until he or she reaches the age of eighteen or so.
   b. It will be immediately apparent at birth.
   c. It will most likely be the same as your primary love language.
   d. It can be used to harm his or her emotional well-being just as easily as it can be used to help it.

4. Which of the following is *not* true of the love language of gifts?
   a. True gifts are not given as payment for "services rendered."
   b. True gifts are not substitutes for emotional involvement in your kids' lives.
   c. True gifts are given in moderation.
   d. True gifts are usually exchanged for items of less sentimental and more practical value.

5. Which of the following is *not* a recommended method for discovering your child's primary love language?
   a. Read his or her journal entries.
   b. Listen to what he or she requests most often.
   c. Give him or her a choice between two options.
   d. Observe how he or she expresses love to others.

Answers: (1) c, (2) b, (3) d, (4) d, (5) a

CHAPTER 11

Teen Speak

(THE FIVE LOVE LANGUAGES FOR TEENAGERS)

SNAPSHOT

Big Mike sat down at the break-room table and poured himself a cup of soup from his Thermos.

"Hey, Mike, how's that son of yours?" Chet asked from across the table.

"Ah, don't get me started on that kid," Mike said with a wave of his hand.

"What's wrong?"

"I'll tell you what's wrong," Mike replied. "He's an ingrate. For his birthday, I got him two tickets to the first night game of the season. A friend of mine gave me a good deal on some seats right behind the visitors' dugout. I figured my son and one of his buddies could go and have a good time—you know, act like big shots down there in the expensive seats."

"I take it that's not what your son had in mind?" Chet asked.

SNEAK PREVIEW

1. Demonstrating unconditional love to your teenager may require a complete overhaul of your communication patterns.
2. Quality time with your teenager involves not only quality activities, but also quality conversations, in which you must communicate with your teen on his or her level.
3. In order to discover your teenager's primary love language, you need to ask questions, make observations, and experiment.

"No," Mike said. "Instead, he asks me if *I* want to go to the game with him. I shouldn't have had to remind him that I have men's league at the bowling alley that night."

"What'd he say when you reminded him?"

"He wanted to know if I could *skip* my bowling league one night!" Mike roared.

"But you're the captain!" Chet exclaimed. "You *carry* that team!"

"That's what I told him!" Mike said.

"Did he understand?"

"Who knows?" Mike said. "He did one of those sad head nods and said he guessed he could find a friend to go with him. Then he said, 'Thanks for the tickets.' But by that time, the whole gift was ruined for me. I don't even know why I bother sometimes."

Chet shook his head sadly and said, "Hey, if a kid can't appreciate his father's love, that's *his* problem."

* * * * * * * * * * * * * * *

Imagine a world in which all teenagers spoke the same love language—for example, words of affirmation. Imagine that the only thing you ever needed to do to show your love for your teenagers was to offer a few simple, heartfelt words of encouragement and guidance. What do you think life would be like in such a world?

Parenting would be easier, that's for sure. But would it be more enjoyable? Probably not. Granted, learning and communicating in five different love languages is a challenge. But challenges are what make life exciting. Besides, when you become fluent in different love languages, not only are you expanding your teenagers' horizons, you're expanding your own.

We've already taken two spins around the love language block in this book, one to show how adults express and receive love (chapters 3–7) and one to show how children do it (chapter 10). So there's no need to go over the lay of the land again in this chapter. If you want to know the basics about love languages, we suggest that you flip back to one of those earlier chapters. In this chapter, we're going to focus on how each love language applies specifically to older children—our teenagers.

A Stranger in the House

Suggesting that the teen years can be difficult for parent and child is like suggesting that the *Titanic*'s maiden voyage didn't go as smoothly as it could have. It's an understatement of biblical proportions. One mother of a fifteen-year-old son summed up the sentiments of many parents when she admitted, "Sometimes I wonder who stole my happy, cheerful, loving son and replaced him with this angry, sullen, antisocial teenager."

Indeed, living with a teenager can be a confusing, frustrating experience. The methods of communication and expressing your love that worked so well when your child was younger may now be met with irritation or stony silence. At times, it may seem as though your home *has* been invaded by body snatchers who stole the inner workings of your child and left only a pimply shell behind.

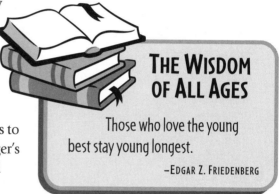

THE WISDOM OF ALL AGES

Those who love the young best stay young longest.

—EDGAR Z. FRIEDENBERG

What you need to understand is that beneath your teen's hardened, defensive exterior is a child who needs your unconditional love every bit as much as he or she did as a baby. Your challenge is to find ways to express that love, using your teenager's primary love language, so that it can be received comfortably and understandably.

Love Language #1: Words of Affirmation

One of the hallmarks of the teenage years is the struggle for identity. Your teenager likely spends a great deal of time comparing himself or herself to peers physically, intellectually, and socially. In many cases, your teen may feel as though he or she just doesn't measure up. Your child's self-esteem will suffer, and there may be intense feelings of insecurity.

This is where you and your words of affirmation can save the day—or at least relieve a little anxiety and insecurity. Even if your teen's love language isn't words of affirmation, he or she will still benefit tremendously from generous portions of praise and affection from you.

Let's look first at how to most effectively offer words of praise to your teenager.

Praise Be

Praising your teenager involves recognizing and giving commendation for accomplishments. Of course, since we're talking about teenagers here, the act of giving praise may not be quite that simple. If you want to do it right, you need to remember three principles.

GLAD YOU ASKED

How can I change the negative communication patterns that have already developed between me and my teenager?

Chances are, your teenager is not responding to you in a positive manner because you're trying to continue the parenting methods you used when he or she was a child. That won't work. As you communicate with your teenager, you need to account for and acknowledge the fact that he or she is becoming more and more complex physically, emotionally, intellectually, socially, and spiritually.

1. Be sincere.

More than almost anything else, teenagers look for truthfulness and authenticity in adults. That's why, when you offer praise to your teenager, you need to make sure that you *really* mean what you say. If your teen suspects that you're trying to flatter, the whole effect will be ruined.

To say something like, "You did a good job cleaning the kitchen last night," when there are still pans soaking in the sink and food residue all over the counters, is an insult to your teenager's intelligence. You both know it's not true, and your teen will resent the fact that you're trying to "fool" him or her with your praise.

2. Be specific.

Along those same lines is the problem of being too broad or general in your praise. Statements like, "You did a good job cleaning out the garage" are rarely accurate in their entirety. Truth is usually better expressed in more specific statements, such as, "I appreciate the way you organized the work bench; now I'll be able to find the exact tool I need exactly when I need it" or "I can't believe you were able to pack all of our Christmas decorations into three boxes!" Those are the kind of specific statements that resonate with teenagers. That's why you should train yourself to look for specifics where your teenager is concerned.

The things you single out will likely be the things your teenager put the most time and effort into. The fact that you pick up on that effort and show your appreciation for it will not go unnoticed (though it will likely go unmentioned).

3. If you can't praise results, praise efforts.

Teenagers suffer from the same strain of imperfection that the rest of us do. The way you respond to that imperfection—particularly in your words of praise—will go a long way toward determining whether your teenager feels loved and affirmed or rejected and bitter.

Many parents make the mistake of sticking a big *but* right in the middle of their praise:

➤ "You did a good job mowing the lawn . . . *but* you missed a couple of patches under the bushes in the side yard."

➤ "That was a great play you made in the fifth inning to get the runner at second . . . *but* you've got to cut down on your strikeouts at the plate."

➤ "I really enjoyed the essay you wrote . . . *but* I noticed two spelling errors that need to be corrected."

Maybe all three of those "but" statements are true. Maybe the teenagers in those scenarios could have done a better job. Maybe they would benefit from the advice that's offered. None of that changes the fact that attaching a caveat to a purported statement of praise will inspire nothing but resentment in your teenager.

There is a time and place for everything. The completion of a task by your teenager is the time for praise. Period. You find the things that are worthy of praise in that completed task and you show your appreciation for them. You praise your teenager's efforts, and then leave it at that.

At some later date—perhaps the next time your teen tackles that task—you might give a couple of helpful tips so that the mistake won't be repeated. Remember, it's all about timing.

Now let's take a look at what you need to know about offering words of affirmation.

THE WISDOM OF ALL AGES

One must not be mean with affections; what is spent of the funds is renewed in the spending itself. Left untouched for too long, they diminish imperceptibly or the lock gets rusty; they are there all right but one cannot make use of them.

—SIGMUND FREUD

Affectionately Yours

Words of praise focus on your teenager's actions. Words of affection, on the other hand, focus on your teenager. Affection is making your teenager aware of your appreciation for who he or she is.

The most common and direct method of expressing affection is found in the three most meaningful words of the English language: *Here's some money.* (Just making sure that you're paying attention.)

Of course, we're talking about the words *I love you.* Some parents use the phrase so often they may wonder if the words still have any impact on their kids. (Memo to those parents: They do.) Other parents resist saying those words for reasons only they understand. Regardless of which camp you fall into, you must understand that your teenagers *need* to hear those words from you. Direct expressions of your love is not a luxury for your teenager, it's an absolute necessity.

You may offer several compelling reasons for withholding those "three little words":

➤ "My son acts like he doesn't even hear me when I tell him I love him."

➤ "After an argument, I always wait for my daughter to say, 'I love you,' to me before I say it to her, so that it doesn't look like I'm giving in to her."

➤ "My father never told me he loved me but I always knew he did. Why should I say it to my kids?"

All of those excuses pale in light of the fact that teenagers who do not hear the words "I love you" from their parents often experience deep emotional pain in adulthood.

So what it comes down to is this: You can't legitimately claim to be concerned about your child's well-being if you are not supplying regular, heartfelt expressions of love. It doesn't matter how your teenager responds or how little you heard those words yourself growing up. What matters is that your teenager desperately needs to hear you say, "I love you"—often and sincerely.

Love Language #2: Quality Time

Quality time means giving your teenager your undivided attention. You can do that in two ways: through quality conversations and quality activities. Let's take a look at what's involved in both of them.

Opening the Channels of Communication

Quality conversation is dialogue between you and your teenager in which each of you feels free to share your experiences, thoughts, feelings, and desires in a friendly, accepting atmosphere. It means speaking *with* your teen instead of *at* your teen.

If you're like most parents, enjoying quality conversations with your teenager will require a radical shift in your approach to communication. Instead of speaking to get your point across and listening to correct, as many parents do when their kids are young, you need to learn to take your teenager seriously in conversation. That involves making a conscious effort to draw out your teen and listen sympathetically to what is said. It involves asking questions—not in a nagging way, but in a way that communicates your desire to understand thoughts and feelings.

If you're really serious about learning how to have quality conversations with your teenager, here are eight tips to keep in mind.

1. *Maintain eye contact.* While your teenager is talking, keep your eyes focused on his or her eyes. This will not only keep your mind from wandering, it will also help your teenager realize that you are giving your full attention to the conversation.

2. *Don't listen and do something else at the same time.* Quality time requires your undivided attention. When your teenager is ready to talk, turn off the TV, put down the newspaper, shut down the computer, and stop doing anything else so that you can give your entire concentration. If it's not possible for

FAMILY TIES

In addition to the little "I love you's" you give your teenager at bedtime or whenever you say good-bye, you need to give periodic, grand "I love you's." Here's what you do. When you have a moment alone, place your hands on your teen's shoulders, look into the eyes, and say, "What I am about to say is extremely important to me. I want you to hear me carefully. I love you very much, and that will never change."

you to stop what you're doing, explain the situation to your teen and schedule a time as soon as possible to have your conversation.

3. *Listen for feelings.* Quality conversations aren't just fact-finding missions to discover the whos, whats, whens, and wheres of your teenager's life. You also want to find out which emotions are being experienced as a result of the things that are going on in his or her life. When you think you spot an emotion in the course of a conversation, ask your teenager for confirmation ("It sounds like you're a little disappointed that I couldn't make it to your game today"). Not only does it give your teenager a chance to clarify feelings, it also demonstrates that you're listening intently to what is being said.

4. *Observe body language.* Look for physical gestures, such as clenched fists, shaking hands, or grimaces, that may give a hint about feelings. If the body language you're seeing contradicts what you're hearing, ask your teenager to clarify the feelings for you.

5. *Refuse to interrupt.* At some point in your conversations with your teenager, you're going to feel the urge to defend yourself or give your teen the "right" answer to a particular dilemma or situation the teen is facing. Resist that urge. Interruptions kill conversations. Besides, the goal of the conversations is not to get your point across, but to demonstrate love to your teenager.

6. *Ask reflective questions.* Don't just *assume* that you know what your teenager is saying. Ask some questions to clear up any potential misunderstandings, questions that summarize and reflect back your teen's words ("Are you saying that you're not sure you want to date Heather anymore?"). Remember, your goal is to understand what's going on in your teenager's head. If you need to ask questions in order to do that, ask away.

7. *Express understanding.* There's a certain amount of vulnerability involved in sharing one's feelings—especially if the person you're sharing with happens to be your parent! You need to recognize and respect that vulnerability in quality conversations by doing everything you can to let your teen know that you understand what he or she is saying ("I can certainly see why you want to devote your time to making your band

successful"). That's not to say you have to agree with everything your teenager says. You just need to let it be known that the message was received loud and clear.

8. *Ask permission to share your perspective.* After your teenager is finished talking, it's your turn. Or, at least, it will be, if your teenager OKs it. The last thing you want to do is hijack the conversation and hold it hostage until you have a chance to unload your thoughts on the matter. That's not how quality conversation works. If you have something to add to the conversation, ask if he or she would like to hear it. If you get an OK, share away. If you get a "Nope," keep your thoughts to yourself.

The art of quality conversations takes a long time to perfect. The rewards will be worth every minute of effort. Your teenager will feel respected, understood, and loved by you. What more could you want?

Quality Time Means Action!

Yes, quality time means action. Teenagers are creatures of action, and often you will find that your best quality conversations take place while you and your teen are doing something together. That *something* may be part of the normal flow of life—school, sports, music, or church events—or it may be a special event designed specifically to give you quality time together.

The key to a successful quality activity is to take your teenager's interests into account. For example, if your son is really into basketball, you might plan a "hoops day" for both of you. Your afternoon could be spent playing one-on-one or just shooting around in your driveway or at a local park. Later the two of you could

GLAD YOU ASKED

Talking to my teenage son is like talking to a brick wall. Is there anything I can do to get him to talk to me?

All teenagers have times when they don't want to talk, for whatever reason. The best thing parents can do during those times is to keep quiet. As for initiating conversation with your son, your best bet is to keep things casual at first and let a quick exchange of "surface" information grow into a deep conversation. One of the best ways to begin such a conversation is by focusing on your teen's mood ("Looks like you had a tough day at school. Anything you wouldn't mind sharing with me?").

attend a local high school or college game together (where tickets are inexpensive and readily available). It doesn't really matter who's playing, as long as the two of you are watching it together. Throughout the day, you could use basketball as a starting point for all kinds of conversations—who you each think is the greatest player of all time, what kind of people make good role models, the best shot each of you ever made in a game, why some people take their natural abilities for granted, and so on.

Love Language #3: Receiving Gifts

Let's get this straight from the top: Gifts, in the context of love languages, are not bribes or rewards for good behavior. They are simply tangible evidence of your love. That's an important distinction to keep in mind, because unless your gifts are presented freely, unearned, and sincerely, your teenager may not recognize them as a love language.

There are two principles you need to keep in mind when it comes to giving presents.

1. Ordinary gifts can be extraordinary.

You probably know the old saying "It's the thought that counts." Maybe you've used it yourself a few times. It's a great justification for anyone who's too cheap to spring for something nice for a loved one. But when it comes to the love language of gifts, it really is the thought that counts. In most cases, the gift itself is almost incidental to the act of giving.

THE WISDOM OF ALL AGES

[Adolescence] is the age of cosmic yearnings and private passions, of social concern and personal agony. It is the age of inconsistency and ambivalence.

–HAIM G. GINOTT

If your teenager's primary love language is giving and receiving gifts, what will matter more than anything is that you find presents *especially* for him or her. A tape of your teenager's favorite songs would make an excellent gift. It's inexpensive, for one thing—especially if you record the songs off the radio or borrow CDs from a friend. It's also meaningful, because it requires attention on your part to discover what the favorite songs are.

And a tape is just one example. Everything from a wildflower you picked in a park to an order of sweet-and-sour chicken from a favorite Chinese restaurant can be a meaningful gift, if it's given in the right spirit.

The perfect gift isn't one that screams, "Look at me, I'm expensive!" The perfect gift is one that says, "I'm here because someone who loves you was thinking of you."

2. Unconditional gifts will speak the loudest to your teenager.

Giving something unconditionally, with absolutely no strings or expectations attached, is extremely difficult to do. There's something inside each one of us that demands recognition, thanks, or compensation for the gifts we give. We may not express those demands verbally, but that doesn't mean they aren't real. The problem is, when we don't get the responses we're looking for, we may be tempted to withdraw from or hold a grudge against the person who received the gift.

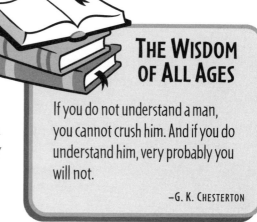

THE WISDOM OF ALL AGES

If you do not understand a man, you cannot crush him. And if you do understand him, very probably you will not.

–G. K. CHESTERTON

In a chapter on meeting your teenager's need for love, do we need to tell you that withdrawing or holding a grudge against your teen is a bad idea? The brutal truth is that if you give your teenager an unconditional gift, you have no right to expect any kind of reaction in return. That's why it's called *unconditional.* If you do receive an expression of thanks or appreciation, consider it "icing on the cake" and go your merry way. If you don't receive any gratitude, don't make a big deal of it. Just start thinking about the next meaningful—and unconditional—gift you can give.

Love Language #4: Acts of Service

Acts of service for teenagers involve doing things for them that they have not yet learned to do for themselves. Obviously, these acts will differ from teenager to teenager, based on age and developmental levels. They could involve everything from cooking meals to sewing torn clothing.

The question that arises most frequently regarding acts of service as a love language goes like this: If I continue to do these things for my teenager as an act of love, how will he or she ever learn to do them for himself or herself? The concern is that acts of service will ultimately cause a teenager to become hopelessly dependent on the parents.

The Guiding Life

To avoid that problem, you need to incorporate the element of teaching into your acts of service. If this represents a shift in behavior for you, you might want to give your teenager a "heads up" that it's coming. Explain that you've enjoyed showing your love by providing acts of service for the past thirteen years or so. If you have special memories of certain acts, you might want to share them. Point out that while you want to continue providing acts of service to your teen, you want to do it in a way that reflects his or her maturity level. Explain that toward that end, you're going to start teaching life skills that need to be learned.

Talk about killing two birds with one stone! Not only are you demonstrating your love using your child's primary love language, you're also preparing your teen to become a responsible adult.

Teenager See, Teenager Do

Your efforts to guide your teenager in learning necessary life skills will require both teaching and training on your part. *Teaching* is giving verbal instructions. *Training* is helping learn by doing.

For example, as an act of service, you may want to teach your teenager to change a flat tire. The teaching process might involve reading together through your car's instruction manual, which should explain where the spare tire and jack are located and offer some safety tips for using the jack and removing the old tire. The training process would involve helping your teenager loosen the lug nuts, find the right place for the jack, remove the tire, and so on.

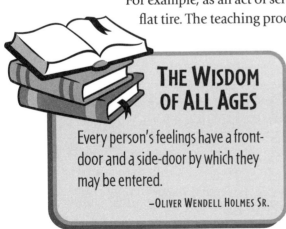

THE WISDOM OF ALL AGES

Every person's feelings have a front-door and a side-door by which they may be entered.

—OLIVER WENDELL HOLMES SR.

This example raises an interesting point. Few teens are going to learn everything they need to know about changing a tire (or any other life skill, for that matter) in one session. For that reason, you should follow up your instructional acts of service periodically with "refresher courses" and "practice time" until your teenager is competent (at least) in the life skill.

If your teenager seems resistant to your teaching efforts, point out that the more life skills acquired, the more true independence there will be. Remember, for teenagers, life is all about freedom and independence. And most of them recognize that they can't legitimately claim to be independent if they have to run home to Mom and Dad every time they need a shirt washed or a tire changed. If you put your acts of service in those terms, it's likely your teenager will buy into the program.

Love Language #5: Physical Touch

As a general rule, teenagers are about as cuddly as rabid porcupines. But that doesn't change the fact that many teens find their primary expressions of love through physical touch. What that means for you, as a parent, is that if you want to meet the emotional needs of your physical-touch-speaking teenager, you have to know the right time, the right place, and the right way to do it.

The Right Time

Finding the right time to offer physical touch to your teenager is tricky for two reasons: (1) The way your touch is received will depend on your teenager's mood, and (2) your teenager's mood is not always apparent. What often happens is that you discover your teen is in a nontouching mood the hard way, after you've already made your move. And the results usually aren't pleasant.

To avoid such uncomfortable situations, you need to study your teenager and learn to gauge moods by behavior. For example, if your teenager starts a conversation with you from across the room, it may be a warning to keep your distance. If he or she stands close to you while talking, it may be an invitation for

FAMILY TIES

As your teenager gets into the spirit of learning adult responsibilities from you, encourage him or her to take the initiative and come up with a list of other things he or she would like to learn. Depending on the eagerness of your teenager, you may get enough service ideas to last for months. You'll also have a teenager motivated to learn.

a loving touch. If you learn to recognize body language, you may be able to spot opportune moments to offer loving touches.

Your safest bet for having your physical touch received in the spirit you intend it is to bestow the touch immediately following a triumph or failure. In the case of a triumph, whether it's an athletic victory, a successful musical recital, or an exceptional test grade, your physical acts of celebration will likely be welcomed (within reason) in the excitement of the moment. In the wake of a failure in your teenager's life, whether it involves receiving a D on a report card, wrecking the family car, or getting dumped by a date, he or she will likely welcome your comforting physical expressions of love.

The one time you should *never* try to offer physical touch is when he or she is angry. Despite your best intentions, your teenager will probably interpret your physical contact as an effort to control and pull away from you.

The Right Place

This part is easy. The best place to give the physical touch he or she needs is in the privacy of your home, when the two of you are alone or in the presence of immediate family members. That's where your teenager will be most comfortable receiving your touch.

What you don't want to do is offer uninvited physical touch in public—especially if friends or peers are around. Your teenager's self-identity is tied up with that of his friends. When you try to enter that world by showing physical affection to your teen, you are threatening self-identity and striking against independence. In your teenager's mind, you're making it look like he or she still needs you. So a good rule of thumb is never to touch your teenager in the presence of friends unless your teen initiates it by touching you.

The Right Way

You have an arsenal of potential touching methods at your disposal, including hugs, kisses, back rubs, pats, tender touches, massages, high fives, hip checks, and out-and-out wrestling. Rather than inundating (and irritating) your teenager with all of them, find the one or two that will be received and learn to employ them as skillfully as possible.

Face it, the kind of touches you prefer to give may not be the kind your teenager prefers to receive. And since the whole point of offering physical touch is to make your teen feel loved, that puts him or her in the driver's seat. Some teenagers like back rubs; others can't stand them. Some teenagers like to be grabbed in headlocks; others prefer more gentle forms of contact. Your teenager will respond well to certain physical expressions and reject others.

> ## THE WISDOM OF ALL AGES
>
> Praise is well, compliment is well, but affection—that is the last and final and most precious reward that any man can win, whether by character or achievement.
>
> —MARK TWAIN

Of course, there will be a trial-and-error period as you learn which touches work and which ones don't. You may ask for guidance, if you think he or she would be of help in narrowing down the list of pleasant touches. Otherwise, you will have to learn to stick with what works as you communicate your love through physical touch.

Discover Your Teen's Love Language

We've covered the topic of recognizing love languages in chapters 3–7 and chapter 10. So let's not beat a dead horse here. Instead, as we wrap up this chapter, let's take a look at a few brief points that apply specifically to the way *teenagers* make their primary love language known.

Chances are, after watching your teenager grow up, you probably already have a pretty good idea what his or her love language is. If, however, you'd like to confirm your suspicions, here are three suggestions for discovering the primary love language.

1. Ask questions.

The only way to know for certain what your teenager is thinking and feeling is to get inside his or her head. The best way to get there is by asking questions that will encourage openness. (You need to take the initiative in asking questions because, as a rule, teenagers aren't known for volunteering information to their parents.)

When it comes to discovering valuable love language information, you can try direct, to-the-point questions ("What is the one thing that you think would improve our relationship?") or more indirect questions ("What would you think about the two of us taking a road trip to Ohio together to see your grandparents?"). Either way, you should avoid the appearance of nosiness and make it clear that you would never use the information you receive from your teenager against him or her in any way.

The more questions you ask, the better able you'll be to narrow down the love language preferences. Remember, moderation is important. Keep your questioning casual and periodic; don't "grill" your teenager.

GLAD YOU ASKED

As a father, I'm not really comfortable touching my daughter as I did when she was younger. Should I?

Some dads don't know how to respond to their daughter's ongoing physical changes; others fear someone may accuse them of sexual touches. But appropriate physical touching by a father will make the daughter feel good about herself as a female, giving her a sense of self-identity and well-being. We strongly encourage you to continue the love language of physical touch during your daughter's teenage years.

2. Make observations.
Make a conscious effort to observe the way your teenager interacts with others. Look specifically for ways love and appreciation are expressed. There's a good chance your teen may be demonstrating his or her primary love language, giving others what is yearned for in return.

You'll also want to pay attention to the things your teen complains about. It seems almost too obvious to say that the things your teenager complains about not having are clues as to what your teen really wants. But don't overlook the obvious, especially when you're searching for the primary love language.

If your teenage daughter has voiced several complaints about your work schedule or having to eat alone or having to find a ride to a game because you're not around, she may be telling you that she needs quality time from you. To miss the cries for love in your teenager's complaints would be a terrible mistake—one that will seriously affect both of you.

3. Experiment.
Concentrate on demonstrating one particular love language to your teenager a week, for five weeks. For example, in Week 1, you might focus on physical touch,

making special efforts to give hugs, kisses, caring pats, shoulder rubs, and any other kind of contact your teenager is comfortable with. In Week 2, you might shift your focus to acts of service, and so on.

Write down your observations of your teenager's reactions each week, identifying evidence of whether a love language is working or not. At the end of your five-week test period, if you don't know for certain which is your teenager's primary love language, you should probably be able to narrow your choices down to two. Then you can run another experiment, this time two weeks in length, to determine a "winner."

THE WISDOM OF ALL AGES

There is nothing sweeter than to be sympathized with.

—George Santayana

A Final Word on Teenage Love Languages

As we suggested at the beginning of this chapter, the teenage years are difficult for parents and kids alike. The inevitable conflicts that arise during this period can do serious damage to your relationship with your child. Unfortunately, there's not much you can do to avoid many of those conflicts. They are inextricably linked to adolescence.

However, by learning your teenager's primary love language, you can establish a communication that supersedes conflict and lets your son or daughter know of the unconditional love that will always be there.

Family Practice

Think you're an expert on the five love languages of teenagers? Here's a quiz to see how much you know.

1. Which of the following is *not* a helpful principle to remember when offering praise to your teenager?
   a. Be sincere.
   b. When you can't praise results, praise efforts.

    c. Be specific.

    d. Be funny.

2. Which of the following is *not* a helpful tip for maintaining a quality conversation with your teenager?

    a. Observe body language.

    b. Interrupt when you hear something you don't like.

    c. Listen for feelings.

    d. Maintain eye contact.

3. Which of the following is *not* true of a sincere love language gift?

    a. It is unearned.

    b. It is given freely.

    c. It is usually lost or thrown away within a week or so.

    d. It doesn't have to cost a cent.

4. Which of the following is true of physical touch?

    a. It's not actually a love language.

    b. Teenage boys are ten times more likely to identify it as their primary love language than teenage girls are.

    c. The ability to have quality conversations with your teenager eliminates the need for physical touch.

    d. The way your touch is received will depend on your teenager's mood.

5. Which of the following is *not* a recommended method for discovering your teenager's primary love language?

    a. Talk to his or her friends and teachers.

    b. Experiment.

    c. Make observations.

    d. Ask questions.

Answers: (1) d, (2) b, (3) c, (4) d, (5) a

"THE WORLD'S EASIEST GUIDE"

Maintaining Relationships

Through Tough Times

Potholes in the Road to Paradise

(DEALING WITH PROBLEMS IN YOUR MARRIAGE RELATIONSHIP)

SNAPSHOT

Debbie walked into the kitchen and saw Bill standing at the sink. "What are you doing now?" she asked.

"Just putting the dishes away," Bill replied as he toweled a plate.

"I was letting them air-dry in the sink," Debbie explained. "I was going to put them away in the morning."

"I know," Bill replied, "but if you don't dry pans right away, you're just asking for rust." He opened a cabinet to his left and put a glass away.

"The glasses go in the cabinet next to the refrigerator," Debbie reminded him.

"I switched things around," Bill admitted. "It makes more sense for the glasses to be next to the sink."

"What if you want something to drink from the refrigerator?" Debbie asked with a hint of irritation in her voice.

SNEAK PREVIEW

1. Minor problems in a marital relationship can escalate into major ones if they are not addressed properly.
2. The key to maintaining a healthy relationship, even in the midst of a conflict or problem, is communication.
3. Marital conflicts are opportunities for growth; every time a couple deals with a conflict openly, honestly, and lovingly, their relationship is strengthened.

Bill stopped and looked at her. "Did I do something wrong?" he asked.

"No, but I feel like I'm doing something wrong," Debbie said. "For the past few weeks, you've been changing and rearranging the way I have everything set up. First, the bedroom dressers, then the closets, and now the kitchen."

"I think I have some good ideas for increasing efficiency in the house," Bill explained.

"Well, that's good news for our stockholders," Debbie said. When Bill didn't laugh, she took a deep breath and said, "OK, if that's what you want to do, knock yourself out. Are there are other efficiency 'red flags' that I should be aware of?"

Bill hesitated for a moment. "Well, yeah, but we can talk about things like folding laundry later in the week."

"Ooooh, I'll be counting the minutes until *that* discussion," Debbie said.

"What's your problem?" Bill asked.

"My *problem* is that I feel like I'm in a stage production of *The Odd Couple*," Debbie told him. "I married Felix Unger without even realizing it."

"Hey, I'm not a clean freak," Bill protested. "I just have a certain system for doing things."

"I suppose next you're going to complain about the way I put toilet paper on the roll."

"I wasn't going to, but since you brought it up . . ."

"I don't believe this!" Debbie cried.

"I'm not complaining," Bill assured her. "I'm just saying that having the roll come over the top makes it easier to use. It also looks better that way."

"Aesthetically pleasing toilet paper—interesting," Debbie said. "I take that back— I didn't marry Felix Unger; I married Martha Stewart in drag."

* * * * * * * * * * * * * *

What do you think of Bill and Debbie's exchange? Would you describe it as a minor difference of opinion? Harmless bickering? Or the beginning of the end of their relationship?

At the risk of sounding overly dramatic, the answer depends on how Bill and Debbie handle the situation. If Debbie begins to take offense at Bill's insistence on reorganizing the house, she may start to make her feelings known a little more strongly. She might tease Bill a little more pointedly. She might start rearranging his rearrangements when he's gone, just to drive him crazy. She might complain to her friends about his seemingly compulsive behavior.

For his part, Bill might take offense at Debbie's objections. He might get tired of her teasing. He might start to resent her "joking" suggestions that he's neurotic and needs to seek professional help for his organizational "obsession."

Over time, Bill and Debbie may start to internalize their feelings and allow their mutual irritation to become bitterness. They may build an emotional wall between themselves and become cold and distant to one another. If one or both of them decide enough is enough, they may make the decision to separate and eventually divorce.

Whew.

That may seem like a long journey from the teasing banter of the opening story, but it's a logical progression. Many couples have seen their relationships start to crumble over lesser issues.

The point of this example is not to make you feel insecure in your relationship, fearful that everything could end over a playful argument you and your spouse have tomorrow. The point is to emphasize the importance of addressing minor issues and complaints about your relationship with your spouse so that they don't become big issues.

In this chapter, we're going to look at eight common complaints husbands and wives have about their spouses. Some of the complaints may seem more serious than others. Some of them may hit closer to home than others. Regardless of whether you or your spouse have made complaints like these in your relationship, you'll probably be able to find a helpful tip or principle in each one that you can apply to your own marriage.

COMPLAINT #1:

"My spouse is causing problems in our relationship."

What's a spouse to do when his or her mate refuses to "get with the program," as far as their marital relationship is concerned? The specific complaints vary from couple to couple, but the basic gist goes like this: "Every time I try to blah, blah, blah, my spouse always yada, yada, yada. I've been patient for a long time, giving my spouse a chance to change, but nothing ever happens. And I'm getting sick of it."

The spoken or unspoken message behind the complaint is that if the "offending" spouse would only get his or her act together, the marriage would be happy and healthy. The spoken or unspoken strategy is to straighten out the offending spouse.

Bad move.

If you really want to solve problems in your marriage, you've got to start with yourself. For many people, that's a tough pill to swallow—especially if their spouses are largely responsible for the problems in their marriage. What you need to recognize is that no one is blameless. If your spouse causes 95 percent of the problems between the two of you, that means you cause the other 5 percent of them. And if you hope to make progress in your marital relationship, you've got to take care of that 5 percent before you start worrying about your spouse's 95. (If that kind of reasoning upsets you or seems unfair . . . wait until you see what's coming next.)

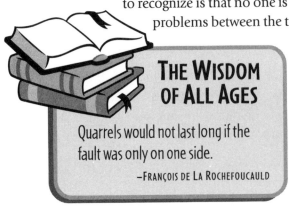

THE WISDOM OF ALL AGES

Quarrels would not last long if the fault was only on one side.

–FRANÇOIS DE LA ROCHEFOUCAULD

The first thing you need to do is ask yourself, "What's wrong with *me*? What are *my* faults as a spouse?" The answers you come up with may include everything from bitterness to unkindness to a lack of love for your spouse. Once you've identified your weaknesses and shortcomings, you can plan strategies for preventing them from disrupting your relationship with your spouse.

Time for Confession . . .

The second thing you need to do is confess your faults and shortcomings to your spouse. Set aside some time to talk about the things you've discovered about yourself. Share in detail the faults and shortcomings you identified and ask for forgiveness for them. The more specific you are in your confession, the better able you'll be to address the problems with your spouse.

You might admit something like this: "It was unfair of me to ask you to get rid of that tree stump right after you mowed the lawn. It was insensitive of me to ignore the fact that you'd already worked most of the morning and afternoon. I know I've done that to you before, and I'm sorry. I want you to know that I'm going to commit myself to correcting that problem."

. . . And a Commitment to Change

The obvious next question is, How will your spouse respond to your confession? The not-so-obvious answer is, It doesn't really matter, as far as your commitment to change is concerned.

Depending on the state of your relationship, your spouse may . . .

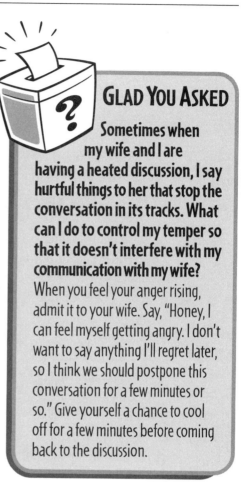

GLAD YOU ASKED

Sometimes when my wife and I are having a heated discussion, I say hurtful things to her that stop the conversation in its tracks. What can I do to control my temper so that it doesn't interfere with my communication with my wife?

When you feel your anger rising, admit it to your wife. Say, "Honey, I can feel myself getting angry. I don't want to say anything I'll regret later, so I think we should postpone this conversation for a few minutes or so." Give yourself a chance to cool off for a few minutes before coming back to the discussion.

➤ fall to his or her knees and confess his or her own faults and shortcomings

➤ say something like, "I've been trying to tell you that about yourself for years"

➤ dismiss your confession with an eye roll and a sarcastic grunt.

Obviously, the more positively your spouse responds, the more inspired you'll be to follow through on your commitment. But even if your spouse laughs you out of the room, you still have a responsibility to address your own faults.

Later, when your spouse sees that you're serious about wanting to improve your side of the relationship, he or she may start to do some soul-searching, too. That's not to say that all of the tension and hard feelings in your relationship will magically disappear overnight. Remember, it took time for those problems to develop, and it will take time for them to be fixed. However, if you commit yourself to taking care of *your* responsibilities to your spouse, you will eventually see positive changes—some of them significant—in your relationship.

COMPLAINT #2:
"Our love for each other is gone."

If your relationship with your spouse is built on the love you feel for each other—the tender emotions that swell up inside whenever the two of you make eye contact—you will have a happy, fulfilled marriage . . . right up to about the third day of your honeymoon.

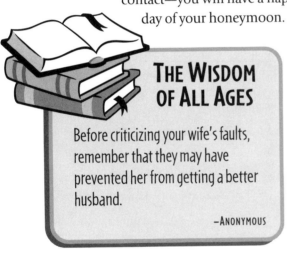

THE WISDOM OF ALL AGES

Before criticizing your wife's faults, remember that they may have prevented her from getting a better husband.

—ANONYMOUS

Unfortunately, relying on those feelings of love to sustain you in your marriage is like relying on your airplane seat cushion (which, your flight attendant will cheerfully remind you, can double as a flotation device) to sustain you in the event of a crash over water. It's just not up to the task.

The problem with the tingly emotion that many people call "love" is that it's unreliable. You never know when it's going to show up or when it's going to disappear. Sure, the feeling might come around when your spouse whisks you away for a romantic week in Jamaica and the two of you are walking hand in hand on a pristine beach, watching a postcard-worthy sunset. But where will that feeling be when your spouse has forgotten to pick up your dry cleaning for the fourth day in a row and is mumbling insincere apologies from the comfort of your bed while you're digging through the clothes hamper, trying to find something that isn't too soiled to wear to work?

Choosing to Love
Love isn't a feeling; it's a choice. It's something you choose to demonstrate to your

spouse regardless of how you "feel." This is an important distinction to make. If love is a feeling, and that feeling disappears, there's not much you can do about it. After all, you can't *force* yourself to feel something that's not there. So you can either resign yourself to living unfulfilled in a "loveless" marriage or you can divorce and start looking for someone else to stir your love feelings again.

If, on the other hand, love is a choice, it is always within your power to maintain it in your relationship. When your spouse whisks you away to Jamaica, you can respond with love. When your spouse forgets the dry cleaning, you can respond with love.

There's no need to ask your optometrist for rose-colored contact lenses. The point is not to overlook your spouse's flaws or the problems in your relationship. The point is to commit to dealing with those flaws and problems in a way that is motivated by love.

Expressing Love

One of the most obvious places to begin demonstrating love to your spouse is through your words. Here are three suggestions for how you can show verbal love to your spouse.

➤ *Build up.* Find something you like about your spouse and express your admiration or appreciation for it. A day or so later, find something else you like and mention that. Then do the same thing again a day or so after that. Develop a pattern of compliments in your relationship with your spouse, and you will be pleasantly surprised by the results.

➤ *Speak with kindness.* Don't allow your emotions to dictate your communication pattern. If you have something to say, even if it involves admitting negative feelings, say it as kindly as possible. Remember what the Bible says: "A gentle answer turns away wrath, but a harsh word stirs up anger" (Proverbs 15:1).

➤ *Don't give orders.* There's nothing loving about making demands. Often all that's needed to make changes in this area is a simple rewording of your desires. Instead of saying, "I want this done today!" try asking, "Is there any chance that you could work this into your busy schedule today?" The same request is being made in both cases; the difference between the two is how they will be received by your spouse.

Obviously, you have no guarantee that your spouse will reciprocate your demonstrations of love. But there's nothing you can do about that. Remember, love is a choice, and you can't make someone else's choice. What you *can* do is make yourself lovable by doing what you can to make your spouse feel loved.

COMPLAINT #3:

"We don't talk anymore."

What is it that kills communication in so many marriages? Is it boredom—spouses getting tired of talking to the same person about the same things over and over again? Is it resentment—spouses withholding information from their

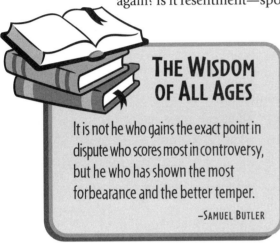

THE WISDOM OF ALL AGES

It is not he who gains the exact point in dispute who scores most in controversy, but he who has shown the most forbearance and the better temper.

–SAMUEL BUTLER

husbands or wives as "payback" for some previous offense? Is it ignorance—just not knowing how to communicate with each other? Is it indifference—no longer caring about what's going on in each other's lives?

In most cases, it's a combination of these and countless other factors, the "little things" that, over time, cause husbands and wives to drift apart and isolate themselves from each other. The unfortunate thing is that, without communication, there's no way for them to get back together.

Many spouses attribute their lack of communication skills to genetics. After all, not everyone is a born talker or a born listener. Some people prefer to keep to themselves, while others prefer constant chatter. That's just the way they're made.

And those would be legitimate excuses for a lack of communication . . . if the primary goal of marriage is to accommodate spouses' personality preferences. But it's not. The primary goal of marriage is to become one. And that can't happen without communication.

With the goal of unity or "oneness" in mind, here are three steps you can take to open the lines of communication with your spouse.

1. Talk to your spouse about your communication patterns.

Find out whether your spouse is content with the present level of communication in your relationship. When he or she is finished talking, share your own thoughts about it. If you both identify areas that need work, discuss them. Let your spouse know that you're willing to sacrifice your time, energy, and comfort level to improve your communication skills; then ask if he or she would be willing to do the same. Chances are, if your spouse sees how committed you are, he or she will be more than willing to contribute to the cause, as well.

2. Learn to ask the right questions.

Instead of putting your spouse on the spot with a request like, "Talk to me," take the initiative to find out the things you'd like to know. Asking questions is especially helpful if your spouse is the "silent type" by nature. Not having to come up with a "conversation starter" tends to take the pressure off of a person who's uncomfortable with talking.

GLAD YOU ASKED

My husband usually gives one-word answers to my questions. He just doesn't open up. What can I do?

When your spouse is giving you one-word answers, don't get discouraged. Continue to ask, keeping the questions as specific as possible. Often the first couple of questions serve to "prime the pump" of conversation. After a few tries, you may find your husband's responses starting to flow more freely, as he becomes more comfortable talking about himself.

To increase your chances for quality conversation, you'll need to make sure that your questions are specific and nonthreatening. The question, "How was your day?" is too broad to initiate any kind of real conversation. Some parts of the day were probably good; some were probably bad. Average them together, and you get the ever-popular, "Fine," as a response. The more specific you get with your questions ("How did Marv react when you told him you were thinking about quitting?"), the better chance you have of getting a substantive response—one that you can work into a full-blown conversation.

3. Look for common interests.

The reason you and your spouse may not be talking is that you don't have enough to talk about. If your personal interests differ significantly from your spouse's, you may not have enough common ground between you to support frequent communication.

If you can't find many common interests with your spouse, take it upon yourself to develop some. Make an effort to learn about the things your spouse is interested in. Not only will it give you things to talk about together, it will also demonstrate to your spouse the lengths you are willing to go to in order to improve your communication.

COMPLAINT #4:

"My spouse expects me to do all the work around the house."

Whose job is it to clean the toilet in your house? You'll note that we didn't ask, "Who cleans the toilets in your house?" We asked whose job it was. And when you answer that question, you'll also need to answer the question, "Why?"

You can probably guess some of the most popular answers:

> ➤ "Cleaning the toilet is woman's work, so it's my wife's job."

> ➤ "Cleaning the toilet is my husband's job because I'm out working all day while he stays home with the kids."

> ➤ "I grew up in a household where Mom did all the cleaning, so that's the model I want to follow in my own home."

FAMILY TIES

If you and your spouse just don't have the time to take care of all of the housekeeping responsibilities in your home, recruit the most convenient underage workers you can find—your kids—to help you. The best way to broach the subject with your kids is to help them see the work as a necessity, instead of a simple "chore." Let them know that you need their help. You'll also want to give them a sense of ownership in the process. Let them have a say in when and how the jobs are done (as long as the jobs get done). Your kids may complain about the work itself, but they will love the idea of having an important responsibility in the family.

No two people enter a marriage perfectly in sync. Everyone brings unique opinions, experience, and personal history to the relationship—some of which may clash wildly with the opinions, experience, and personal history of the spouse. And while it's safe to say that those differences are what make the marital relationship exciting, it's also safe to say that those differences lie at the root of most marital conflicts. If you can't agree on which of you should clean the toilet, it's probably because you have differing opinions on how your marital relationship should work.

Your choice is either to discuss your differences of opinion and work together to come up with a solution that's agreeable to both of you . . . or to buy a lot of air freshener for your home to disguise that smell coming from your bathroom. Allow us to recommend the first option.

You might start your conversation by sharing with each other the housekeeping patterns in your own home when you were a kid. After you have a better appreciation of where each other is coming from, you can begin to ask some logical questions that may shed light on a solution. For example, you might ask . . .

➤ Which of us has the most time during the day to devote to housekeeping responsibilities?

➤ What are your favorite (or least objectionable) chores around the house? Where do you excel?

➤ What are your least favorite chores around the house? What would you prefer to eliminate from your list of responsibilities?

➤ What kind of compromise can we reach so that one of us doesn't get stuck with all of the tough, nasty jobs, like cleaning toilets?

Before we wrap up this section, we need to make one final point. Any household job that you refuse to do because it's too difficult or time-consuming or disgusting will fall to your spouse. If that thought doesn't inspire you to do something to lessen your spouse's burden—or, at the very least, stir up feelings of empathy—you may need to reread the section earlier in this chapter on choosing to love your spouse.

Complaint #5:

"My spouse makes all the decisions in our house."

One of the most important things a couple can do to ensure the health of their relationship is to establish a pattern for decision making as early as possible in their marriage. Otherwise, what tends to happen is that the dominant personality asserts itself and begins taking over the decision making in the family.

Many couples base their decision making models on their spiritual beliefs, citing biblical exhortations for the husband to be the leader of the home. And there's certainly nothing wrong with that perspective. It should be pointed out that the biblical model of the family does not prohibit the wife from being involved in the decision making process.

Ideally, all of the major decisions that are made in your home should be the result of a collaboration between the two of you. That means you must sit down together and discuss the pros and cons of each side of the issue at hand. Each of you should feel free to offer your honest opinions and preferences. You should also feel free to question—but not dismiss—each other's points of view. Once each has had a chance to make your feelings known, you can vote on the issue.

If it turns out that you're split on the matter, take some time to rethink the issue. Examine your motives for feeling the way you do about it. After you've had a few days to contemplate, meet again to talk about your ideas. If you're still split after that, continue discussing the matter until you can reach a mutual agreement.

If you're making decisions without considering each other's opinions or point of view, you're not demonstrating the unity—not to mention the personal respect and affirmation—that is essential to a healthy marital relationship. What you're doing is sending the message that his or her opinion ultimately doesn't matter. So instead of becoming one with an equal, in a sense, you're becoming "parent" to a "child."

GLAD YOU ASKED

In our house, my wife always says, "That's how we did it growing up, so that's how we do it now." It's exasperating. What should I say?

When it comes to housekeeping decisions, spouses tend to fall back on the family models they were exposed to as children. If you grew up in a home in which your father was an autocrat, you will likely enter the marriage expecting that the husband will make all important decisions in the household, with little or no input from anyone else. If you (or your wife) grew up in a matriarchal environment, you may expect that the wife will take the reins of the family. The solution is a collaboration. Read on.

COMPLAINT #6:
"Sex life? What sex life?"

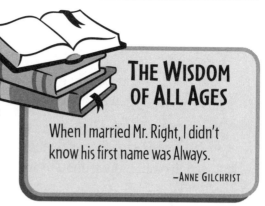

THE WISDOM OF ALL AGES

When I married Mr. Right, I didn't know his first name was Always.

—ANNE GILCHRIST

One of the biggest obstacles to sexual fulfillment in many marital relationships is unrealistic expectations. Thanks to Hollywood, many people enter marriage believing that the simple coming together of two bodies will produce all of the requisite sexual fireworks and mutual satisfaction. They find out very quickly that that's not the case.

The fact is, sexual oneness is not achieved easily. It requires the same degree of commitment and effort that intellectual and social oneness require. That's not to say the work is without its benefits. (Actually, as far as many people are concerned, you couldn't ask for a more desirable task.) But effort is required nonetheless.

One of the most helpful things you can do for your relationship is to make your intimate desires known. If there are things that will enhance your physical and emotional pleasure, by all means, let the other know. Satisfy each other.

For example, a husband might make the following requests of his wife:

➤ "I would like it if you would wear something attractive at bedtime instead of baggy pajamas."

➤ "I would like you to be the aggressor sometimes."

➤ "I would like to hear you express your pleasure."

➤ "I would like you to clear your mind of daily things when we're being intimate, so that you can relax and enjoy the experience."

The wife, on the other hand, may give these requests to her husband:

➤ "I would like you to talk to me and show me affection after we have intercourse."

➤ "I would like it if you gave me compliments throughout the day and not just right before sex."

➤ "I would like you to call me from work sometimes just to say, 'I love you.'"

➤ "I would like it if you'd initiate lovemaking at times other than right before bed."

That's not to say that you should expect every desire to be fulfilled. Remember, love is a *choice.* But if you make your desires known, there is material to work with in your mutual quest to achieve sexual oneness.

GLAD YOU ASKED

What can I do to let my parents know that I still need them, even though I'm married?

Seek their advice. Though your parents are at least a generation removed from you, chances are they've experienced many problems and situations in their marriage from which you can learn. The fact that you think enough of their wisdom and knowledge to consult them will be all the evidence they need to be assured that you want them involved in your married life (within certain boundaries, of course).

COMPLAINT #7:

"I didn't know I was marrying my spouse's family, too."

Dealing with in-laws in your marriage requires you and your spouse to walk a fine line between two important responsibilities: leaving your parents and honoring them.

On the one hand, you have the responsibility to *leave* your parents. Remember, marriage is the process in which *two* people become one. That leaves no room for anyone else in there. That's why it's important to separate yourself from your parents, physically and emotionally, when you dedicate yourself to each other.

Marriage involves a change of allegiance, from an allegiance with your parents to an allegiance with your spouse. What some call "cutting the apron strings" is really undoing the psychological ties to your parents. Depending on how long you lived with your parents and how strong their influence was in your life, this cutting process may be fairly traumatic for them and you.

The flip side of your responsibility to leave your parents when you marry is your responsibility to *honor* them. Honoring your parents involves recognizing their contributions to your life and showing your appreciation for what they've done. It involves recognizing the wisdom and knowledge they've accrued and tapping into it from time to time. It involves making your spouse a part of your parents' lives and making your parents a part of your lives. It does *not,* however, involve turning over the reins of your marital relationship to them. Remember, parental advice is good; parental control is bad.

Honoring your parents—and especially your spouse's parents—requires you to accept them for who they are. It's not your job to try to change your in-laws, no matter how badly they may need to change. Your job is to look for their positive qualities and learn to love them.

FAMILY TIES

Maintaining a healthy relationship with both sets of in-laws is important for your kids' sake. Assuming that your in-laws pose no physical danger to them, you will be doing your kids a favor by encouraging regular visits and one-on-one interaction with grandparents, aunts, uncles, and cousins. Not only will it increase your kids' circle of loved ones, it will also give them a better sense of who they are. Grandparents in particular have a knack for sharing memorable anecdotes and vital information about family history.

COMPLAINT #8:
"We can't seem to agree on finances."

Money may make the world go round, but it sure doesn't do married couples many favors. It's safe to say that most arguments between husbands and wives involve money. Tensions or disagreements over money can have a negative impact on almost every area of a couple's life, from the spiritual to the sexual.

While we may not be able to give you million-dollar stock tips to eliminate your worries about money, we can give you a tip for dealing with money in your marriage. And we won't even charge you commission for it.

Here's the tip: *Think in terms of "ours."*

When you get married, there's no such thing as "your money" and "my money"; it's all "our" money. The same thing holds true for debts. It doesn't matter who brings what to your marriage, when you and your spouse accept each other as partners, you also accept each other's assets and liabilities. It's all part of the "oneness" that is your ultimate quest.

Since it is "our" money, "we" ought to agree on how it's spent. Remember the decision-making process we described earlier in this chapter? This is where it comes in handy. Before any financial decision is made, you should talk about it openly. If you don't agree, continue talking until you do.

THE WISDOM OF ALL AGES

Men often bear little grievances with less courage than they do large misfortunes.

—AESOP

You should think seriously about including all major purchases—anything over $50—in your discussions. That means neither would be able to buy anything that cost more than $50 without first consulting the other. Imagine how many impulse buys—the kind that later make you kick yourself and ask, "What was I thinking?"—could be prevented by this strategy.

If you find yourself balking at the idea of sharing your financial decision-making responsibilities, you need to figure out why. Is it because . . .

➤ you don't trust your spouse to act wisely with the money?

➤ you feel "cheated" for having brought more money into the marriage?

➤ you're not used to sharing?

Whatever the cause, you need to discuss your feelings and work through the issues that are preventing you from becoming "one" financially.

A Final Word About Relationship Problems

For each relationship problem we listed in this chapter, there were dozens left out. When two people share one life, conflicts are going to arise—lots of them. The fact that you have conflicts—even frequent conflicts—is not a problem. Indeed, it might be healthier for your relationship if you started thinking of conflicts as opportunities for growth. Every time you deal with a conflict openly, honestly, and lovingly, you strengthen your relationship.

That's not to say that every conflict you face will be easily resolved. Some may never be fully resolved. But if you commit yourselves to not letting anything come between you—to keeping the lines of communication open no matter what—you will know what it means to live "happily ever after."

Family Practice

Think you're an expert on dealing with the minor irritations of family life? Here's a quiz to see how much you know.

1. If your spouse is causing 95 percent of the problems in your relationship, what should you do?
   a. Focus on taking care of the 5 percent of the problems you're responsible for.
   b. Increase the amount of problems you cause in order to make the percentages a little more equal.
   c. Continue to remind your spouse of how few problems you're causing until he or she gets the message.
   d. Demand that your spouse cut his or her problem causing by at least half.

2. Which of the following is true of marital love?
   a. It's based on feeling.
   b. It will continue to lessen over the years until it finally disappears.
   c. It cannot be demonstrated verbally.
   d. It's a choice.

3. Which of the following is *not* a step you can take to open the lines of communication with your spouse?
   a. Learn to ask the right questions.
   b. Look for common interests.
   c. Demand that your spouse talk to you.
   d. Talk to your spouse about your communication patterns.

4. Which of the following is true of sexual oneness?
   a. It's something that occurs naturally when two people are in love.
   b. It requires very little communication.
   c. It requires the same degree of commitment and effort that intellectual and social oneness require.
   d. If it's not there at the beginning of your relationship, it will never be there.

5. Which of the following tips will be most helpful in creating unity between you and your spouse on financial matters?
   a. Insist that your spouse take care of his or her debts, while you take care of your own.
   b. Think in terms of "ours."
   c. Make sure that the two of you spend exactly the same amount on yourselves.
   d. Let an accountant handle your finances.

Answers: (1) a, (2) d, (3) c, (4) c, (5) b

CHAPTER 13

Reality Living

(WORKING THROUGH PATTERNS OF DESTRUCTIVE BEHAVIOR IN YOUR RELATIONSHIP)

SNAPSHOT

"Did you hear about Dean and Edna?" Millie asked as she passed the bread basket around the table.

Nancy grabbed Millie's arm, almost knocking over her water glass. "Yes!" Nancy exclaimed. "Isn't that unbelievable?"

"How could he do that to her?" Millie asked.

"How could she *let* him do that to her?" Nancy countered.

"Do you think they'll get a divorce?" Al chimed in.

"What else could they do?" Millie asked. "Could *you* stay married to someone who did that to you?"

"I always knew Dean was capable of something like that," Roland observed.

"I know what you're talking about," Al agreed. "I always noticed that there was something a little 'off'

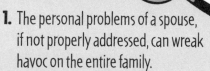

SNEAK PREVIEW

1. The personal problems of a spouse, if not properly addressed, can wreak havoc on the entire family.

2. Reality living involves taking responsibility for one's own actions and allowing others to take responsibility for their actions.

3. Tough love is essential in dealing with a spouse's destructive habits or patterns of behavior.

about their relationship."

"What do you mean by 'off'?" Nancy asked.

"Well, it always seemed like there was something going on under the surface," Al explained, "something they never wanted anyone else to see. Their relationship wasn't—"

"Like ours," Roland finished, looking around at his wife and their two married friends.

"Here's to strong marriages," Millie proposed, raising her water glass in salute.

"And to couples who never have to worry about the things that Dean and Edna are going through right now," Nancy added.

Almost in unison, all four of them knocked on the oak wooden table.

* * * * * * * * * * * * * * *

In chapter 12, we identified eight minor problems that can damage a marital relationship if not handled properly. In this chapter, we're going to look at more serious threats to the marital relationship—namely, seven different patterns of destructive behavior that can devastate the health of a family.

You don't need to be a math major to figure out that covering seven different behavior patterns in one chapter doesn't leave a lot of room for exploring each pattern. What you'll find in this chapter are the bare necessities—identifying features of each behavior, vital information about the behavior, and tips for addressing the problems the behavior causes in your marriage. (For further information about these and other dangerous behavior patterns, pick up a copy of my book *Loving Solutions*.) We will look at case studies of seven kinds of destructive behaviors and look at possible responses to each one.

DESTRUCTIVE BEHAVIOR #1:
The Irresponsible Spouse

My husband has been fired from four jobs in the past six years. He doesn't seem to have any desire to build a stable career or provide steady income for us. I figured that since he's not working, the least he could do is take care of some repair jobs around the house. For almost two years now, I've told him that we need shelves installed in the laundry room. And for almost two years, he's told me he'll get around to it. Unfortunately, the only thing he ever seems to get around to is surfing the Internet and playing softball with his friends. We've talked about having kids in a few years, but I sometimes feel like I'm already living with one.

Few things are more disappointing than discovering that your spouse isn't the person you thought when you got married. Think about it. What are you supposed to do when it turns out that the ambitious, conscientious, hardworking person you married turns out to be considerably less than ambitious, conscientious, or hardworking? What if you discover that you're married to someone with no sense of responsibility—to you or anyone else?

Analyze the source of the problem.

If you live with an irresponsible person, the first thing you need to do is try to understand why your spouse is so irresponsible. There are four common possibilities that you need to consider.

1. *Your spouse is following the model of parents.* We follow our models. What you consider laziness or irresponsibility your spouse may be considering as freedom or personal liberty—because that's what was modeled.

2. *Your spouse is rebelling against a negative model.* If your spouse grew up with a workaholic father who never had time for his kids, he or she may believe it's better to err on the side of irresponsibility than workaholism.

3. *Your spouse may have developed a self-centered attitude.* There's also the possibility that irresponsibility is pure selfishness—the need to do whatever, whenever. The unspoken sentiment is that it doesn't matter if his or her personal freedom disappoints or causes problems for you; individual happiness is all that matters.

> ### THE WISDOM OF ALL AGES
>
> Though the wisdom or virtue of one can very rarely make many happy, the folly or vice of one man often make many miserable.
>
> —SAMUEL JOHNSON

4. *Your spouse may be expressing resentment toward you.* If you do a little investigation, you may discover that your "irresponsible" spouse is actually quite responsible in areas that don't include you, such as involvement in committees at church. Dig a little deeper, and you may discover that your spouse is more responsible in those areas because he or she receives frequent praise and affirmation for the things he or she does—praise that's missing in your relationship.

Taking Action

After you discover the cause of irresponsibility, there are three steps you can take to address it.

1. *Acknowledge your own imperfections.* Be honest about areas in which you've failed, either through nagging ("When are you going to get a job?") or criticism ("You are the laziest person I've ever seen in my life"). Let it be known not only that you're sorry for your failures, but also that you're committed to improving in those areas.

2. *Express your love.* Give some heartfelt words of encouragement and affirmation regarding the positive characteristics or traits you see. Express your appreciation for the things done around the house. Then leave it at that. Don't follow up your affirmation with a nag ("I just wish you would . . .").

3. *Ask for suggestions on how to be a better parner.* Ask for areas in which a change in your attitude or behavior could improve your relationship. Rather than asking for an on-the-spot analysis, give your spouse some time to think about it. You might even ask for a list of suggestions for you. Those suggestions may include things like, "Instead of complaining about the things I *don't* do during the day, I'd like you to spend a couple minutes noticing the things I *do.*"

Armed with that information, you can start making changes to your attitude and behavior in order to fulfill your spouse's needs. Your willingness to take suggestions to heart and make changes in your attitude and behavior should inspire reciprocal behavior.

Tough Love

If you don't notice a difference in behavior, you may need to shift your focus from trying to change to trying to get help from a counselor. The fact is, your spouse's problems may be too complex for the two of you to handle by yourselves.

There may be an attitude of refusal, so you need to be firm, insistent, and understanding. (You might say, "I know that you're dealing with a lot of issues with your father, and I think the only way you're going to be able to put those issues behind you is to work through your feelings with someone who knows what he's doing.") Emphasize your love. Do whatever is necessary to make your relationship healthy again.

> **THE WISDOM OF ALL AGES**
>
> Work expands to fill the time available for its completion.
>
> —C. NORTHCOTE PARKINSON

DESTRUCTIVE BEHAVIOR #2:

The Workaholic Spouse

My husband is a tax accountant, so I've always known that during the two months or so before tax day, he would be working a lot of hours. That's the nature of his business. Since he's become a partner in his firm, it's like every day is April 15. He never gets home before eight at night, after the kids are in bed. He works at least ten hours on Saturdays, and he's even gone in on Sundays to work. When I ask him to take a day off, he looks at me like I'm crazy.

Workaholism is an especially insidious threat to family relationships, not only because it separates the workaholic from the rest of the family for long stretches of time, but also because the workaholic appears to *choose* his or her job over the family. Let's take a look at what you can do if you live with a workaholic.

Understand what drives the workaholic.

A workaholic is someone who's put all the eggs in one basket. The workaholic's vocation is life. The workaholic is obsessed with the job. In order to understand the workaholic, you have to understand the motivation of life. There are two major reasons for workaholism that you need to know.

First, there are feelings of inferiority. The seeds of workaholism are usually planted in childhood. Most workaholics grow up believing or being told by their parents that they're not as good or as smart as their siblings. As a result, they work themselves ragged trying to perform at a higher level than everyone else to overcome their feelings of inferiority. Many workaholics also feel unloved. It's their need for "love"—in the form of accolades in the workplace—that drives them.

Second, there is avoiding one's feelings. Many workaholics use the busyness of their jobs to avoid getting in touch with their own feelings or the feelings of others. This is especially true of those whose spouses communicate that the workaholics are incompetent as a husband or wife or parent. On the job, workaholics can convince themselves that they're successful by virtue of their hard work. If that illusion is shattered when they come home, it follows that they will try to put off coming home as long as possible.

Taking Action
Once you've identified the motives behind your spouse's workaholism, you can take the necessary steps to begin addressing the problem.

1. *Meet emotional needs.* Give your spouse the encouragement and affirmation needed. Instead of nagging and complaining about the job, take an interest in it. Make a habit of sharing affirming statements such as, "Your boss must say a prayer of thanks for you every morning" or "It's no wonder your employees like you so much." Make your house a pleasant, popular place.

2. *Use tough love.* Believe it or not, your workaholic spouse may not be aware of what the obsession is doing to your family. Perhaps there's the notion that you enjoy reaping the benefits of all the work. That's why you may need to shock your spouse into recognizing what he or she is giving up. We're not talking about a guilt trip. We're talking about lovingly and honestly confronting with concrete examples of events that have been missed because of work. These events might include everything from your child's first words to the first ride on a two-wheel bike.

The Controlling Spouse

My husband does not trust me to make decisions in our household. He gives me money for groceries and expects me to keep the kids clothed and fed. I'm like his employee. I have no say in anything that goes on in the house.

Living with a controlling spouse is difficult because he or she likely views questions about or objections to his or her way of doing things as personal attacks, thus making communication extremely difficult. Let's take a look at what you can do if you live with a controlling spouse.

Understand the reasons behind the behavior.

The behavior likely has one of two origins: his or her childhood or personality.

Many controlling spouses are simply following the examples set by their own parents. They are doing the things that seemed to work in their own childhood homes. Of course, as kids, they were too young to recognize the downside of controlling behavior, so their views of running a family are decidedly one-sided.

Meanwhile some people are born with a dominating or controlling personality. These are the "Type A's," the movers and shakers, the "go to" people. They produce results and get the job done. However, they are rarely in touch with emotions—their own or others'.

Avoid the wrong kind of reaction.

You need to know that there are two ways *not* to deal with a controlling spouse: using a power play or becoming a submissive servant.

The "power play" approach is to fight every attempt to control you. Inevitably the results of this approach are frequent arguments and an unhealthy sense of wariness.

The submissive servant approach is to do whatever it takes—even yielding personal freedom—in order to maintain peace in the family. The result is an extremely unhealthy master-slave relationship.

Taking Action

Dealing with a controlling spouse won't be easy, but it can be done. You need to keep three things in mind:

1. *Respond to the need for freedom.* Control is the need for freedom run amok. You must acknowledge your spouse's need for freedom in your efforts to craft a healthy relationship. That means you should not restrict his or her input giving at all. Your spouse must always feel free to offer his or her opinions.

2. *Respond to the need for significance.* Keep in mind that your spouse's self-worth is likely tied to performance. The more goals are reached—including family-oriented goals—the more positive feelings.

3. *Work to influence by agreeing.* Don't try to argue with a controlling spouse; it only adds fuel to the fire. Instead, try influencing through agreement. That means you agree with arguments, but don't allow yourself to be controlled by them. In practical terms, it means acknowledging the positive elements and reasoning, but countering with specific reasons as to why you need to pursue another course of action ("I think your idea for saving money makes a lot of sense; unfortunately, I don't always have the time to . . .").

DESTRUCTIVE BEHAVIOR #4:

The Uncommunicative Spouse

My wife usually lets me know I've done something wrong by "freezing me out"—that is, not talking to me—until I figure out what I've done wrong and apologize for it. Usually the silence lasts for a day or two, but on a couple of occasions, it's lasted almost a week.

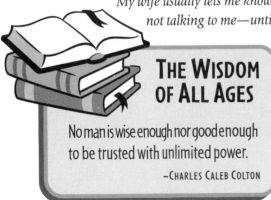

THE WISDOM OF ALL AGES

No man is wise enough nor good enough to be trusted with unlimited power.

–CHARLES CALEB COLTON

Living with an uncommunicative spouse can be extremely frustrating, because it forces you to guess at what's going on in your spouse's head. Unfortunately, the result is usually more misunderstandings. Let's take a look at what you can do if there's no conversation.

Look for the reasons behind the lack of communication.

If your spouse is prone to giving you the "silent treatment" for real and imagined offenses in your marriage, it may be fear—the fear of expressing his or her feelings or the fear of your response to those feelings.

Your spouse may not feel right about expressing anger. He or she may have been raised to believe that only "bad" or "weak" people allow their negative emotions to show. So rather than owning up to negative thoughts and emotions, your spouse may choose to let them dissipate quietly.

Or your spouse may remain silent because he or she doesn't want to deal with your response to his or her feelings. If you have a tendency to criticize or "pounce on" the things your spouse says, he or she may decide that talking just isn't worth the hassle.

Recognize your spouse's needs.

Your spouse's lack of communication may actually be speaking volumes. There may be a lack of a basic need, such as love, freedom, significance, recreation, or peace. To help narrow the list of possibilities of what's missing in life, ask yourself these questions:

➤ Does my spouse genuinely believe that my love is unconditional?

➤ Have I done or said anything that may have been interpreted as a threat to his or her freedom—including freedom of expression?

➤ Have I done or said anything that may have been interpreted as a dismissal or condemnation of something significant to him or her?

➤ Does my spouse view me as a hindrance to recreation or relaxation?

➤ Does my spouse view me as a hindrance to spiritual peace or growth?

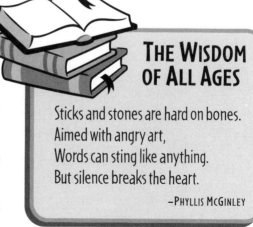

THE WISDOM OF ALL AGES

Sticks and stones are hard on bones.
Aimed with angry art,
Words can sting like anything.
But silence breaks the heart.

—PHYLLIS MCGINLEY

Taking Action: Changing Your Negative Patterns of Communication

A large part of bringing change in your spouse is to bring change in your negative patterns that contribute to the behavior. Here are a few ideas to consider when it comes to making changes to the way you communicate with your spouse.

➤ Cut back on your complaining.

➤ Don't interrupt or correct when your spouse speaks.

➤ Instead of expressing dissatisfaction about how things are, talk about how you'd like things to be.

➤ Give space when he or she needs it.

➤ Maintain confidences; don't tell others what your spouse shares with you.

In addition, work on developing your listening skills. Make sure that you give your undivided attention when he or she is talking. Turn off the TV, put down your newspaper, do whatever you need to do in order to show that what is said is of great importance to you.

DESTRUCTIVE BEHAVIOR #5:

The Verbally Abusive Spouse

Last week, my wife called me a "pathetic excuse for a husband" and said she would have been better off staying single for the rest of her life—all because I didn't take out the trash in time for the garbage truck to pick it up. It's been like this since we got married. At first, I tried to ignore her criticism, but that's getting harder to do. Sometimes I wonder if she's right about me.

Victims of verbal abuse often describe the criticism and cutting remarks they endure in *physical* terms—as "crushing" or painful "blows" to their emotional well-being. The good news is that if you are married to a verbally abusive spouse, you can take steps to address the situation.

Understand the source of the abuse.

Low self-esteem lies at the heart of most verbal abuse. Abusers may appear to be supremely confident on the outside, but inside they are desperately trying to prove their worth. Most verbal abusers were themselves victims of verbal abuse. They learn to direct their anger in the way their parent's anger was directed at them. If your spouse is a verbal abuser, you need to understand these underlying issues before you can effectively address the problems in your relationship.

Taking Action

There are four steps you can take to improve your relationship with your verbally abusive spouse. Let's take a look at them.

1. *Affirm the need; reject the behavior.* There are needs for self-worth, purpose, and fulfillment, among other things. Learning to recognize and affirm those needs is one of the keys to healing the damage of your spouse's verbal abuse. That's not to say that you should accept destructive efforts to meet his or her needs. You should never "take" verbal abuse, but neither should you lash back in self-defense. Instead, you should incorporate the emotional needs into your response to the verbal abuse.

   For example, you might say something like, "I know you must be extremely frustrated to say things like that to me. I would like to help you work through your frustrations, but not in this way. Your words are hurting me right now. Perhaps we can talk about the things that are bothering you after your anger subsides."

2. *Believe in the worth of your spouse.* Regardless of how nasty things get during verbal rants, there is still something of value in his or her character. Don't lose sight of that. After all, you had to have seen some attractive qualities before you got married, right? Your job is not to bring those positive qualities and attributes to the surface again, but simply to *believe* that they're still there—and to let your spouse know that you believe they're still there.

   For example, during a "quiet time" in your relationship, you might say something like, "Remember how we used to communicate when we first started dating? We were awesome together! I liked not having to worry about saying the wrong thing around you or worrying about when

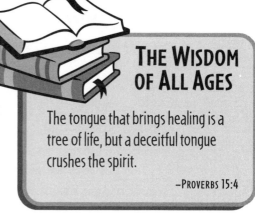

THE WISDOM OF ALL AGES

The tongue that brings healing is a tree of life, but a deceitful tongue crushes the spirit.

–PROVERBS 15:4

you were going to say something hurtful to me. I know the kind of person you are deep down inside, so I know that we can have that great communication again. That's the goal I want us to work toward together."

3. *Share your own feelings.* Acting as though your spouse's verbal assaults have no effect on you is not the answer. Instead, you need to make your spouse aware of just how deeply words cut you. Your spouse needs to live with the awareness that you are hurting and that you need to do something about your pain—specifically, that you need to talk to a counselor.

4. *Agree on a strategy.* Once the problem of verbal abuse has been discussed, the two of you need to develop a strategy for addressing it. If your spouse agrees to go with you for counseling, your counselor will help you develop a strategy for ending the cycle of verbal abuse in your home.

This fourth action step is important, but what if your spouse is unwilling to seek help with you? Then you will need to develop a strategy on your own. One strategy you may want to consider is removing yourself from your spouse's presence. For example, you might explain that because the verbal abuse causes you so much pain that you will make a practice of leaving to spend time elsewhere each time your spouse lashes out at you verbally. You may go spend a day with a close friend or a couple of days at your parents' house. It doesn't matter where you go, as long as you make your spouse aware that that's what you'll be doing.

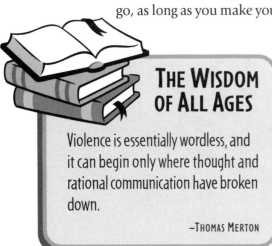

THE WISDOM OF ALL AGES

Violence is essentially wordless, and it can begin only where thought and rational communication have broken down.

–THOMAS MERTON

Of course, after you come up with a strategy, you must follow through with it. This isn't an area for "second chances." You must never allow verbal abuse to work for your spouse.

DESTRUCTIVE BEHAVIOR #6:
The Physically Abusive Spouse

Three weeks after our wedding, my husband and I were having an argument. When I said something about how much time he spends at the gym, he gave me a shove. I fell backwards over a chair and almost smashed my head on our glass coffee table. My husband seemed as shocked by what he'd done as I was. He started crying and apologizing and saying it would never happen again. A couple of months later, in the middle of another argument, he grabbed me by my hair and threw me out of our bedroom. Afterward, he apologized and said it would never happen again. Well, it's happened three other times since then. What should I do?

Physical abuse in your home must be addressed immediately. Left unchecked, it will devastate not only your relationship with your spouse and your children's relationship with their parent, but also your children's relationships with their own future spouses and kids.

Ending the cycle of physical abuse in your home will not be easy, but it can be done. And the first thing you need to do in order to address the problem is to look at yourself.

Understand why the abuse has continued.

Chances are, if you've experienced physical abuse at the hands of your spouse, it's happened more than once. The question you need to ask yourself is why you've allowed yourself to be victimized more than once. Here are some of the common reasons spouses stay with their batterers:

> **GLAD YOU ASKED**
>
> **What can I do to counteract the effect of my spouse's verbal abuse on my kids?**
>
> Your first step should be to schedule appointments for your kids to talk to a child counselor. The effects of verbal abuse can be devastating—and permanent—if they're not addressed properly. In the meantime, make an effort to "trump" your spouse's criticism of your kids with some positive comments of your own. For example, if your spouse tells your child that he or she is stupid, you might point out that "stupid" people don't score 92 on their American history final exams.

1. *The abused spouse blames herself.* In the beginning, it's surprisingly easy for an abused spouse to convince herself that the violence is her fault. (Though some husbands are physically abused, the vast majority of victims are wives, so we'll use the pronouns *she* and *her.*) The victim thinks, *"He wouldn't have hit me if I hadn't . . ."* Over time, as the abuse continues, she will likely come to recognize the truth. Unfortunately, by that time, the pattern has been established and becomes difficult to break.

2. *The abused spouse is a "rescuer."* Some battered spouses find their identity in helping people in need. They see their spouse's need for nurturing in nonviolent moments and are willing to endure the abuse in order to provide it. In other words, the abused spouse loves Dr. Jekyll so much that she's willing to live with Mr. Hyde.

3. *The abused spouse feels isolated.* As a result of the shame they feel about their abuse, many battered spouses isolate themselves from friends, family, and neighbors. When the time comes to do something about the abuse, the victims often feel as though they have no place to go. So they continue in their relationship, hoping against hope that something will change.

4. *The abused spouse is afraid.* Many battered spouses are scared that if they talk to someone about what's going on, the abuse will worsen. Others are so emotionally and financially dependent on the abuser that they are frightened of what might happen if they were to do something about the problem.

Taking Action

Is there hope for a relationship torn apart by abuse? Absolutely! If you are an abused spouse, you *can* become a positive change agent in your marriage. But you can't do it alone. You will need the help of a trained counselor and the support of family and friends. Your first order of business should be to locate a professional counselor immediately, if not sooner. If you don't know where to look, ask your pastor to recommend one for you.

Reality living probably will be part of a counselor's approach. Reality living involves taking responsibility for one's own actions and allowing others to take responsibility for their actions.

There are four aspects to reality living you need to be aware of in order to properly address the physical abuse in your home:

1. *You are responsible for your own attitude.* If you've resigned yourself to the fact that your only options are abuse or divorce, it's time for a reality check. Instead of approaching your relationship with your spouse with a sense of dread and resignation, you need to approach it with a sense of purpose and determination. Something must be done to save your

relationship. If you don't search for what that something is, who will?

2. *You can't change your spouse's behavior.* Your spouse is who he is primarily because of his personal history and his unique psychological makeup. And there's nothing you can do to change either of those things. Accepting that fact will help you resolve your feelings of guilt and responsibility for your abuse.

A word of hope about this second reality: While you can't change your spouse's behavior, there are certain steps you can take that have the potential to *influence* your spouse's behavior. Married couples influence each other every day through their actions and attitudes. You may not be able to keep your spouse from physically abusing you, but you can learn to recognize growing tensions in your relationship and take proactive steps to address the problem—either by discussing things or leaving the house. This lets your spouse know that the present situation is intolerable and confronts him with his own need for change.

FAMILY TIES

Your first responsibility as a parent is to remove your children from harm's way. Even if your kids are not the targets of your spouse's abuse, they are being victimized by it just the same. Don't imagine for a second that your abuse is going unnoticed by your kids. It's not. And the psychological damage that's being done may not become apparent until it's too late. So not only do you need to find a safe house for your kids to stay, you need to get them into counseling as soon as possible so that they can work through the emotional damage caused by the abuse.

3. *Your negative emotions need not control your actions.* It's one thing to admit that you are afraid to do something about the physical abuse in your marriage. It's quite another thing to allow that fear to prevent you from doing something about it. You need to know—and admit to yourself—that the situation will not improve on its own. Physical abuse isn't something that just "goes away" over time. The abuse will continue, and will likely become more and more severe, until you take action.

4. *Love, particularly tough love, is the greatest weapon for good at your disposal.* One of the strange ironies of physical abuse is that many battered wives

THE WISDOM OF ALL AGES

When cheated, wife or husband feel the same.

—EURIPIDES

are reluctant to take action because they don't want to "hurt" their abusive husbands. A common objection might go something like this: "My husband may not be perfect, but I love him, and I could never do anything to embarrass or humiliate him. When I said I would love him for better or worse, I meant it."

What you need to understand is that the tough decisions you make—whether it's to start seeing a counselor or to move out of the house for a while—may be the motivation your spouse needs to start making necessary changes in his life. Your tough love may be the only thing that can save your relationship.

DESTRUCTIVE BEHAVIOR #7:

The Substance-Abusing Spouse

My husband has been unable to keep a job for more than eight months since we got married. The reason is his drinking. Before we got married, I knew he liked to have a few beers with his friends on the weekend, but I thought that was it. Unfortunately, things have gotten much worse in the past three years. He now comes home drunk at least two or three nights a week. He doesn't think he has a drinking problem, but everyone who's close to him knows better.

Alcoholism and drug addiction are not just personal problems; they're family problems. Few things damage family relationships more severely than substance abuse. A substance abuser lives in an egocentric world. He or she is concerned only with easing his or her pain and finding pleasure. That leaves little room for concern about the effect pleasure seeking might have on loved ones.

If you're married to an alcoholic or a substance abuser, you can find help—not only for your spouse, but also for you, your kids, and your family relationships.

Stop the enabling.

One of the first things you need to do is recognize your role in your spouse's addiction. You'll note that we did not use the term "your responsibility" in that previous sentence. This is an important distinction to make. You are not *responsible* for your spouse's addiction problem. However, you may be playing a role in the addiction without even realizing it.

You may be unwittingly *enabling* your spouse's addiction through behavior that you consider to be loving and caring. If you're concerned that you may be enabling your spouse, your best bet would be to start attending Al-Anon support meetings in your community. (You can find information about Al-Anon in your local phone book.)

At Al-Anon, you'll learn the two most important steps in ending your pattern of enabling: (1) taking responsibility for your own actions, and (2) letting your spouse take responsibility for actions.

Concerning enabling, answer these questions: How many times have you lied for your spouse regarding substance abuse? How many times have you cleaned up after him or her? How many times have you chauffeured your spouse home? All of these actions are examples of enabling. And if you're guilty of any of them, you need to acknowledge that and start working to correct your actions.

That's not to say that any of those actions are *causes* of substance abuse. But they do make life easier for the substance abuser. And the last thing you want to do for an addicted loved one is to make life easier.

FAMILY TIES

Honesty and sensitivity are the two most important qualities you need to demonstrate when you talk to your kids about your spouse's substance-abuse problems. Honesty requires you to admit to your kids that your spouse is sick and needs help. If he is in a treatment program, explain that he won't be coming home until he gets better. Sensitivity compels you to withhold some of the more sordid details of your spouse's addiction.

Let the abuser take responsibility for his or her actions.

The only thing that ultimately makes a substance abuser choose to change his or her lifestyle is suffering the consequences of that lifestyle. What that means for you is that you must learn to allow your spouse to *experience* those consequences.

Specifically, it means . . .

➤ refusing to lie to your spouse's boss about why your spouse didn't show up for work

➤ refusing to clean up your spouse's messes

➤ refusing to sugarcoat the truth about your spouse's substance abuse for your kids and other family members

➤ allowing your spouse to spend the night in jail instead of posting bail.

GLAD YOU ASKED

What should my spouse and I look for in a substance-abuse treatment program?

There are seven elements that characterize a successful treatment program: (1) a commitment to a drug-free environment and a goal of total abstinence, (2) competent medical and nursing care, (3) a strong emphasis on one's personal spiritual life, (4) educational sessions that provide understanding of the effects of drugs, (5) both group and individual therapy sessions, (6) involvement of the larger family in the treatment process, and (7) a strong commitment to getting the patient into a support group after the initial treatment program.

Taking a hands-off approach to your spouse's "problem" may be difficult, but it's absolutely essential. Only when an addict comes to despise the lifestyle will there be motivation to seek treatment.

The Art of Tough Love

If your spouse's substance abuse continues or worsens, at some point it will become necessary to separate yourself and your kids. If you have family or friends you can stay with, go there. If not, see if you can make arrangements through your church.

This act of separation will likely serve as a wake-up call. His or her initial reaction may be to beg for forgiveness and "another chance," and to ask you to return home. Don't do it.

Until your spouse is enrolled in (and attending) a legitimate substance-abuse program, you should not even consider returning home. The temptation to fall back into old patterns may be too strong to resist.

After completion of substance-abuse counseling, the two of you will need to undergo extensive marital counseling before you move back in together. If that seems excessive to you, you may be underestimating the damage caused by substance abuse.

Family Practice

Think you're an expert on working through destructive behavior in your relationship? Here's a quiz to see how much you know.

1. Which of the following is *not* a likely cause for irresponsibility in your spouse?
   a. Rebellion against the model of his or her parents
   b. His or her Christian beliefs
   c. The desire to follow the model of his or her parents
   d. A self-centered attitude

2. Which of the following is generally *not* true of workaholics?
   a. They are driven by insecurity.
   b. They are not in touch with their own feelings or the feelings of their spouses.
   c. Their jobs receive more of their attention than their spouses and children do.
   d. Most of their behavior patterns can't be changed.

3. Which of the following is a recommended strategy for dealing with a controlling spouse?
   a. Power plays
   b. Understanding the emotional needs behind the quest for control
   c. Servantlike submission
   d. Expressing doubt about his or her ideas

4. Which of the following statements does *not* apply to an uncommunicative spouse?
   a. Constant nagging and whining will get him or her to open up.
   b. He or she may be afraid of expressing negative emotions.
   c. He or she may be following the example that one or both of his or her parents set.
   d. He or she needs to have his or her emotional needs met.

5. Which of the following is *not* an example of letting an abusive spouse take responsibility for his or her actions?
   a. Leaving your spouse lying on the bathroom floor where he or she passed out
   b. Refusing to confirm your spouse's excuse for his boss about why he or she missed four straight days of work

c. Telling your kids that Daddy is acting "silly" because he's really tired

d. Letting your spouse spend the night in jail on a disorderly conduct charge

Answers: (1) b, (2) d, (3) b, (4) a, (5) c

CHAPTER 14

Temper, Temper

(Dealing with Anger in Your Family Relationships)

SNAPSHOT

"Hi, Honey; I'm home," Kent said as he walked into the bedroom and set his briefcase down.

"Yeah, I can see that," Darla replied without turning around from the dresser where she was putting clothes away. "Do you think I'm stupid or something?"

"No," Kent said. "Actually, you're one of the smartest—"

"Don't patronize me," Darla warned as she threw a pair of his boxer shorts into a drawer.

"Uh . . . Honey?" Kent said carefully. "Is something wrong?"

Darla slammed a drawer shut in response.

"Is it something I did?" Kent asked.

"Hmmph," Darla replied as she grabbed some more clothes from the laundry basket and started folding them.

SNEAK PREVIEW

1. Anger is a normal, healthy emotion. It is productive when it's expressed in a positive manner.

2. In order to deal with conflict positively and effectively in a marital relationship, spouses need to develop anger-management strategies before conflicts arise.

3. In order to teach children how to deal with their anger in a positive way, parents need to model proper anger-management techniques, as well as giving guidance and instruction.

"I'll take that 'Hmmph' as a 'yes,'" Kent said. "So that's two questions down, eighteen to go."

"I'm glad you find this so amusing!" Darla snapped as she furiously folded the clothes in her hands.

"Honey," Kent replied, "I just wish you would tell me why you're angry."

"Who said I was *angry?*" Darla snapped. "I don't *get* angry! What makes you think I'm angry?"

"Well, aside from the fact that you just used the word *angry* three times in a row," Kent said as he pointed at the clothes in Darla's hands, "I notice that you're tying that laundry awful tight."

"I always tie your socks in pairs so you don't lose them," Darla reminded him.

"I know, Honey," Kent replied, "but that's my dress shirt you're knotting up there."

* * * * * * * * * * * * * * *

Does that scenario sound familiar? Do you and your spouse ever play "Twenty Questions" to get to the root of a conflict between you? Do one or both of you ever resort to the "silent treatment" to demonstrate your anger? Or do you prefer to get everything out in the open—at 120 decibels?

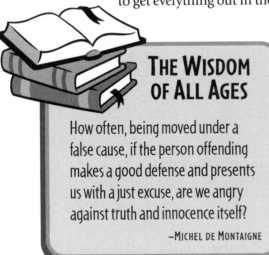

THE WISDOM OF ALL AGES

How often, being moved under a false cause, if the person offending makes a good defense and presents us with a just excuse, are we angry against truth and innocence itself?

–MICHEL DE MONTAIGNE

There are many different ways to express anger. In this chapter, we're going to look at the healthiest methods for you and your family to use.

Exploding a Few Anger Myths

Before we tackle the dos and don'ts of expressing anger, we need to get a handle on what anger is—and what it isn't. Contrary to popular opinion, anger is not . . .

➤ a sign of emotional weakness

➤ a nonphysical form of violence

➤ a sin

➤ evidence of a lack of personal control

➤ an inappropriate response to frustrating situations

➤ an indication of problems in a relationship.

Anger is an emotion that rises in us when we encounter something we perceive to be wrong. The fact that we feel anger demonstrates that we have some concern for justice and righteousness. Our capacity for anger reveals our concern for fairness. The experience of anger is evidence of our nobility, not our depravity.

To cease to experience anger is to lose one's sense of moral concern. Without moral concern, the world would be a dreadful place indeed.

That's not to say that the more angry a person gets, the more moral he or she is. What matters is not what a person feels, but how the feelings are expressed.

For the purposes of this chapter, the issue is not whether anger in a relationship is good or bad, but whether that anger is expressed in a way that brings about positive or negative results.

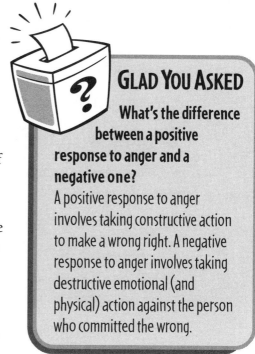

GLAD YOU ASKED

What's the difference between a positive response to anger and a negative one?

A positive response to anger involves taking constructive action to make a wrong right. A negative response to anger involves taking destructive emotional (and physical) action against the person who committed the wrong.

When Your Sweetie Pie Gets Sour

All married couples experience anger in their relationship. A significantly smaller percentage of those couples actually know how to process that anger productively. What usually happens in marital conflicts is that spouses edge toward one of two extremes. They either explode in verbal tirades that do nothing but make the situation worse or they suffer in silence, isolating themselves by withdrawing.

After a few hours (or days), when the anger has subsided, they pick up the pieces

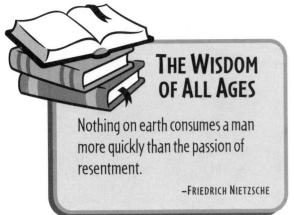

of their relationship and continue on—until the next conflict arises and the whole thing starts all over again. The problem is, until a couple can deal with their anger properly, they will never have a truly satisfying relationship. Love cannot coexist with unresolved anger. Love causes you to seek the well-being of your spouse; uncontrolled anger causes you to want to hurt and destroy your spouse's emotional well-being.

The good news is that you can learn to deal with your anger in a proper manner. The bad news is that it won't be easy.

Dealing with the Anger

In order to develop sound anger-management principles in your relationship, there are six things you need to do *before* you get angry with each other:

1. Acknowledge the reality of anger.

2. Agree to acknowledge your anger to each other.

3. Agree that verbal or physical explosions against the other person are not appropriate responses to anger.

4. Agree to seek an explanation before passing judgment.

5. Agree to seek a resolution.

6. Agree to affirm your love for each other.

Let's take a closer look at each of these ideas.

1. Acknowledge the reality of anger.
No matter how well you get along or how much you enjoy each other's company, anger is inevitable in your relationship. In fact, the absence of anger in a relationship would suggest seriously flawed communication patterns.

Keep in mind that anger is not wrong; it's simply evidence that one has a concern for fairness and justice. If you acknowledge the legitimacy of anger from the start in your relationship, you'll have no reason to condemn each other for feeling angry from time to time. You'll also have no reason to *deny* feeling angry, for fear of looking bad.

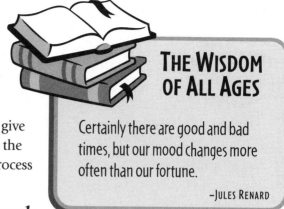

To give your spouse the right to feel angry is to give the right to be human. Once you acknowledge the right to feel angry, you can begin learning to process your anger in a positive way.

2. Agree to acknowledge your anger to each other.

Don't make your spouse play "What's My Emotion?" with you. You know: "Question One: Are you mad? Question Two: Are you mad at me? Question Three: Are you mad at me for something I've done in the past couple of hours?" Instead, if you're angry with your spouse, just say so.

Whether your anger is due to something your spouse said, did, or forgot, you need to make a resolution to reveal your feelings as soon as possible. That means resisting the urge to keep your anger to yourself, nursing and feeding it until just the right time when you can spring it on your spouse for maximum effect.

When you are treated unkindly, unfairly, or inappropriately, a barrier goes up between you. If your spouse isn't aware of wrongdoing or your feelings about it, there's nothing he or she can do to correct the situation and eliminate the barrier. And as long as that barrier is up, your relationship will suffer.

3. Agree that verbal or physical explosions against the other person are not appropriate responses to anger.

Venting your anger at top volume or with your emotions revved to the red line is unhealthy and destructive. Unfortunately, it's also natural. Many people allow their emotions to dictate their reactions. When something makes them a little mad, they respond in a fairly controlled manner. When something drives them crazy, they explode in a frenzy of yelling and accusations. The more intense the anger, the more intense the reaction.

Since that kind of response does nothing but harm, you need to create a strategy

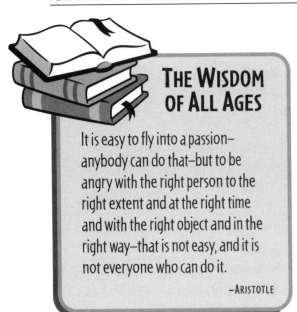

THE WISDOM OF ALL AGES

It is easy to fly into a passion–anybody can do that–but to be angry with the right person to the right extent and at the right time and with the right object and in the right way–that is not easy, and it is not everyone who can do it.

—ARISTOTLE

for nipping verbal explosions in the bud. That doesn't mean you should set as your goal the elimination of all such outbursts in your marriage. As long as you remain fallible, that kind of goal is not going to be attainable for you.

Instead, you should commit yourselves to taking a proactive stance against verbal outbursts. You might agree on a "walking away" strategy whenever one of you overheats during an argument or confrontation. Here's how it works. If one of you starts to get loud or obnoxious in expressing your anger, the other will just walk away. If the angry one continues verbal assault, the other spouse will keep walking out the door and down the street. If the angry outburst continues, the spouse being yelled at will head to a neighbor's house or hop in the car and leave for a while.

If you set this as your strategy before you find yourself in an angry situation, you will know that when one of you starts walking away during a conversation, it will be a sign for the other to stop and reflect. After a few moments of "cooling down," the angry spouse may be ready to apologize for the outburst. At that point, the two of you can put the outburst behind you and begin focusing on the cause of it.

4. Agree to seek an explanation before passing judgment.

When you get angry with your spouse, it's because you assume there has been a wrong done. Until you verify that assumption, it's best to keep your mouth shut. You'd be surprised (or maybe you wouldn't) at the number of arguments that are caused by misunderstandings or misinterpretations.

Instead of exploding at your spouse for an imagined offense, it's important to give a chance to explain. In doing so, you may discover . . .

➤ extenuating circumstances

➤ motives you may have misread

➤ misunderstandings that are your own fault.

By getting that information in advance, you can avoid not only the embarrassment of being wrong, but also the damage of detonated anger.

5. Agree to seek a resolution.

If and when you discover that there is a legitimate conflict or hurt feelings, you're faced with a choice. You can either hold on to your anger, at the expense of your relationship, or you can work through your anger with your spouse to resolve the situation.

Working through your anger is the obvious choice, but that doesn't mean it's the easiest one. Resolving conflict with your spouse requires a hefty chunk of work and sacrifice on your part. Remember, pouting is easy; talking is hard. What's more, some conflict solutions may not be immediately obvious. That's OK. What's important is not how quickly you reach a resolution, but how committed you are to reaching the resolution in a healthy manner.

6. Agree to affirm your love for each other.

After the anger is resolved, let the loving begin. Affirming your love immediately after a conflict sends a powerful message—namely, that you will not allow anger (or any emotion, for that matter) to come between you.

As you affirm your love, talk about what the two of you did together in working through your anger. As a couple, you heard each other out, resolved the issue, learned from the experience, and prepared yourselves to move on in your relationship together. As bonding experiences go, you really can't do much better than that.

In the end, you'll see that what could have divided you ended up bringing you closer together. If that's not a testimony to the strength of your relationship and the depth of your love and commitment, what is?

Making It Work

You'll notice that this strategy for anger management calls for a lot of agreement (so much so that you may feel like you're drafting a resolution for the U.N. instead of dealing with heated emotions). Obviously, agreeing is easy to do when everything's copacetic between you and your spouse. But what about when anger gets a foothold in your relationship? Won't your first order of business be to rip up the list of strategies into six hundred pieces? Not if you make a *concentrated* effort to hold each other accountable to these principles.

In the heat of the battle, it may be tempting for you to "take off the gloves" and go at it. But by maintaining a cool head and sticking to these anger-management strategies, you'll find that the resolution you reach together will be infinitely more satisfying than anything a temper tantrum might achieve.

For the Kids' Sake

And how about your children's anger feelings? Few of your parental responsibilities will have a longer-lasting effect on your kids' lives than teaching them how to process anger in a positive and healthy way. In fact, your instruction and guidance can literally mean the difference between healthy relationships and unhealthy relationships in your kids' futures. (Pressure, anyone?)

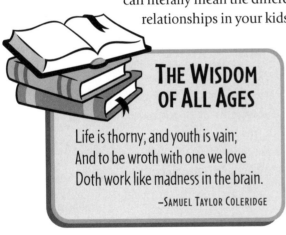

THE WISDOM OF ALL AGES

Life is thorny; and youth is vain;
And to be wroth with one we love
Doth work like madness in the brain.

–SAMUEL TAYLOR COLERIDGE

No matter how effective your teaching strategies are, there's one thing you *can't* do for your kids. You can't eliminate anger from their lives. You shouldn't even try. Remember, anger is a normal, healthy emotion. Your job is to help your kids learn to *respond to it* in a positive way.

Toward that end, the first thing you need to focus on is meeting your kids' need for emotional love. Before you can influence their responses to anger, your kids need to know that your love for them is unconditional. (For more information on how to demonstrate unconditional love to your kids, check out chapter 10.)

After your kids are secure in the knowledge of your love, you can start helping them process their emotions in a healthy way. There are three primary methods for teaching your children to handle their anger positively:

1. Model proper behavior.

2. Take an active role in guiding them through their own anger episodes.

3. Give instruction.

Let's take a closer look at each of these methods.

1. Model proper behavior.

Like it or not, most kids learn to deal with their anger by watching their parents handle anger. If the thought of your child mimicking your typical response to anger scares you, do something about it. Learn to change your destructive methods of dealing with anger. The example you set for your kids in committing yourself to developing healthier ways of dealing with your anger will likely make a big difference in their lives.

Most kids respond positively when they hear their parents admit that their own method of handling anger needs to be improved. When kids see the actual changes taking place in their parents' behavior, they will be motivated to examine and improve their own anger-management skills.

2. Take an active role in guiding your kids through their own anger episodes.

In addition to modeling the proper way to handle anger, you can take an active role in guiding your children through their own anger episodes. We're talking about using the same approach you use in teaching your kids to ride a two-wheeler or mow the lawn or drive a car. You can't expect kids to learn anger management on their own. What's more, in guiding your kids through their anger, you first have to accept their present level of development and then help them grow from there.

You need to recognize that kids have two ways of expressing their anger: through their words and through their actions. Each method can be used positively or negatively.

A child might express anger negatively by . . .

FAMILY TIES

Involve your kids in your anger-management efforts by encouraging them to come up with a list of things you can do when you feel angry in order to keep from blowing your top. One obvious suggestion would be to count to ten. Given the right encouragement, your kids will likely come up with some considerably less obvious ideas ("Chew a piece of gum until all of the flavor is gone before you respond to someone who has made you angry"). Choose one suggestion from the list each week and report back to your kids on how well it worked for you.

➤ hitting someone,

➤ throwing things, or

➤ slamming doors.

FAMILY TIES

For young children who are just old enough to understand the difference between positive and negative expressions of anger, consider using cartoons as a teaching tool. Watch some of your kids' favorite animated programs with them. Pay particular attention to scenes in which characters get mad or try to resolve conflict. Ask your kids to identify what the characters did right and what they did wrong in each situation. Later, you can apply the principles your kids pick up to their own real-life responses to anger.

You'll notice that these expressions are knee-jerk reactions—immediate and inappropriate responses to feelings of anger.

On the other hand, a child might express anger positively by . . .

➤ leaving the room before tensions become unbearable,

➤ counting to one hundred before responding to an angry person, or

➤ taking a walk around the block to get his or her head clear.

These expressions all demonstrate the wisdom of "cooling off" before reacting.

On the verbal side, a child might express anger negatively through . . .

➤ name-calling,

➤ swearing, or

➤ screaming.

You'll note that these expressions are aggressive, attacking responses to anger.

On the other hand, a child might express anger positively by . . .

➤ admitting that he or she is angry,

➤ asking for an opportunity to discuss the problem, or

➤ agreeing to talk about the situation later.

As you work to guide your kids through their anger, you may be frustrated by the fact that they opt for negative expressions of anger more often than positive. Don't let it bother you. Perfection is not your goal. Helping your child understand the difference between a negative expression of anger and a positive one is your goal.

What you *don't* want to do in helping your child respond properly to anger is miss the message behind the anger. That means if your child is screaming at you in an angry voice, you need to listen to what is being said. Don't get distracted or upset by the screaming. In a calm voice, ask questions to find out why your child is feeling this way. The more questions you ask—the more intently you try to figure out what's going on with your child—the more likely it is that the screaming will stop and positive discussion will continue.

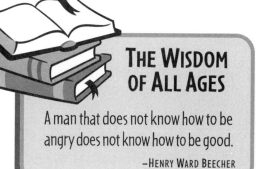

THE WISDOM OF ALL AGES

A man that does not know how to be angry does not know how to be good.

—HENRY WARD BEECHER

Don't focus on trying to get your child to settle down; instead, focus on trying to find out what it is that seems unfair or wrong. You may not agree with what your child says, but that's not the point. The point is to "hear" your child out. If your child believes there is wrong, that anger won't go away until you have heard and understood what neeeds to be said. You need to let your child know that his or her feelings are important to you.

After your child has had a chance to cool down, make a point of talking about your confrontation. Admit that you don't always handle angry situations well, either. See if the two of you can reach some mutual decisions about how you will handle your next angry situation together. Above all else, make it clear to your child that you always want to hear about thoughts and feelings, regardless of how they are expressed.

Your child may not always be happy with you or the parental decisions you make, but you have earned respect in future confrontations.

Each time you're able to guide your child through an anger episode, there is growth in expressing anger. Over time, you may also see a noticeable reduction in yelling and screaming. Here's why. If your child becomes convinced that you're interested in listening to thoughts and feelings, there will be no need to resort to extreme measures to get a point across.

3. Give instruction.

This is the most tempting place to start for most parents ("Let me tell you how you should handle your anger"). In reality, instruction is best used as a supplement to modeling and guiding anger-management principles.

The kind of instruction you use will depend on the age of your kids. For younger kids, reading and discussing stories in which a character experiences and reacts to anger may provide the instructional opportunities you need.

For older kids, informal conversation may be your best instructional strategy. You might ask, "What do you think of the way I deal with anger?" By putting the focus on yourself, you give your child a chance to speak openly and honestly. After the two of you have identified your weaknesses, you can start talking about more positive ways to deal with anger.

If you're feeling especially adventurous, you can share some examples of times when you let your anger get the better of you and later regretted it. Revealing your own struggles with anger will capture your kids' attention. Hearing you address your faults when it comes to anger may encourage them to do the same with their own anger issues.

If you want to go for the whole enchilada, try apologizing to your child for a recent blowup caused by your allowing your anger to get the better of you. You may be surprised at what an apology will do to your child's level of respect for you. Your child will likely already know what you've done wrong. Admitting it yourself will restore your relationship. You'll be setting an important example when your child has to apologize.

GLAD YOU ASKED

My son tends to throw or slam things when he's mad. What can I do to help him?

Focus on the anger first and the behavior second. You might say something like, "I can see that you're angry, and I'd like to hear what's bothering you. But we can't have a meaningful discussion while you're throwing things. Would you like to take a walk and talk about it?" What you're doing is acknowledging both your son's anger and his destructive manner of expressing it and giving him an opportunity to end his negative expression on his own terms.

Remember, a combination approach to teaching anger-management skills that includes a positive parental model, loving parental guidance, and non-condemning instruction will go a long way toward shaping your child's emotional health.

THE WISDOM OF ALL AGES

No man is angry that feels not himself hurt.

—FRANCIS BACON

A Final Word on Anger

The key to preventing anger from damaging your family relationships is knowing how to respond to an angry person. Here are seven tips for you to use the next time you're confronted with a fire-breathing loved one, whether spouse, offspring, sibling, or other relations.

1. *Listen to the person.* The best thing you can do for an angry loved one is listen. As you become aware of what triggered anger, you begin to gauge the depth of angry feelings.

2. *Listen to the person.* Second verse, same as the first. After you've heard the angry person's story, ask to "repeat, please"—not in an effort to make the person angry, but in order to demonstrate that this is serious. Let the person know that you really want to understand what happened.

3. *Listen to the person.* No, this isn't a typo. After the story is repeated, ask some questions to make sure that you understand it—and to let the person release those feelings. You'll find that it takes three (and sometimes even four) rounds of listening for the angry person to get out all of the concerns and frustrations.

4. *Seek to understand the person's situation.* As you try to understand what stimulated the person's anger, ask yourself, "Would I be angry in the same situation?" Try to identify with the person by putting yourself in his or her place.

5. *Express your understanding of the situation.* Explain to the person what you understand from listening to the story three times or more. Make sure that you maintain a spirit of compassion and empathy as you relate your understanding of what caused the anger. Even if the person has some facts

wrong, don't try to modify or challenge the details of the situation. You can do that later. At this point, you just want to make sure that you affirm the person's feelings. You might say, "I can see why you would be angry about that. If I were in your shoes, I probably would feel angry also."

6. *Share additional information that may shed light on the subject.* If you have information or a point of view that will alter the angry person's perception of the situation, present it in a kind, straightforward manner. If you give the person time to let the anger subside, this new information will be less likely to embarrass or offend. Depending on the information you share, the person may realize at this point that you have done no wrong, and apologize for getting angry.

7. *Confess any wrongdoing and make things right.* If you come to the realization that the person's anger with you is justified, own up to your wrongdoing and apologize to him or her. Then take the necessary steps to right your wrong.

Your responsibility is not to prevent anger. Your responsibility is to make sure that something positive results from the expression of your anger.

Family Practice

Think you're an expert on dealing with anger? Here's a quiz to see how much you know.

1. Which of the following is true of anger?
   a. It's a sign of weakness.
   b. It's a form of violence.
   c. It's a healthy emotion.
   d. It's a sin, according to the Bible.

2. Which of the following is *not* a sound anger-management principle for couples to apply to their relationship?
   a. Agree to seek an explanation before passing judgment.
   b. Agree to discuss only conflicts that you both consider important.

c. Agree to affirm your love for each other.

d. Agree to acknowledge your anger to each other.

3. Sound anger-management principles can do all of the following for a marital relationship except:

a. Reduce heated arguments between spouses

b. Open lines of communication between spouses

c. Create a bonding experience for spouses

d. Prevent spouses from getting angry

4. Which of the following is *not* a suggested method for helping your child deal with anger in a positive way?

a. Give him or her legitimate reasons to be angry.

b. Take an active role in guiding him or her through anger episodes.

c. Model proper behavior.

d. Give instruction.

5. How do most kids learn to deal with their anger?

a. By watching the way their parents deal with anger

b. By mimicking what they see on TV

c. By experimenting with different kinds of responses until they find one that feels right to them

d. By reading self-help books on anger management

Answers: (1) c, (2) b, (3) d, (4) a, (5) a

the ONE and ONLY!

The Power of One

(HELP FOR THE SINGLE PARENT)

SNAPSHOT

Janice waited until she and Kyra were out of earshot of the other walkers on the trail. "So how are you doing?" she asked.

"I'm fine," Kyra replied.

Janice gave her a sharp look. "Hey, this isn't the nosy old lady down the street asking. It's me, your best friend. So how are you *really* doing?"

Kyra sighed. "When I was a kid, I used to watch reruns of *Alice* and *The Courtship of Eddie's Father* all the time. You'd think that I would have learned *something* about being a single parent from them."

Janice laughed. "I remember, right after my divorce, thinking that all the other parents in my neighborhood were talking behind my back about what a bad mother I was. It seemed that everywhere

SNEAK PREVIEW

1. Single parents must employ the efforts of others, including family members, friends, teachers, and church members, in meeting the emotional needs of their children.

2. Assisting children and teenagers in recovering from the aftershocks of divorce or the death of a parent involves helping them work through the various stages of grief, including anger, denial, and bargaining.

3. Noncustodial parents must take it upon themselves to learn their children's primary love language so that they can make the most of their limited time with their kids.

I went people were trying to give me advice or encouragement."

Kyra groaned in recognition.

"Have you ever run into those well-meaning types who say things like, 'You're better off without him' or 'A pretty gal like you won't stay single for long'?" Janice asked.

"Oh, yeah!" Kyra exclaimed. "And then there are the people who say, 'Just let me know if there's anything I can do for you.' Sometimes I feel like saying, 'Well, you could come over to my house at 9:30 every night to help me comfort my seven-year-old daughter while she cries herself to sleep because her dad isn't around to kiss her good night. Or you could help me come up with a response for my nine-year-old son when he tells me that his father would probably still be around if I'd been a better wife.'"

"If you ever did say something like that, most of your would-be helpers would be out of there so fast, they'd leave skid marks," Janice said.

Kyra laughed and added, "But as they left they'd probably offer to drop off a tuna casserole or a pan of lasagna."

* * * * * * * * * * * * * * *

As a single parent, when was the last time you felt . . .

➤ lonely? ➤ desperate? ➤ guilty?

➤ scared? ➤ overwhelmed? ➤ underqualified?

➤ unpopular? ➤ trapped? ➤ underappreciated?

If we were to suggest that successful single parenting can be achieved in three easy steps, you'd probably throw this book across the room in frustration. Taking care of the physical and emotional needs of your kids, while at the same time trying to provide financially for your family and maintain order in your household, is an exhausting, never-ending process. There is no easy way to do it.

The purpose of this chapter is to help you understand that the work can be done—and that the rewards of a job well done are worth the tremendous effort you put into that job. As a single parent, you can develop strong family relationships. Here are ways to aid in their emotional and social growth.

Help for Grieving Children

The first, and perhaps most obvious, thing we need to point out is that you're not the only person in your family struggling with your one-parent status. Don't forget that your kids will be able to match you woe for woe when it comes to your family situation. Researchers have discovered that children of divorce struggle with feelings of fear, anger, and anxiety as much as ten years after their parents split up.

You'll find that the process of helping your kids deal with your divorce is similar to the grieving process after the death of a loved one. Responses such as denial, anger, and bargaining are common as kids work through the reality of their parents' divorce.

The good news is that eventually most kids are able to come to grips with the loss of family unity. Some will do it quicker than others. Some will do it more painfully than others. What will make the difference in *your* kids' lives is your willingness to communicate with them openly about their loss.

In order for you to help your kids, you first need to be aware of the different stages of the "grieving process." Let's take a look at some of the things they may be experiencing.

THE WISDOM OF ALL AGES

Only solitary men know the full joys of friendship. Others have their family; but to a solitary and an exile his friends are everything.

–WILLA CATHER

Denial

The first response to your divorce will likely be denial. No child wants to believe that the parents are splitting up for good or that one parent has abandoned the family. You may find that your kids talk as though you and their other parent are simply temporarily separated, and that you'll get back together eventually.

In this stage, your kids will likely be very frightened and feel a deep sense of sadness and loss. They may cry a lot, hoping that it may inspire you and your spouse to reunite. Your kids may also feel a profound sense of rejection.

Anger

Your kids' denial stage will likely be followed (and perhaps even accompanied) by an intense period of anger. The anger comes from their perception that the absent parent has failed to fulfill the parental duties. This anger may be expressed through words or actions, or it may be held inside, because of the fear of making the family situation worse.

Your kids will get angry because they feel powerless in their situation. As a result, they may feel the need to lash out—at their missing parent, at you, or at friends or other family members. And while you may be tempted to take offense at the anger directed at you, keep in mind that beneath the angry exterior is a deep sense of loneliness and frustration over their inability to talk about their problems with anyone who matters to them.

> ### THE WISDOM OF ALL AGES
>
> When you have shut your doors and darkened your room, remember, never to say that you are alone; for you are not alone, but God is within, and your genius is within.
>
> –Epictetus

What your child needs is to feel loved, to know that someone really cares. And since it's not likely that they will feel that love from their departed parent, that places the burden on your shoulders.

Bargaining

After denial and anger, you may start to see evidence of "bargaining" in behavior. Your kids may get it in their heads that they can bring you and your ex back together. They may talk to you and your ex separately or together, begging you to put aside your differences and reunite, for the sake of the family. As added incentive for you, your kids may promise to behave or get straight A's or something else remarkable if you will get back together.

If that doesn't work, your kids may resort to bad or even dangerous behavior. Depending on the child, this misbehavior might involve anything from drug use to sexual promiscuity, from vandalism to attempted suicide. Not all bad behavior is used as a "bargaining chip." Many kids of divorce use misbehavior as a way of testing their parents' concern for their well-being.

More Anger

When bargaining doesn't work, your child will probably resort to more anger. For at least a year after the divorce, there will likely be struggles with feelings of anger, guilt, fear, and insecurity. The results may be . . .

➤ lower grades in school

➤ more aggressive negative social behavior

➤ lessened respect for all adults

➤ intense loneliness.

It's within this hotbed of emotions that you have to meet your kids' need for love and create some semblance of a normal home life for them.

Whew.

Reading Is Fundamental

If you have young kids, you may find that reading books with them helps them work through some of the negative emotions they're experiencing—or at least helps them achieve some peace of mind. One of the characteristics of a child overwhelmed by the breakup of his or her parents' marriage is an inability to think clearly. Reading can help focus, so that they can begin to process their feelings of pain and loss.

Make sure that you choose age-appropriate books to read with your kids. You want books that your kids can understand. You also want books that will encourage reactions. As you read together, periodically ask what they are thinking. Take advantage of every opportunity for discussion.

GLAD YOU ASKED

How can I give my son the love he needs when he blames me for the divorce that split up his father and me? You may not be able to bridge the gap between you and your son right away. Until you're able to restore that relationship, then, you may need to find other family members, such as grandparents, aunts or uncles, or teachers or church leaders to help fill the void. If you make those "significant others" aware of your son's primary love language, you will help them be more effective in meeting his needs.

For example, if the book you're reading involves a character who is lost or has lost something valuable, you can talk about what it feels like to be lost or to lose someone dear to you. That discussion could then lead to another discussion about the specifics of the other parent.

Using the characters of the book as a starting point, you can begin to explore feelings about the separation from their parent and help them work through some of their feelings.

Help!

You can't meet the need for love by yourself. Whether that reality causes you to panic or gives you a sense of relief will depend on the "support group" (or lack of one) you have in place around you. If you don't have a support group, you need to build one for yourself. In order to do that, you may first need to take a gulp of your pride.

Don't make people come to you. Don't wait until someone asks if you need any help. Some potential helpers may be holding back, not wanting to interfere with your family, waiting for you to indicate that you need assistance. Others may not even be aware of your need for help. If you wait for volunteer help to arrive, you—and your kids—may be waiting a long time.

That's why you need to take the initiative in finding stable, reliable, trustworthy, and caring people. The first place to look is to your extended family. If your relationship with your family is strained, you need to do what you can to become close again. The time for proving a point or holding a grudge is past. You need your family to be involved in your lives. Your kids need the love that grandparents, aunts, uncles, and cousins can give. (The exception, of course, would be cases in which members of your immediate family pose a physical or emotional risk to the children.)

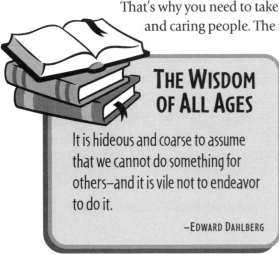

THE WISDOM OF ALL AGES

It is hideous and coarse to assume that we cannot do something for others—and it is vile not to endeavor to do it.

—EDWARD DAHLBERG

Beyond your immediate family, you can find a surprising number of people willing to help single parents simply by making your needs known. At times, a neighbor or teacher is ready to listen to you and show care to your children. One of the best places to make your needs known is the church. Make an appointment to talk to your pastor or one of the other leaders of the church. Explain the situation and your needs carefully. Many churches have established ministries specifically designed to meet the needs of single parents. If that's true of your church, you can expect to hear from caring people who want to make a difference in your life and the lives of your kids.

Again with the Love Languages

You don't have to be a math major to understand that your child's need for love, minus one parent, equals more work for you. And if you're working and trying to run your household at the same time, that doesn't leave a lot of opportunity for giving the one-on-one "loving time" they need.

That's why it's vital that you make the most of the time you do have. The way to do that is to learn your child's primary love language. Specific information about the five love languages can be found in chapters 3–7 of this book. Tips for applying those principles can be found in chapters 10 and 11. We're not going to rehash the principles of those chapters here. We're not even going to list the highlights. Instead, we're going to reiterate the importance of becoming fluent in your child's primary love language.

If your daughter's primary love language is quality time, but you insist on showering her with words of affirmation, you're directing your precious time and energy in the wrong place. You may still see results from your efforts, but they will not be as profound or as dramatic as they could be otherwise. Speaking your

GLAD YOU ASKED

My daughter's husband recently left her for another woman, leaving her and her twin sons alone. I'm retired and live nearby. What's the best thing I can do for her?

Aside from giving her a listening ear and a shoulder to cry on, the best way to help your daughter right now is to take care of some of the everyday logistics for her. That may mean running errands for her, picking up groceries, taking your grandchildren to soccer practice, making dinner for them, and so forth. Beyond that, you can help her by establishing a bond with your grandchildren and filling their lives with unconditional love.

child's primary love language will make your interactions more intensely satisfying and fulfilling for both of you.

Learning to demonstrate love effectively—and efficiently—is an absolute must for single parents.

Welcome to the Teen Years

As your kids become teenagers, you may begin to notice some things that you have never seen. Feelings that you thought had been dealt with in their younger years may come roaring back for a dramatic encore when they hit their teens. Emotions such as hurt, anger, and rejection, which your kids may not have expressed at all in childhood, can team up to devastate teenagers' self-esteem. The results can include anything from feelings of inadequacy to depression to destructive behavior.

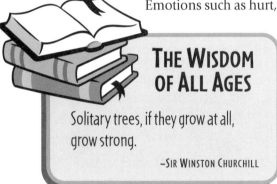

THE WISDOM OF ALL AGES

Solitary trees, if they grow at all, grow strong.

–Sir Winston Churchill

Compounding the problem for you is the fact that your teenager may not exhibit these feelings, or the resulting behavior, in front of the other (noncustodial) parent. Your teenager may be wary of disrupting a relationship already considered fragile. Or there may be concern about the noncustodial parent's opinion.

Whatever the reason, you will still be the odd person out. You will be the one who feels the brunt of your teenager's emotional onslaught. And that's a tough thing to accept—especially when you consider the fact that you're the one who's sacrificed and worked hard to care for your teenager.

What you need to know is that the disappointment, hurt, and anger you may feel as a result of your teenager's seeming unfairness is normal. What you also need to understand is that it's nothing personal. Your teenager's strong emotions are part of the quest for independence. As your teen edges closer to the adult world, he or she will be forced to deal with life's inequities. The resulting emotions can be tough for parent and teen alike. The good news is that as your teenager learns to process these emotions, maturity will come. The bad news is that the maturation process doesn't happen overnight.

Responding to Your Teenager

Finding a way to deal with your teenager's emotional jags can be difficult. A method of communication that seems to work one day may be met with stony silence the next. There are, however, three strategies that can improve your chances for connecting with your teenager. Let's take a look at each one.

1. Focus on your teenager's emotions.

Let's say your teenage son spends roughly 90 percent of his nonschool time in his room, watching TV, listening to music, and just generally sulking. He seems to have little interest in anything except moping.

How would you respond? If you're like most parents, your first instinct would probably be the "get a life" response. You might encourage him to call up some friends and go out. You might tease him about his ghostly pallor and suggest that he spend some time in the sun. You might even demand that he get a job.

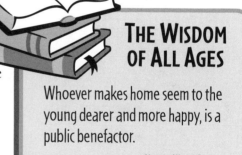

THE WISDOM OF ALL AGES

Whoever makes home seem to the young dearer and more happy, is a public benefactor.

–HENRY WARD BEECHER

All of those responses are perfectly understandable. None of them get to the heart of the matter. Those approaches deal with the teenager's *behavior.* In order to truly reach your son, you need to focus on his *feelings.*

The truth is, your son is probably moping because he's feeling depressed or rejected. Instead of telling him to stop moping, try asking him what's causing his feelings. Give him a chance to share what's going on in his life.

That's not to say you should expect your teenager to open up like a book just because you ask what's wrong. Most teenagers aren't wired that simply. You may have to conduct your investigation over the course of several conversations, putting together grunts and one-word answers like pieces of a jigsaw puzzle until you have a complete picture.

The best thing you can do is to create an atmosphere in your home in which he or she feels comfortable talking, particularly about the events and emotions surrounding the divorce, death, or abandonment that created your single-parent family. In allowing your teenager to express feelings, you're also paving the way for emotional healing. Until everything is out into the open and understood, there will still be struggles with negative feelings.

2. *Listen and tell your teenager the truth.*

Teenagers are bombarded with lies every day. From the false claims of advertisers to the unreal world of models and celebrities to the slippery promises of friends and romantic partners, teenagers are surrounded by untruths. For that reason, people who actually speak the truth to them—regardless of how hurtful that truth may be—earn a place of respect in their lives.

Sooner or later, your teenager is going to lob some tough questions at you regarding the absent parent. Answers that may have sufficed when your child was younger will not be enough.

Depending on the nature of your separation from the other parent and the individual interests of your teenager, he or she may ask you . . .

> ➤ what life was like when your family was intact

> ➤ why you and your "ex" decided to split up

> ➤ how you feel about your "ex"

> ➤ whether your "ex" really loves him or her

> ➤ what your "ex" used to say about him or her.

Those aren't easy questions to answer, but they must be answered just the same. Your teenagers deserve the truth, and they deserve it from you. This isn't the place for excuses or a whitewashing of the facts.

If your teen finds out later that you lied or withheld information, he or she will be less likely to trust you in the future. The emotional healing requires knowing the truth. And while the truth may hurt sometimes, it also has a tremendous ability to heal.

3. Respect your teenager's unrealistic desires.

Most of your teenager's unrealistic desires and expectations will center on the absent parent ("I wish Dad would come home for Christmas"). Knowing what you know about your ex, your first reaction may be to blow your teenager's expectations out of the water ("Your dad will be spending Christmas, not to mention his Christmas money, on his new wife and kids"). A far better approach is to acknowledge and affirm the desires ("You'd like your dad to spend Christmas with you—I understand that; I'd love for you to see him Christmas Day, too").

By responding positively to even your teenager's most unrealistic desires, you're affirming him or her as an adult. You're accepting a way of thinking instead of trying to change it. Remember, your goal is continued sharing of his or her thoughts and feelings with you. The way to do that is to respond positively. Besides, you'll often find that your teenager knows the desires are unrealistic, and that dreaming is part of a way of coping with the situation.

A Word to Noncustodial Parents

If you're not your kids' primary caregiver, you can still be a positive influence in their lives. In order to develop the kind of relationship your child needs, though, you're going to have to learn to avoid some common parenting pitfalls. Let's take a look at them.

Pitfall #1: The "Disneyland Daddy" Syndrome

This is where you spend the time you have going to amusement parks or ball games or video arcades or movies. Being a "Disneyland Daddy" (or a "Magic Mountain Mommy," if you prefer) casts you in the role of entertainer instead of parent. Your time becomes a quest for fun instead of an opportunity for bonding.

Don't misunderstand; there's nothing wrong with having fun. It's just that fun shouldn't be your *sole* focus. If your time is limited, you need to make the

THE WISDOM OF ALL AGES

To dare to live alone is the rarest courage; since there are many who had rather meet their bitterest enemy in the field, than their own hearts in their closet.

—CHARLES CALEB COLTON

most of it—in every sense. If you're unacquainted with the everyday problems and situations your kids are facing, you need to make time to acquaint yourself with them.

Your children will enjoy the fun things you do with them, but they will *thrive* on the moments you spend meeting their emotional needs.

Pitfall #2: Taking Advantage of Your Teenager

If you and your new spouse plan your social schedule around your teenager's availability as a baby-sitter for a child, you need to adjust your thinking regarding the purpose of the visit. Your teenager is not cheap labor, someone who makes your life a little easier once a week by doing things around the house you don't want to do, or don't have a chance to do, yourself.

That's not to say there should be no work during the visits. In fact, working together in the yard or doing things like grocery shopping as a team can be great bonding experiences.

But if you view the teenager's visits as opportunities for you to take care of the things you need to do, your child will know it—and will resent it. If life in high school teaches kids anything, it's how to know when they're being used.

Pitfall #3: Assuming Your Teenager Is Emotionally Stable

The fact that your teenager *seems* OK doesn't mean that he or she feels OK. As we mentioned earlier in this chapter, many teenagers are reluctant to let their noncustodial parent see their negative emotions. What that means for you is that if you want to be involved in your teen's emotional life, you need to look beyond surface expressions.

When it comes to sharing emotions, atmosphere is everything. So if you want your teenager to open up to you, you need to create an environment in your home

GLAD YOU ASKED

What should I do if my teenage daughter starts criticizing her father in front of me—especially if I agree with why she is complaining?

Keep your thoughts to yourself. Listen to what your teenager is saying, but don't join in the criticizing yourself. Stay above the fray. Ask your teenager's advice on what you can do to help, but don't butt in with ideas of your own. Your teenager needs the listening ear of a caring adult, not a fellow grumbler.

that encourages sharing. One of the best ways to create such an environment is to make a point of inviting your teenager to share. Lay your cards on the table. Acknowledge that the decision to split with your "ex" was devastating and that it probably caused all kinds of emotional turmoil. Let your teenager know that you want to hear what's going on inside—good or bad—and that his or her emotional well-being is your highest priority.

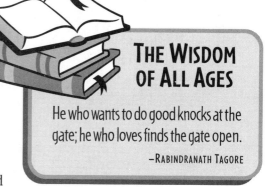

THE WISDOM OF ALL AGES

He who wants to do good knocks at the gate; he who loves finds the gate open.

—RABINDRANATH TAGORE

The most important thing you can do as a noncustodial parent is to make the most of your visits, phone calls, and E-mail messages. Share the things that are going on in your life, both good and bad, and *invite* your teenager to do the same. Being honest and vulnerable will likely inspire him or her to take the same approach with you.

Take the time to probe thoughts, feelings, and desires. Ask questions about things you don't understand. Make your interest in your teenager's life apparent.

Create a relationship in which there freedom to talk about or ask you anything. You need not have all the answers. You will earn more respect if you readily acknowledge that you don't have all the answers. Just being willing to help discover the answers will be enough.

Finally, in keeping with the unofficial theme of this book, learn your teenager's primary love language. The time you spend together is short. Make the most of it by learning to express your love in a way that speaks directly to his or her heart.

Five to Grow On

Whether you're a custodial or noncustodial parent, there are things you can do to make the best of your less-than-perfect family situation. Here are five tips you'll want to keep in mind:

FAMILY TIES

With a little preparation, you can create a bonding experience—and get some work done around your house— each time your teenager comes to visit. Choose a project around the house for the two of you to work on together. One week it might be washing your car. Another week it might be sealing your driveway. Another week it might be painting a bedroom. Just make sure that the projects you choose allow you to be in close proximity to your teenager. For added effect, you might even let your teenager choose the music you listen to while the two of you work. You may not like the tunes you hear, but they will give you starting points for conversations with your teenager.

1. Listen.

2. Teach your teenager to handle anger in a positive way. (For more information on healthy anger management, check out chapter 14.)

3. Give unconditional love.

4. Consider joining a single-parent support group.

5. Kindly but firmly keep boundaries in place.

A couple of thoughts about tip 5. As hard as it may be to believe, and as much as there may be protests, your teenager *wants* boundaries in place in your household. With your family situation in a state of instability, there is a need for something solid and unchanging. That's why it's important that you not let your guard down when it comes to the things your teenager is allowed to do.

Though your child will likely never admit it, there is the need for the security of knowing that you will prevent him or her from doing anything that may be harmful or detrimental to their well-being.

If you and the other parent can agree to form a united front in this area—if you can both commit to the same set of rules—you will communicate that you both care equally about his or her well-being.

A Little Help from Your Friends

As we close this chapter, we'll emphasize this point one more time: You should enlist the help of extended family and friends.

If your extended family lives nearby and you believe they would have a positive impact on your teenager's life, take the initiative to ask for their help. A grandfather, uncle, or older cousin (or a grandmother, aunt, or older cousin) can pick up the slack for a missing parent and give your teenager the kind of balanced interpersonal interaction needed.

If your extended family does not live in the immediate area or if you're concerned about the influence they may have on your teenager, look for help from friends, neighbors, and church members you can trust.

You will always be the most important positive influence in your teenager's life. But you shouldn't be the *only* positive influence. That means you shouldn't try to be everything, all the time. It also means you shouldn't be too proud to ask for help.

Raising kids as a single parent may be the most difficult job in the world. And, though it may not be a job you applied for, you can rise to the task. If you commit yourself to providing the guidance, direction, and unconditional love your kids need, you will succeed as a parent. And, in the process, you will set an example that they will be able to draw strength from for the rest of their lives.

FAMILY TIES

If you're the product of a single-parent family, take some time to write a letter to your father or mother, expressing your love and appreciation for the sacrifices he or she made in order to raise you. Let your parent know what qualities, characteristics, or elements of his or her parenting style you're going to adopt in raising your own family. In short, let your parent know that the hard work was not in vain.

Family Practice

Think you're an expert on healthy single parenting? Here's a quiz to see how much you know.

1. Which of the following is true of raising a family as a single parent?
   a. The parent's own emotional needs are more important than those of the children.
   b. The parenting is actually much easier than most so-called experts would have you believe.

c. The strong parent can meet the needs of the kids alone, without the support of others.

d. The parenting will likely become more difficult when the kids enter their teen years.

2. Which of the following is *not* one of the stages of grief your kids may experience in the aftermath of a divorce or the death of a parent?

a. Bargaining

b. Denial

c. Security

d. Anger

3. Why is reading important for children in the aftermath of a divorce or the death of a parent?

a. It helps them work through some of the negative emotions they may be experiencing.

b. It helps them understand that imaginary worlds are much more satisfying than the real one.

c. It's a good way to kill time when you and your children are home together.

d. It will earn you "brownie points" in your battle with your ex for your kids' affection.

4. Which of the following is *not* a good way to respond to your teenager?

a. Focusing on his or her emotions

b. Warning him or her not to become like his or her absent parent

c. Telling him or her the truth

d. Respecting his or her unrealistic desires

5. Which of the following tips would be least helpful for a single parent?

a. Listen to your teenager.

b. Consider joining a single-parent study group.

c. Give your teenager unconditional love.

d. Give your teenager a lot more freedom, as far as house rules go, than he or she is used to.

Answers: (1) d, (2) c, (3) a, (4) b, (5) d

CHAPTER 16

Together but Apart

(SUSTAINING YOUR RELATIONSHIP DURING A SEPARATION)

SNAPSHOT

"Don't look now, but I think those two women at the concession stand are giving us the eye," Lionel said between mouthfuls of Cracker Jack.

Tim shifted the hot dog and soda on his lap, but didn't look up. "I don't think I'm allowed to respond to things like that," he said.

"How do you know?" Lionel asked. "Do you have a copy of the official rules for men who are separated from their wives? Or did your wife tell you you're not allowed to look at other women?"

"No, actually that's one of those gray areas that no one seems to talk about," Tim explained. "There are a lot of gray areas like that when you're in my situation."

"Such as?" Lionel prompted.

"Such as filling out forms," Tim replied. "I was filling out a credit application the other day, and it said,

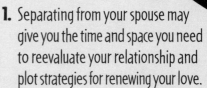

SNEAK PREVIEW

1. Separating from your spouse may give you the time and space you need to reevaluate your relationship and plot strategies for renewing your love.
2. Examining your own personality is a necessary step in evaluating your marriage, because it forces you to look at the strengths and weaknesses you bring to your relationship.
3. The true test of whether your marriage is salvageable is not how much love you *feel* for your spouse, but how willing you are to demonstrate loving actions.

'Marital status: Single, Married, Divorced, or Widowed.' I didn't know which box to check."

"You should have just cast a write-in vote for 'Separated'," Lionel suggested.

"I hate that word," Tim replied as he took a bite of his hot dog and checked the scoreboard. "It makes it sound like I lost a couple limbs in an industrial accident. I'm *separated.*"

"So, tell me, what's it like to be . . . *separated?*" Lionel asked.

"I don't know," Tim admitted. "I feel like I'm in limbo. It's not the heaven of a happy marriage, but it's not quite the living hell of divorce."

Lionel chuckled. "So when the IRS asks you for your marital status, you'll just say—"

"Purgatory," Tim replied.

* * * * * * * * * * * * * *

"We need to spend some time apart."

Depending on the state of your marriage, those words, spoken by your spouse, may send chills down your spine or they may start you dancing in the aisles. Separation—physically removing yourself from your spouse's daily life—is a radical step, but one that's been successful in saving countless marriages.

Whether separation can work for your marriage will depend on how you approach it. You need to understand what it is and what it isn't—as well as what it means and what it doesn't.

Think of this chapter as your handbook to separation. (Like most chapters in this reference book, you may not need to read it. But if you do [or aren't sure] . . . read on.) We may not address every question you have about separating from and reconciling with your spouse, but we will try to cover the major areas in order to help you understand what separation can mean for your marriage.

To Separate or Not to Separate—That Is the Question

Most couples separate out of frustration. They're tired of living together and need some time apart. That's certainly an understandable feeling. It's not a healthy reason for separating, but it's an understandable feeling.

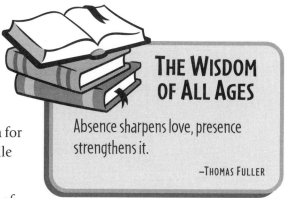

THE WISDOM OF ALL AGES

Absence sharpens love, presence strengthens it.

–THOMAS FULLER

If you are committed to your relationship, but believe that you need to separate, for whatever reasons, it's important that you have an agenda for what you want to discover and accomplish while you're apart.

Separation is like standing at a fork in the road of your life. You need to choose which path you will follow in the weeks or months that you're apart. If you choose the path of reconciliation, you must follow it to its end. If you choose the path of divorce, you must consider where that path will eventually lead and who will be lost along the way. (You'll find more information on the topic of divorce in chapter 11 of *Hope for the Separated,* by the author.)

Regardless of which path you choose, you need to understand that your spouse is not your enemy in this process. Your enemies are the forces that are threatening to destroy your marriage. Indifference, anger, and distrust are enemies. Your spouse is your fellow warrior.

Making Separation Work for You

If you and your spouse choose to separate for the sake of your marriage, you need to be aware of certain things to make sure that your separation doesn't cause devastation in your relationship.

The first thing you need to be aware of is that separation often brings a misleading sense of emotional peace. When embattled husbands and wives finally get some time alone, one of the first things they notice is the serenity of solitude. They get a taste of the peace that comes from being alone. If they're not thinking clearly, they may assume that the peace they feel is an indication that they're meant to be away from each other for good. And, suddenly, divorce becomes a more appealing option to them.

What you need to understand is that the peace people experience in separation is the result of removing themselves from the battlefield of their marriages. Let's put it this way: If your relationship with your spouse has been marked by frequent battles, arguments, and outbursts, of course some peace and quiet are going to seem appealing to you. But that's not a sign that you need to leave your spouse. It's simply a taste of what you can work toward in your marriage.

That's where separation may prove to be useful. Away from the conflicts and pressures of everyday life with your spouse, you can think clearly about what's missing in your relationship and what can be changed.

The second thing you need to be aware of is that there are no simple cures for a marriage that has deteriorated to the point that spouses feel like they need to be away from each other. The solutions offered in this book will require a great deal of sacrifice and work on your part. If you and your spouse are willing to make those sacrifices and do that work, you can save your marriage. In fact, you may be able to make your marriage better and stronger than it's ever been.

The question you need to ask is, *"Will* I work on reconciling with my spouse?" You'll note that we didn't ask, "Do I *want* to work on reconciling with my spouse?" The answer to that question may very well be, "No."

Think about it. If you've been beating your head against a wall for years trying to improve your marriage, only to have your spouse disregard or ignore your efforts, you're probably pretty close to being burned out. The last thing you may want to do is continue trying to reconcile.

When you remove the question from the realm of personal preference, the issue comes into clearer focus. By asking, *"Will* you work on reconciling with your spouse?" we're asking you to determine how important your relationship is to you. If your marriage is high on your priority list, you're going to work on it, regardless of whether you *want* to or not.

So let's put the question to you again: *Will* you work on reconciling with your spouse? Will you spend your time, energy, and effort finding out what can be done to save and improve your marriage? Will you take the constructive actions necessary to build a closer and stronger relationship?

If the answer is yes, keep reading. If the answer is no, skip ahead to chapter 17— specifically, to the section on divorce.

Keeping Your Eyes on the Goal

There are no hard and fast rules regarding the dos and don'ts of separation. There are some things you'll want to keep in mind if your ultimate goal is restoring your relationship.

We've come up with six guidelines. They are . . .

1. Guard your attitudes and actions.

2. Avoid or abandon any romantic relationship with another person.

3. Realize divorce will not lead to personal happiness.

4. Understand that marital difficulty is caused by the marriage partners, not by someone outside the marriage.

5. Do not date during the separation period.

6. Move slowly in completing any legal separation papers.

Let's take a look at the difference each of these principles can make in your relationship with your spouse.

1. Guard your attitudes and actions.

You can't prevent yourself from feeling things like jealousy, resentment, and betrayal. You can choose the actions and attitudes you exhibit to your spouse. If you allow your negative emotions to dictate the way you communicate, chances are you will not send the kind of signals that will make the idea of getting back together an appealing prospect.

That's not to say you shouldn't make your spouse aware of how you're feeling. You just need to choose the right place and the right way to do it. You've got to admit, there's a big difference between saying something like, "I feel hurt and a little angry when I hear that you've been telling our friends I'm the reason we're separated," and saying, "If you think I'm going to put up with the lies you've

> **THE WISDOM OF ALL AGES**
>
> Ever has it been that love knows not its own depth until the hour of separation.
>
> –KAHLIL GIBRAN

been spreading behind my back, you must not know me very well. But, of course, that's been obvious since the day we got married."

Those two statements illustrate the difference between admitting your emotions and being controlled by them. Being honest about your emotions—without thrusting them in your spouse's face—may inspire openness as well. It wouldn't be stretching the point to say that an open line of emotionally honest communication is an important step toward reconciliation.

GLAD YOU ASKED

What's the best way to break off an affair?

First you need to make the other person aware of your concern. After you've done that, confess your wrong in violating your marriage commitment. Firmly explain your decision to work on reconciliation with your spouse. You may choose to make your feelings for the other person known again, but you must emphasize your decision to do what's *right* rather than what feels good to you.

2. Avoid or abandon any romantic relationship with another person.

Many marital separations are the result of an affair by one (or both) of the spouses. The reasons for the affairs may differ from couple to couple ("She makes me feel young again" or "I can talk to him about things that I can never talk about with my husband"). But the result is almost always the same: unhappiness. The pressures and tension that result from breaking up a marriage for the sake of an affair practically doom the affair from the start.

Obviously an affair, regardless of its nature, causes tremendous damage to a marriage. If you have any interest in salvaging your marriage, you must abandon any romantic entanglements with anyone other than your spouse. Your best interests are served by returning to your spouse, resolving your conflicts, learning to love, and rediscovering the joy in your relationship.

3. Realize divorce will not lead to personal happiness.

In the wake of an affair—or any circumstances in your marriage serious enough to cause you to separate from your spouse—you may give serious consideration to divorce. Many spouses approach separation with an eye toward divorce. They reason that the short-term pain caused initially by the divorce will eventually be followed by long-term happiness.

Research indicates that that's not the case at all. Studies have shown that divorce does not lead to greater happiness or more fulfillment for the couple or their children. In fact, the damaging effects of divorce tend to plague the couple and their children for life.

Those statistics could also be used to argue the previous point regarding extramarital affairs. If you are engaged in such an affair, your wisest course of action—from a moral and scientific standpoint—is to end it immediately, while showing dignity, respect, and kindness to the other person involved. Breaking off the relationship makes divorce a less likely possibility and reconciliation a more likely one.

4. Understand that marital difficulty is caused by the marriage partners, not by someone outside the marriage.

For the "odd" spouse out in an extramarital affair, deciding how to respond to the infidelity may prove to be more difficult than can be imagined. The one response you (either as the faithful or unfaithful spouse) want to avoid is blaming the "other person" for the problems in your marriage.

The brutal truth is that your marital difficulties were caused by both of you, and by no one else. Unresolved conflict, unmet needs, and stubborn selfishness are just a few of the problems that can eat away at a marriage and make conditions right for an extramarital fling.

The second part of that equation is that since you both created the difficulties in your marriage, both must work toward repairing them. Unfortunately for you, waiting for your spouse to come crawling back to you is not an effective reconciliation strategy.

> **THE WISDOM OF ALL AGES**
>
> Sometimes, when one person is missing, the whole world seems depopulated.
>
> —ALPHONSE LAMARTINE

Assuming that your separation was caused in part by your spouse's infidelity, the question you need to consider is how you will respond to the affair. Your options are plentiful. You could . . .

➤ confront your spouse with heated accusations

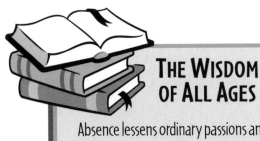

THE WISDOM OF ALL AGES

Absence lessens ordinary passions and augments great ones, as the wind blows out a candle and makes a fire blaze.

–FRANÇOIS DE LA ROCHEFOUCAULD

➤ try to persuade the other person to bow out of the picture gracefully

➤ use your kids to make your spouse feel guilty

➤ hire a private detective to obtain incriminating evidence

➤ embark on an affair of your own.

Chances are, none of them would be effective in bringing about reconciliation. That's why we recommend a more straightforward, but potentially difficult, alternative.

This alternative can be broken down into three steps. Let's take a look at each one.

1. *Explain to your spouse how deeply hurt you are.* Without letting your emotions overwhelm you or resorting to guilt-trip strategies, help your spouse understand the effect the affair has had on you and your emotional well-being.

2. *Acknowledge your past failures in your relationship.* Don't let yourself get drawn into a pass-the-blame exchange. However, you should identify the areas in which you've failed your spouse and apologize. You may not get the response you're looking for—at least, not at first—but that's not the point. The point is that you've taken the initiative in working to correct the past mistakes in your relationship.

3. *Ask for reconciliation.* Express to your spouse your hope and confidence that the two of you can reconcile your differences and put the pieces of your relationship back together. You'll need to be realistic in sharing this hope. You don't want to take a let's-just-pretend-that-none-of-this-ever-happened-and-go-back-to-the-way-things-used-to-be approach to reconciliation. You need to acknowledge the fact that restoring your relationship won't be easy. At the same time, you need to maintain the belief that the end result will be well worth the effort.

Obviously, if your spouse is still engaged in an affair, your request for reconciliation may cause an awkward situation. So be it. That's not to say you should intentionally try to put your spouse on the spot. In fact, you shouldn't look for any response at all. The hope you hold out for your relationship may inspire a similar hope in your spouse. Be sensitive to the timing of things. Remember, you can't force reconciliation; you can only make the prospects look bright.

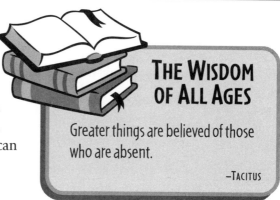

THE WISDOM OF ALL AGES

Greater things are believed of those who are absent.

—TACITUS

5. Do not date during the separation period.

A period of separation from your spouse can be an extremely lonely time. And, since you may consider yourself "technically" unmarried during your separation, you may be tempted to find solace and companionship with a charming and attractive member of the opposite sex.

Before you make that leap back into the dating pool, you need to think about the consequences it will have on your marriage. Here's what happens: The more you date, the more difficult reconciliation with your spouse will become.

Getting dating relationships off the ground requires a lot of time and effort, not to mention a hefty investment of emotional energy. And the more time, effort, and energy you devote to others, the less you will have to devote to your marital relationship.

During your period of separation, what you need more than a dating partner is a friend, a trusted individual (or two or three) in whom you can confide. The ideal friend is someone who can help you keep your eyes on what's really important in life—namely, your marriage and your family—and then help take your mind off your problems for a while by getting you out of the house and to a ball game, a movie, a restaurant, or someplace else.

The kind of friend you need in your life will not only listen to your worries and concerns, but will also help you shoulder the load. And that's not the kind of person you find in most dating circles.

6. Move slowly in completing any legal separation papers.

Separation papers are simply legal agreements drawn up by spouses to ensure that certain elements of their relationship—most often their children and their finances—are taken care of while they're apart.

Some couples prefer to have separation papers because of the legal security they provide. Other couples prefer to avoid them because they seem too much like divorce papers. Your decision will depend on your situation.

Before you decide, take into consideration the nature of your separation. Is it likely or even possible that you will reconcile within a few weeks? If the answer is yes, you may want to hold off on the separation papers. Why spend money for an attorney?

If you and your spouse can come to a mutually satisfying agreement on your own about who is responsible for what and how you will interact with your children, you're better off going that route. If you can't agree on an arrangement that works for both of you, or if you don't see much progress in your reconciliation after a couple weeks of being apart, you may need to have separation papers drawn up. This is especially important if your financial situation gets tight or if your children are being neglected as a result of the separation.

Keep in mind that separation papers need not be forerunners of divorce proceedings. Many couples make a celebration of burning their separation papers when they reconcile.

Personality Plus . . . and Minus

Here's a tip that may surprise you. One of the most beneficial things you can do during your separation is to examine your own assets and liabilities, and, based on your examination, to take positive steps toward personal growth.

Glad You Asked

There's a guy at my office who seems really concerned about me. He says he'd like to take me out to get my mind off my marriage problems. Should I take him up on the offer?

No. Whether you realize it or not, you're in an extremely vulnerable place, emotionally speaking. Unfortunately, there are many people of the opposite sex who prey on that kind of vulnerability. Their objective is to use you to satisfy their own desires–all the while pretending to be concerned about you and your needs. Don't put yourself in a position to be used like that. The guy at work may be sincere, but more likely he's not.

If developing your own personality during your separation from your spouse seems like an odd concept to you, let us suggest that the notion of married people living apart for the sake of their union seems a little odd, as well. But that doesn't mean there isn't merit in it.

Obviously you'll need to do a fairly comprehensive study of your personality if you hope to understand anything about yourself. Your personality plays a major role not only in the way you live, but also in the way you interact with and respond to other people—most notably, your spouse.

Unfortunately many people believe that their personality is part of their DNA code, that it's wired into the very core of their being at birth and can't be changed. As a result, some of them may feel trapped by the less-than-appealing aspects of their personality —they believe there's nothing they can do to change their behavior patterns.

They're wrong.

It's true that certain people have certain tendencies to act in certain ways, but it's also true that those tendencies are quite changeable. Don't allow yourself to be enslaved by your personality. Take a long, hard look at who you are and what you're like. Identify your strengths and learn to use them for your benefit and the benefit of others. Then identify your weaknesses and focus on ways in which you can grow and improve in those areas.

> **FAMILY TIES**
>
> To avoid any inadvertent self-delusion on your part, you might want to put these same questions to your kids ("Would you say that I'm more critical or complimentary?"). Few people know you better than your kids. And few people will be more eager to tell you the truth about yourself than they will. Listen to what they have to say about your personality. You may learn a thing or two about yourself.

If you're stumped about where to begin in this self-understanding process, try answering the following questions:

➤ Would you describe your outlook on life as positive, negative, or indifferent?

➤ Are you more critical or complimentary of others?

THE WISDOM OF ALL AGES

When one is a stranger to oneself then one is estranged from others too.

—ANNE MORROW LINDBERGH

➤ Are you more critical or complimentary of yourself?

➤ Are you more extroverted or introverted?

➤ Are you talkative or quiet?

➤ Are you patient or impatient?

➤ Do you tend to keep your feelings to yourself or make them known?

➤ Do you think your attitude or behavior patterns contributed to the breakdown of your marriage? If so, how?

That last question is the key. Remember, your goal is not to become self-aware for the sake of knowing yourself. Your goal is to apply your self-awareness to your relationship with your spouse. You want to identify the strengths you can bring to your marriage and minimize the negative effects your weaknesses have on it.

You should also use your period of separation to improve some of your weaknesses. If you know (or learn) that you have a tendency to keep your feelings to yourself, you may want to use your time of separation to become comfortable with sharing your thoughts and emotions. Find a counselor or a trusted friend to help you. When you become comfortable communicating with that person, you will be comfortable communicating with your spouse. And that may prove to be important in your reconciliation.

Making the First Move

If you've reached a stalemate, with both of you ensconced in your respective headquarters, unwilling to venture into "enemy territory," you're as good as divorced. Putting distance between you and your spouse is understandable and even constructive under certain conditions. Putting walls between you, on the other hand, will do nothing but keep you apart.

Since reconciliation is the name of the game in this chapter, let's take a look at what you can do to tear down the walls that are keeping the two of you from connecting. The good news is that it only takes one person to break the silence and start dismantling the walls. The bad news is that, because you're reading this book, you're the most likely candidate.

Let the objections begin: *Me? Why should I be the one who makes the first move? This separation is all my spouse's fault. If he or she had been more committed to our marital relationship, we wouldn't be in the situation we're in! If anyone should make the first move, it's my spouse!*

If that criticism roughly summarizes your own feelings, you probably have a very good reason for expecting your spouse to come to you for reconciliation, rather than the other way around. However, we have an even better reason for ignoring your expectations and doing what needs to be done: Your marriage may not survive otherwise.

While we're on the subject, let's address one other point in this argument. There's no such thing as a blameless spouse. If you are having problems with your relationship, it's because both of you have failed.

Identifying your spouse's failures will likely be pretty easy for you. This is especially true if your spouse's failures are egregious, such as those that involve infidelity or financial chicanery. On the other hand, identifying your own failures may be a little more difficult. Your faults may not be readily apparent to you because you've lived with them for so long.

To help you in your search, let us suggest that marital failure usually occurs in two areas:

> ➤ failing to meet the needs of your partner

> ➤ doing and saying things that are meant to hurt them.

Spouses fail to do what they *should* do for each other and end up doing what they *shouldn't* do to each other.

If you think long and hard about your own relationship, especially your conflicts with your spouse, you'll likely be able to pinpoint several areas in which you failed. And when you do, you can join the rest of us imperfect spouses here in the real world.

"My Fault"

It's not enough to simply recognize your faults and failures; you need to confess them to your spouse. Many couples have found that the act of confessing their marital "sins" acts as a catalyst for reconciliation. In other words, confession gets the ball rolling toward a renewed relationship.

Make a list of the faults, failures, and weaknesses you identify in yourself. Be as specific as possible in sharing them. Instead of saying something like, "I'm not very patient," it would be much more effective to say, "I never give you a chance to explain your point of view when we argue."

After you've laid your negative characteristics bare, you can ask for forgiveness for them. This doesn't have to be a dramatic scene. You don't need to throw yourself sobbing at your spouse's feet and beg for forgiveness. A simple, heartfelt, "I'm sorry for the hurt I've caused you and our relationship; will you forgive me?" will suffice.

Despite the confessions of the couples mentioned three paragraphs earlier, we need to emphasize that admitting your wrongs and asking for forgiveness will not guarantee a reconciliation. It will give you a clear conscience. Your spouse may or may not choose to forgive you. There may be no interest in reconciliation at the moment. Those issues are out of your hand, though. After you ask for forgiveness, you will have done everything you can do to correct the past.

FAMILY TIES

If your pride or stubbornness is preventing you from taking the initiative in seeking reconciliation with your spouse, give your kids a say in the matter. Ask them if they think the possibility of a restored family unit is worth swallowing your pride over. Ask them if they think having their mother and father together again is worth your doing something that you don't believe is your responsibility. Chances are, your kids will be more than willing to help you set your priorities straight.

You also can't force your spouse to follow your lead and confess to you. Your example may inspire your spouse to do the same—or it may not. Unfortunately, you can't reconcile until there is confession of past wrongs.

Until that happens, all you can do is wait, pray, and continue to show love to your spouse—even if it means doing those things from a distance.

And Then Comes Love

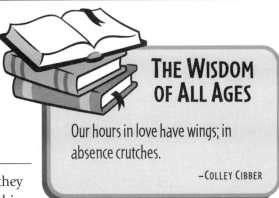

THE WISDOM OF ALL AGES

Our hours in love have wings; in absence crutches.

–Colley Cibber

If you were to ask most estranged spouses why they separated, you'd probably hear a response like this: "After all that's happened, I just don't love my husband (or wife) anymore. I wish I could say that I do, but I don't." The assumption behind a response like that is that love is something that's *felt*. The reasoning follows that when you no longer have loving feelings, there's nothing you can do about it.

As we've pointed out elsewhere in this book, that's faulty reasoning. Love is not something we *feel*; it's something we *choose*. To love your spouse is to decide that his or her interests are your highest priority—higher than even your own. Once you've made that decision, then you will take the appropriate actions to demonstrate your love.

If you're separated, chances are you're harboring feelings of disappointment, hurt, rejection, loneliness, anger, frustration, or hostility. You need to understand that none of those feelings can—or should—prevent you from demonstrating love to your spouse.

From a practical standpoint, you may be wondering how you can demonstrate love when you're separated from each other. We're here to tell you that long-distance love is possible. All that's required is a commitment on your part.

Here are a couple of ideas for demonstrating love for your spouse during your separation. If any of them work for you, great. If not, take it upon yourself to come up with some ideas that do.

If you're serious about showing love to your spouse, you can . . .

> ➤ demonstrate patience by not setting a time limit on your reconciliation
> Let your spouse know that you're willing to wait as long as it takes to
> restore your relationship.

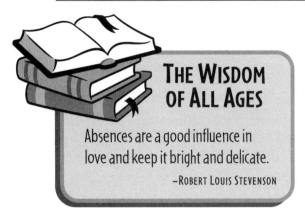

THE WISDOM OF ALL AGES

Absences are a good influence in love and keep it bright and delicate.

–ROBERT LOUIS STEVENSON

➤ demonstrate kindness by doing necessary chores in an effort to make life easier. If doing physical tasks isn't feasible or advisable, you might consider showing kindness by calling or sending an E-mail message just to express your concern and interest.

➤ demonstrate interest in your spouse by arranging a series of dates for the two of you—assuming that your spouse is comfortable with the idea.

Do things that the two of you can enjoy. While you're together, be courteous and respectful. Do the "little things" you know are appreciated.

As we pointed out earlier, reconciliation with your spouse will require a great deal of sacrifice and effort from you. That's why it's important to remind yourself that the end result—a renewed, loving marital relationship—is worth every bit of the work and trouble it causes.

In this chapter, we've looked at the logistics of marital separation and strategies for working toward reconciliation with your spouse. Eventually, you and your spouse will have to answer the Big Question: *Are we going to get back together or divorce?* We will explore both options in chapter 17.

Family Practice

Think you're an expert on sustaining a relationship during a separation? Here's a quiz to see how much you know.

1. Which of the following is *not* true of a marital separation?
   a. It works equally well for healthy and unhealthy relationships.
   b. It often brings a misleading sense of emotional peace.
   c. It does not always succeed in bringing reconciliation to spouses.
   d. It can help you see the problems in your relationship with clearer focus.

2. Which of the following guidelines would be least helpful in making sure that your separation accomplishes what you want it to accomplish?

a. Do not date during the separation period.

b. Get as far away from your spouse as possible.

c. Move slowly in completing any legal separation papers.

d. Guard your attitudes and actions.

3. Which of the following is *not* a productive response to your spouse's infidelity?

a. Asking for reconciliation.

b. Acknowledging your past failures in your relationship.

c. Giving your spouse a taste of his or her own medicine by embarking on an extramarital affair of your own.

d. Explaining to your spouse how deeply hurt you are.

4. Which of the following questions would be least helpful to you in your quest for self-development?

a. "Am I a patient person or an impatient person?"

b. "Am I more likely to compliment or criticize someone?"

c. "Am I more likely to stay silent when my feelings are hurt or let someone know about it?"

d. "Am I more of a dog person or a cat person?"

5. Which of the following is a true statement?

a. Love doesn't have to be felt in order to be shown.

b. Until you feel love deep in your heart, there's no reason for you and your spouse to attempt reconciliation.

c. If you and your spouse have allowed your relationship to degenerate to the point that you need to separate, it's likely that you never really loved each other in the first place.

d. Love means never having to say you're sorry.

Answers: (1) a, (2) b, (3) c, (4) d, (5) a

CHAPTER 17

Is That Your Final Answer?

DECIDING THE FATE OF YOUR MARITAL RELATIONSHIP

SNAPSHOT

Rex gave Elaine a nervous smile as he handed her a menu. "So this is it, huh?" he asked. "Crunch time. The big night. The day of reckoning."

"The night of a thousand clichés," Elaine added.

"Does your mother still call you every day to see if I've moved back?" Rex asked.

"What do you think?" Elaine replied as she scanned the appetizers.

"I guess we have taken this separation business to its logical extreme," Rex said. "What's it been, two and a half months?"

"No, it hasn't been that long," Elaine said. "I'd say it's probably been closer to seventy-three days, thirteen hours, and eleven minutes."

Rex looked up from his menu.

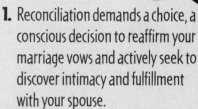

SNEAK PREVIEW

1. Reconciliation demands a choice, a conscious decision to reaffirm your marriage vows and actively seek to discover intimacy and fulfillment with your spouse.

2. The decision to return to your spouse is a step of faith because you may not be able to envision your emotional love returning, your differences being resolved, or your intimacy being restored.

3. Reconciliation is not always possible because it requires the response of two people, and neither can force the other to return.

"Not that anyone's counting," she added.

"So what do you want to do?" Rex asked.

Elaine laughed.

"What's so funny?"

"I was going to ask you the same question," she explained. "Then it occurred to me that we haven't come very far from when we first started dating. If you remember, most of our earliest conversations consisted primarily of two sentences: 'What do you want to do?' and 'I don't know, what do you want to do?' We spent most of our time together trying to figure out what we were going to do."

Rex laughed. "I was always afraid that if I made the wrong decision, I'd ruin everything, and you'd never want to see me again."

Rex paused for a moment as he thought about the implications of his last sentence. Elaine looked at her watch. "So our first awkward moment comes about four and a half minutes into the meal," she announced.

"Just like the early days," Rex said, lifting his water glass in a toast.

"The kids have weighed in with their decisions, in case you hadn't guessed," Elaine said.

"And what was the vote?" Rex asked.

"It turned out to be unanimous," Elaine explained. "But only after some serious debate."

"Who was the dissenting voice?" Rex asked.

"Jeremy," Elaine said. "He's been sitting in your place at the dinner table so that he can see the TV while we eat, and he's a little reluctant to give that up."

"The sacrifices one must make for one's family," Rex said with a laugh and a shake of his head.

"Rachel and Greg talked to him for about an hour about how important it is for all of us to be together, and how the three kids need to do everything they can to make life easier for the two of us."

"That was nice of them," Rex said.

"And when that didn't work, they held him down and rubbed his face on the carpet until he finally agreed with them," she continued.

Rex smiled and then gave Elaine a long look. "So what do *you* want to do?" he asked.

"I don't know," she replied. "What do *you* want to do?"

＊ ＊ ＊ ＊ ＊ ＊ ＊ ＊ ＊ ＊ ＊ ＊ ＊ ＊ ＊

In chapter 16, we explored the ins and outs of marital separation. In this chapter, we bring the matter to its logical conclusion. At some point, after weeks or even months of separation, you will have to make a decision about the future of your marriage. Will you give your relationship another chance or will you end it permanently through divorce?

Obviously it's not a question to be taken lightly. The decision you reach will deeply affect your lives—and especially the lives of your children. In order to help you make this tough decision, let's take a look at the factors and consequences involved in each option.

Option #1: Reconciliation

If you decide that reconciling is the right thing to do—regardless of what's happened between the two of you in the past or how you may be *feeling* about each other at present—you deserve a great deal of credit. Divorce is an extremely appealing option for people who are fed up with their marriages. It takes a lot of courage, commitment, and dedication to resist the urge to "wipe the slate clean" and start life over without the baggage of a problem spouse.

Let's not kid ourselves. You'll probably find that it's much harder to stay together than it is to remain separated—at least for awhile. If you have lost your loving feelings for each other, your difficulties will likely be compounded.

It's one thing to reconnect with someone you're still crazy about deep down inside. It's quite another thing to try to rebuild a relationship with someone who doesn't stir much passion in your soul anymore.

Reconciliation demands a choice. If you wait until you're *inspired* to reconnect with your spouse or until you feel *motivated* to work on your relationship, you'll probably be eating alone for quite some time. You must *choose* to reaffirm your marriage vows and actively seek to discover intimacy and fulfillment again in your relationship.

Making the decision to reconcile with your spouse is an act of faith. You have no guarantee that your emotional love will ever return. You have no guarantee that you will be able to resolve your differences with each other. You have no guarantee that you will ever be able to restore intimacy to your relationship.

> ### THE WISDOM OF ALL AGES
>
> Life is not a static thing. The only people who do not change their minds are incompetents in asylums, who can't, and those in cemeteries.
>
> –EVERETT M. DIRKSEN

The bad news is that taking those first couple of steps in faith can be a scary proposition. The good news is that real commitment to reconciliation is usually rewarded.

Keep in mind that you're not choosing to go back to the kind of relationship you had when you separated. Reconciliation isn't a matter of making the best of a bad situation. Reconciliation isn't a matter of giving up your happiness and suffering for the rest of your life. When you choose to reconcile with your spouse, you're committing yourself to working toward creating something meaningful and fulfilling in your relationship.

When Your Mind Is Made Up to Reconcile

All right, you've made the decision to reconcile. Now what? How do you go about restoring your relationship? Where do you start?

If you're uncertain about what to do next, there are three steps you should consider: (1) pray; (2) tell your spouse; and (3) give your spouse time to reach a decision. Let's take a look at each one.

1. Pray.
If you believe in the power of prayer and God (I do), you'll want to make sure that

your every move is grounded in prayer. If you're a Christian, the closer you hold your faith and your spiritual values, the better equipped you'll be to make the difficult choices required in a reconciliation.

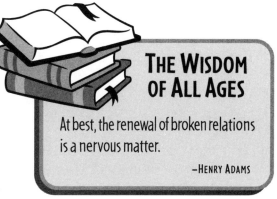

THE WISDOM OF ALL AGES

At best, the renewal of broken relations is a nervous matter.

–HENRY ADAMS

Spend some quality time in prayer unburdening yourself of your doubts, concerns, and fears regarding your relationship. Confess the areas in which you've failed and ask for God's forgiveness. Share your positive and negative feelings about reconciliation. Thank the Lord for giving you a second chance to make your marriage work.

Ask God to change you into the person He wants you to be. Ask for strength and endurance to accomplish the things that need to be done before you can reconcile. Ask for patience, wisdom, and empathy as you communicate with your spouse and attempt to restore your damaged relationship. Ask for God's guidance as you make your way toward reconciliation.

2. Tell your spouse.
Most relationship experts would probably agree that it's good etiquette to let your spouse know if you intend to reconcile. The question is how do you break that kind of news?

The exact method you use will depend a lot on the unique circumstances of your separation. If possible, your first discussion about reconciliation should be conducted in person, rather than over the phone or across computer lines.

Your best bet would probably be to invite your spouse to dinner. When the time is right, either during the meal or after it, express that you've been doing a lot of thinking and praying about your marriage. Talk about some of the things you've come to realize about yourself, specifically areas in which you've allowed your emotions and attitudes to dictate your behavior. Let it be known that you've determined not to be a slave to your emotions and have committed to making changes in your attitude. Admit that you've failed in many ways and ask forgiveness for those failures.

Disclose that you've been reading material that has helped you come to the conclusion that you want to work toward restoring your marriage. Make it clear that you know you can't do that alone. Share your desire to work hand in hand to create something truly special and meaningful in your relationship.

3. *Give your spouse time to reach a decision.*

Make it clear that you don't expect a response right away. If your announcement comes as a surprise, or if reconciliation is the last thing on his or her mind, responding might take some time.

Your best bet is to ask your spouse to think and pray about the situation. Give a copy of the book *Hope for the Separated* by the author of this book. Be open to talk about any questions or concerns regarding reconciliation.

And then back off. Give your spouse all the time and space needed to think, read, and pray about your relationship. Ask your spouse to call you and arrange to get together again to discuss the next step.

We'll pause here for a quick reality check.

Regardless of how receptive your spouse is to the idea of reconciliation, your relationship problems will not vanish over the course of one evening together. Introducing the idea of working to restore your relationship is only the first step on the long road to reconciliation.

GLAD YOU ASKED

What if my spouse doesn't want to meet with me in person?

Keep trying. It's extremely important that you have a face-to-face conversation with your spouse about reconciliation. If he or she seems reluctant to get together or demands to know why you want to meet, keep emphasizing that you would prefer to talk about it in person. Whatever you do, don't demand that your spouse meet with you—and don't use ambush tactics, either. Just make your desire known and give your spouse a chance to respond to it. If you maintain a positive spirit while continuing to make your wishes known, sooner or later your spouse will agree to a face-to-face meeting.

The Road to Reconciliation

Let's assume that your spouse likes your idea of reconciliation. Let's say there is agreement to the thought of restoring your relationship. Let's say your mate expresses a willingness to work with you in changing the things that need to be changed in your relationship and strengthening the things that need to be strengthened. Let's say your spouse is excited about getting back together with you.

End of the story, right? You move back in together, hold a tearful reunion with your kids, take a family trip to Disney World, and then live happily ever after.

> **THE WISDOM OF ALL AGES**
>
> You cannot step twice into the same river, for other waters are continually flowing in.
>
> —HERACLEITUS

If Hollywood ever decides to make a movie about your relationship, that may be the way things work out. Until then, you'll need to accept the fact that reconciliation won't happen quickly—or easily.

The one thing you want to avoid is rushing back into the union. Your objective is not to "get back together." Your objective is to create a new relationship. And in order to do that, you have to examine and resolve the conflicts, misunderstandings, frustrations, and unmet needs that sent Relationship One hurtling to the ground in flames.

Let a Professional Handle This

The most important thing you can do for your postseparation relationship is to involve a trained counselor in the reconciliation process. If you don't know any counselors in your area, ask your pastor (or a local minister) to make a recommendation for you. If the pastor has training in marriage counseling, he may be able to help you himself.

You'll likely find that meeting with a pastor or counselor to develop your communication skills brings a sense of freedom to your relationship. You will learn to reach agreements on issues that previously might have been left unresolved. You will also learn to give each other leeway to disagree on certain issues while maintaining a spirit of kindness and love toward each other.

Let your counselor set the timetable for your moving back together. Some counselors may decide after three or four sessions that you're ready to cohabitate. Other counselors may want you to wait until you've completed twelve or more sessions. It's important that you follow your counselor's instructions on this matter. Don't jump the gun. Remember, slow and steady wins the race.

That's not to say that cohabitation is the "finish line" of your reconciliation. Your responsibilities for creating a new relationship won't end when you move back in together. With physical closeness comes added pressures on your relationship. Your counselor will be able to help you maintain open, loving channels of communication during this critical time.

For the sake of your relationship, it's important that you incorporate the strategies for resolving conflict and communicating openly and honestly into your everyday life. Make a habit of reading relationship-building books and articles together and discussing additional strategies and principles that you can add to your marriage.

True reconciliation is achieved only by making the continued health and growth of your relationship your primary priority.

GLAD YOU ASKED

How long should my spouse and I continue to see a counselor after our reconciliation?

Ideally the decision to end your counseling sessions will be a joint agreement reached by you, your spouse, and your counselor. It would be a tremendous mistake to end your counseling prematurely. Continue until you feel you have adequately dealt with unresolved conflict and developed skills in handling disagreements.

Option #2: Divorce

If you decide that divorcing your spouse is the right thing to do, think again. Consider the emotional toll that divorce takes on both parties. Consider the financial hardship that inevitably follows divorce. Consider the legal wrangling that's required for terminating a marriage. Consider whether separating permanently from your spouse is the best thing for you and your children.

Look beyond the appeal and convenience of leaving your marital problems behind once and for all and consider the big, bleak picture of divorce.

If you've done all that and you're still convinced that divorce is your only real option, keep reading.

If you're committed to reconciliation, but are dealing with a spouse who has ruled out the possibility, you're going to have to face the specter of divorce, whether you like it or not. For better or worse, reconciliation requires the participation of two people. You can't force your spouse to get back together with you.

There are some things you will need to consider in order to prevent your divorce from being any more devastating than it has to be.

No Contest

If your spouse has ignored your personal pleas for reconciliation, you may be tempted to try to block the divorce through legal channels. There was a time when a spouse who contested a divorce stood a decent chance of preventing it—or at least making it much more difficult to obtain. Today, divorce laws have become more and more liberal, making it easier to terminate the marriage—regardless of how the other person feels about it. It's safe to say that the only thing you'll accomplish in contesting your divorce is padding your lawyer's wallet.

Even if you could prevent your divorce in court, that wouldn't change the fact that your spouse has no interest in reconciling with you. Unfortunately, the nature of marriage dictates that if one spouse desires to reunite and the other desires to disunite, the dissenter will always have the upper hand. Trying to prevent that disunion legally will only prolong your misery.

The Law and You

Divorce severs not only an emotional and physical relationship, but also a legal contract. And where there are legal contracts, there are lawyers.

You've got three choices when it comes to your legal representation for divorce proceedings. You can . . .

➤ forgo a lawyer completely

➤ use your spouse's lawyer

➤ retain the services of your own lawyer.

Let's take a look at the pros and cons of each option.

First, consider forgoing a lawyer. So-called "no fault" divorce laws have been created to streamline the legal process involved in terminating marriages. In order to qualify for a no-fault divorce, a couple must meet some fairly strict standards. Even then, the process is more complicated than one might imagine.

As a general rule, it's a good idea to retain the services of an attorney for divorce proceedings.

Second, consider having one lawyer. If you and your spouse can agree on an equitable settlement—if you're willing to work together to make the best of a bad situation—you may be able to use one attorney to represent you both. Doing so will eliminate most of the fractious elements that usually accompany divorces.

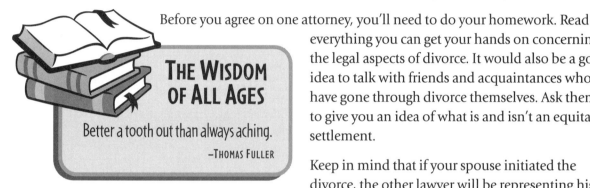

THE WISDOM OF ALL AGES

Better a tooth out than always aching.

–Thomas Fuller

Before you agree on one attorney, you'll need to do your homework. Read everything you can get your hands on concerning the legal aspects of divorce. It would also be a good idea to talk with friends and acquaintances who have gone through divorce themselves. Ask them to give you an idea of what is and isn't an equitable settlement.

Keep in mind that if your spouse initiated the divorce, the other lawyer will be representing his or her interests. If you have had problems agreeing on finances, property, or child custody, you will definitely need a lawyer to represent your own interests.

Third, consider having two lawyers. Your best bet for securing the kind of settlement you need in order to take care of yourself and your children is to retain the services of your own lawyer. Your goal is not to take your spouse for everything he or she is worth—no matter how much you might want to or how much your lawyer insists that you should—but to do what's right and fair for everyone involved.

Kids First

Your first instinct may be to shield your kids from the unpleasant realities of divorce by lying or keeping important information from them. That's a mistake you want to avoid at all costs. Eventually your kids will learn the truth, and if they discover that you were dishonest with them, their confidence in and respect for you will be diminished.

Though it may be the hardest thing you ever have to do, you owe it to your kids to sit them down and give them a complete explanation of what's going on in your marriage. Ideally, this is something you and your spouse will do together.

After explaining what the divorce will mean for your family, you'll need to assure them of two things: (1) The divorce does not change your love for them at all; and (2) they are in no way responsible for your breakup.

It is extremely important that your kids feel your love at this critical point in their lives. Keep in mind that your kids' sense of security is tied directly to the love they receive. If, in the midst of your divorce proceedings, you neglect to demonstrate your love for your kids, the result may be a lifetime of emotional insecurity for them.

As we've emphasized throughout this book, demonstrating your love for your kids involves more than saying, "I love you." It involves finding out exactly what makes your kids feel loved and giving it to them. That's right, it involves speaking to them in their primary love language.

In addition to love, your kids will need rules and consistent discipline in the wake of divorce. The boundaries you establish will go a long way toward helping them feel secure. With so many things changing, they need the constancy that rules provide. If you relax your rules, even with the best of intentions, you may be sending the wrong message to your kids.

Ideally, you and your spouse will work together to create a uniform set of rules regarding things like . . .

> ➤ bedtime

> ➤ study habits

FAMILY TIES

In the early days of your separation from your spouse, try to keep your kids' everyday routine as normal as possible. If it's feasible for you, try to stay in your present home or apartment for at least several months after the divorce. Remember, divorce is traumatic enough. You don't want to add to your kids' stress level by making them deal with things like moving to a new neighborhood, leaving friends, or changing schools.

FAMILY TIES

If your spouse refuses to express love for your kids, don't try to convince them of that love. Kids place importance on actions, not words. If your spouse doesn't have obvious love for them, they will know. The best thing you can do in this situation is give them a chance to talk about their feelings. If they ask, "Why doesn't Dad love me?" you might ask, "What would you like your father to do to show his love for you?" You could then pass on their response to your spouse.

➤ allowance

➤ curfew

➤ music

➤ movies

➤ television.

What often happens after a divorce is that one spouse relaxes the house rules in order to be seen as the "fun" parent. And while the kids may enjoy the freedom given by that parent, the ultimate result is a sense of insecurity.

Facing the Future

Regardless of the option you choose—reconciliation or divorce—it's important that you not allow your past failures to dictate your attitude toward the future. If you choose to reconcile with your spouse, you can discover the joy of a relationship reborn.

As you and your spouse learn to forgive the past, share your feelings, commit to understanding, and develop love for each other again, you will find an intimacy and fulfillment in your marriage that you've never before experienced.

Let's emphasize this one more time. Achieving intimacy and fulfillment with your spouse will not be easy. In fact, dealing honestly with past emotions may prove to be painful for you. You may find yourselves occasionally reverting back to old, destructive habits in your relationship. That's only natural. The key to successful reconciliation is recognizing those tendencies in yourselves and addressing them before they have a chance to interfere with the health of your marriage.

As we pointed out earlier in this chapter, your best efforts cannot *guarantee* reconciliation. Your spouse always has the freedom to reject your efforts to rebuild your relationship.

So where does that leave you? Guilt-free, as far as your relationship is concerned. Having confessed your past failures, to your spouse and to God, and made every effort to reconcile, you will be able to face your future with a clear conscience—and unlimited opportunities for personal growth and happiness.

THE WISDOM OF ALL AGES

Time heals griefs and quarrels, for we change and are no longer the same persons.

–BLAISE PASCAL

That's why it's important that you not allow your past to spoil your future. To help prevent you from doing that, here are a few important "don'ts" to keep in mind:

1. Don't give depression a foothold in your life by dwelling on negative feelings about your marriage.

2. Don't allow bitterness to overwhelm your outlook on life.

3. Don't allow expressions of self-pity to occupy your thoughts.

4. Don't refuse the fellowship of friends.

5. Don't cut yourself off from others by maintaining an attitude of doom and gloom.

6. Don't torture yourself by asking "What if . . .?" questions about your marriage.

7. Don't lose today worrying about tomorrow.

The only sensible way to live your life in the wake of divorce is one day at a time. Your plate is full enough with today's worries and opportunities. It makes no sense to pile on concerns about what will happen to you tomorrow or ten years from now. Let tomorrow and ten years from now take care of themselves.

THE WISDOM OF ALL AGES

Most folk are about as happy as they make up their minds to be.

–ABRAHAM LINCOLN

THE WISDOM OF ALL AGES

Yesterday is not ours to recover, but tomorrow is ours to win or lose.

–LYNDON B. JOHNSON

For now, you've got more important issues to think about—questions such as . . .

➤ What can I do today to improve my personal situation?

➤ What do I need to pray about today?

➤ Who do I need to talk to today?

➤ What do I need to get done today?

➤ Whose life can I touch today?

Here's what it comes down to: You can't change the past and you can't predict the future, so you might as well do all you can with the present.

Remember, you are responsible for what you do with your life. You may try to blame your spouse or the "other person" or your parents, but the responsibility for your success or failure in life ultimately falls on you.

This is important to understand, because it means you don't have to be miserable simply because someone has treated you miserably. You can choose your response to both the positive and negative events in your life.

If you learn to adopt this attitude, in time, you will begin to feel less and less like a victim of your circumstances. Eventually you will be able to demonstrate to yourself that, with God's help, you can build a life that is productive and fulfilling.

Family Practice

After a marital separation, what? Here's a quiz to see how much you know about the possible next steps in the marriage relationship.

1. Which of the following is *not* true of reconciliation?
   a. It requires the efforts of only one spouse.
   b. It is almost always preferable to divorce.
   c. It is often much more difficult than divorce.
   d. It requires the involvement of a trained counselor.

2. Which of the following is *not* a recommended strategy after you decide to seek reconciliation with your spouse?
   a. Tell your spouse about your decision face-to-face.
   b. Wait until your spouse brings up the topic before you mention your decision.
   c. Pray.
   d. Give your spouse time to reach a decision of his or her own.

3. Which of the following is true of divorce?
   a. Its effects usually last no more than a year in the lives of most kids.
   b. It always requires the services of a lawyer.
   c. It severs not only an emotional and physical relationship, but a legal contract as well.
   d. Attempts to contest it are often successful.

4. Which of the following strategies will *not* be helpful to your kids if there is a divorce?
   a. Maintaining a consistent and fairly strict set of household rules
   b. Communicating love to them through their primary love language
   c. Being honest with them about what's going on
   d. Moving to a new house or apartment right away in order to give them a fresh start

5. Which of the following statements is important advice for someone recovering from divorce?
   a. Don't refuse the fellowship of friends.
   b. Don't allow bitterness to overwhelm your outlook on life.
   c. Don't allow expressions of self-pity to occupy your thoughts.
   d. All of these.

Answers: (1) a, (2) b, (3) c, (4) d, (5) d

Appendices

FAQs About Love, Marriage, Family . . . and In-Laws

Here are answers to twenty FAQs (frequently asked questions) I hear while leading conferences and counseling sessions.

1. How can I get my husband to really talk to me?

Take "baby steps." Don't overwhelm him by saying, "I wish you'd talk more." He can't respond positively to that. It comes across as condemnation. Begin by asking little questions, and be content to get little answers. He has to crawl before he can walk. When he gets used to hearing his own voice, then he can talk more.

Become a good listener. When your husband talks, give him your undivided attention. Don't respond to his ideas with condemnation. Rather say, "That's an interesting idea; how do you think that would work if we applied it to our lives?" Give him your opinion, but only if he asks for it. If he finds that he gets a sermon every time he shares an idea, he will stop sharing his ideas.

After a few weeks, try the following:

1. Ask if he would be willing to have a daily "sharing time" in which each of you shared two things that happened in your life today and how you feel about them? If he complains that these times are taking too long, then set time limits, such as no more than ten minutes each.

2. Try sharing a book. Find a book that you think would be of interest to him, and ask if he would be willing to read a chapter each week and you will read the same chapter. At the end of the week, each of you will share with the other one thing you liked or learned from the chapter.

2. When do I address my spouse's irritating habits, and when do I "let it go"?

Because we are human, we are different. Some of these differences can be terribly annoying. I believe you should find a way to address these and ask for change. But begin with yourself. I suggest that once a week, you ask your spouse, "What one thing could I change in my life that would make life better for you?" Then to the best of your ability, work on making that change. After a few weeks of this, your spouse will likely begin asking you the same question. Now you have a chance to ask for change—but never more than once a week.

Remember, you cannot make your spouse change. However, you can create a climate where change is a way of life. Arguing, demanding, and manipulating are not positive ways to seek change.

3. We are both working full time and when I get home I start dinner, but my husband comes in and sits on the couch. How do I encourage him to participate in household chores?

Set fire to the couch! Then hand him the fire extinguisher. Do this every two days for one week. He will no longer sit on the couch. Well, that's one approach, but not one that I recommend. Nor do I recommend yelling at him and calling him a lazy slob.

All of us have patterns of behavior which we have developed through the years. Some of these are helpful to the marriage (for example, your starting dinner), and some are detrimental to the marriage. The problem is, we are not always aware of what these are until they are brought to our attention. But how you bring them to your spouse's attention is the important thing.

I suggest you initiate a "marriage improvement month." Say to your spouse, "I've been thinking about us, and I don't want us to drift into a dead marriage. I don't want to just be an ordinary wife. I want to be an exceptional wife. Would you be open to giving me one suggestion each week for the next month on how I could be a better wife? I would give you one suggestion on how you could be a better husband, and both of us could grow. Would you be open to this?" If he is, then you are on the road to positive change. One of those weeks, you can share with him what you would like him to do when he arrives home. He will not take it as nagging, because you have made it a part of your month of improvement.

4. I have tried, but I really don't enjoy sex. I am just doing it to be obedient. What can I do?

Lack of interest and enjoyment in the sexual part of marriage is a common problem. Usually such lack of enjoyment is rooted in one of several factors. Sometimes it is rooted in sexual abuse as a child. Adults who were abused as children almost always struggle with sexual fulfillment. Sometimes it is rooted in the way the couple handled sex before marriage. For example, individuals who felt taken advantage of sexually before marriage, or felt forced into a marriage because of pregnancy, will often struggle with sex after they're married. Sometimes it is rooted in the way the spouse handles sex. Crude words or behavior with little attention to the spouse's concerns may emotionally turn the other person off to any interest in sex.

The best thing you can do is to find a Christian counselor with expertise in this area of counseling and begin to identify the problems and look for solutions. Sex is an important part of marriage and must not be ignored. I also recommend reading *The Gift of Sex*, by Clifford and Joyce Penner, published by Word Publishing.

5. How can I get her/him to have sex more often and make sure we both enjoy it?

Finding mutual sexual fulfillment is a process. It does not happen automatically. God told ancient Israel to take the first year of marriage and learn to pleasure each other (see Deuteronomy 24:5). One of the best ways to learn is to expose yourself to good information. I suggest that the two of you read one chapter per week in the book *The Gift of Sex*, by Clifford and Joyce Penner. At the end of the week, discuss the ideas presented in the chapter. The goal is to understand male and female sexuality and to discover how to pleasure each other sexually.

Your attitude should always be one of love, looking out for each other's pleasure. Share your desires with each other, but never force any sexual expression on your spouse. How often your spouse desires sex will be influenced by how you treat him/her. Open communication in an atmosphere of love will lead to mutual sexual fulfillment.

6. How do I nurture the spiritual dimension of our marriage when I don't feel comfortable praying out loud?

Pray together silently. It's simple: You hold hands, close your eyes, pray silently, and say "Amen" aloud so your spouse will know you are through. Continue to hold your spouse's hand until he/she says "Amen." If you will do this for six months, one night one of you will slip up and pray out loud. You will have broken the sound barrier and from then on you will pray out loud; but if you never pray out loud, it still will help your marriage to pray silently. If you sit together in church, you can also hold hands and pray silently as the pastor leads in prayer.

7. I recently got married but have been on my own for many years. How do we build a life together? How do I submit to my spouse's decisions after making my own decisions for so long?

In this question, you have hit upon one of the big differences between being married and being single. As a single, you do what you want to do when you want to do it. As a married, that is impossible. Why? Because "two have become one." It is no longer "your business" and "my business," but rather "our business." Now you must consider how your actions will affect your spouse. Remember, love is looking out for the other person's interest.

This doesn't mean that you must spend every waking hour together, but it does mean that you must keep each other informed. You are now a team, and team members must work together. It is not a matter of one making all the decisions. Rather, it is making decisions together, so that each of you feels good about what is happening. If all of this seems costly to your independence, you are correct. Intimacy and independence are mutually exclusive.

8. We got married because I was pregnant and now I feel like I have made a big mistake. Can I get a divorce or do I have to stick it out? If so, where do I start?

Your assumption seems to be that you have only two alternatives: Stay in the marriage and be miserable the rest of your life, or divorce and be happy. I suggest that there is a third alternative which offers far more hope: Work to build a successful marriage. Many people get into marriage in less than ideal circumstances. Yours was pregnancy. For others it was emotional dependency, dreams of getting out of a bad home situation, misguided romantic feelings, and any number of other factors. Getting off to a rocky start, or getting married for the wrong reasons, does not mean that you cannot have a good marriage.

Any couple can build a successful marriage if they will seek God's help. Through prayer, Bible and supplemental reading, and wise counsel, there is hope. Realize that the Scriptures lay down the principles for building a godly marriage. Books based on the Judeo-Christian perspective also can be extremely helpful. In addition, professional counselors and ordained ministers are also available. God can bring healing to past failures and supply hope for the future. Use the right resources, and yours can become the marriage you always wanted.

9. After being married one year, I'm not sure I'm "in love" anymore. Where could we have gone wrong?

This is the same question I was asking the first year of my marriage. I had been told that if you are really "in love" it will last forever. I was misinformed. The fact is that the emotional obsession that we commonly call "falling in love" is a temporary experience. Research indicates that the average lifespan of this "in love" phase is two years. Since we fall in love before we get married, most couples are coming down off the high within the first year of their marriage. We no longer feel those warm bubbly feelings, and we no longer think that our spouse is perfect. In fact, we are realizing that we are so different, and we are wondering, *How did we ever get together?*

Then begins the second and more important phase of love: learning how to speak each other's love language. In order to keep emotional love alive after we come down off the "in love" high, we must learn to speak each other's language. Remember, those five love languages are words of affirmation, gifts, acts of service, quality time, and physical touch. Once you make this transition, you will each feel loved, and you will hardly even miss the "in love" high. Your emotional love tank will be filled by your spouse's regular expressions of love.

10. My spouse is emotionally abusive. My friends are all telling me not to stay. When is it OK to leave?

Emotional abuse, which is often the result of verbal abuse, seldom goes away with the passing of time. Neither is the problem solved by simply leaving your spouse.

You need a plan and support system to help you take constructive steps of tough love. (My book *Loving Solutions* is written to people who are in difficult marriages. The theme is helping you to be a positive change agent in such a marriage.) Tough love may eventually require a temporary separation, but this should be done as a therapeutic move, not as an act of abandonment. Such a step should never be taken without the guidance of a Christian counselor or a minister. Don't try to do this on your own. Reach out for the help of those who are professionally trained and have had experience in helping others in such marriages.

11. I feel strongly about certain types of discipline with our children, but my husband just laughs it off and does not support me. How do I handle this situation?

Disagreements over styles of discipline are fairly common for one simple reason: We each grew up in different families. We tend to discipline like our parents did, or believing that they treated us unfairly, we tend to do the opposite of what our parents did.

How do we resolve these differences? It is not likely that you will ever totally agree on this matter, but you can find a workable solution. It begins by each of you making a list of the basic rules you think you should have for the child and what the consequences should be if these rules are broken. With these lists in hand, you have a parental conference in which the two of you work through your lists. Check off the ones on which you agree and negotiate agreement on the others. (Both must be willing to find common ground. Don't insist that your way is the only way.) With these in place, it is then a matter of making sure the child understands the rules and the consequences, and consistently applying the discipline when rules are broken. Kindness but firmness is the key in applying discipline.

12. I feel like I am always the one who has to discipline our children, and my spouse comes out looking like the good parent. How can we come together to agree on this issue?

Because we grew up in different homes, we often come to parenting with different perspectives. Nowhere is this demonstrated more than in patterns of discipline. Most parents will have conflicts over discipline of children. The answer lies in recognizing this reality and finding a plan to deal with the conflict.

One place to begin would be to share a book on discipline. Both of you would read the book, a chapter per week, and discuss the content. This will expose you to sound principles of discipline. You might try *Making Your Children Mind Without Losing Yours,* by Kevin Leman, published by Fleming H. Revell Co. A second step is to call a parent conference and focus on your present struggles with discipline. Such a conference might involve listing the rules you feel are appropriate for the children, and discussing what each of you feel is appropriate consequences for breaking the rules. If you don't agree on consequences, then negotiate. Be willing to meet each other in the middle. Once the rules and consequences are in place, these should be shared with the child. Then each of you knows what will happen if a rule is broken. This keeps either of you from overreacting in the heat of anger. Kindness, firmness, and consistency are three key words in administering discipline.

13. Is it right to spank my children? If so, in what circumstances?

Physically spanking a child is only one way of discipline, and not always the most effective way. Remember, the purpose of discipline is to teach the child the wisdom of following rules, by demonstrating that disobedience always has negative results.

Spanking should never be the first step in correcting a child. It should be administered only after all else has failed. If a parent uses spanking as the usual way of treating all disobedience, the child will likely be hardened by the spankings and become even more rebellious.

The first principle of discipline is that the punishment must fit the crime. Spanking for minor infractions is irresponsible parenting. Also, spanking administered out of parental anger will almost always engender resentment in the child. Such angry behavior often leads to child abuse. The best way to avoid such parental failure is to decide ahead of time what punishment the child will receive if he violates a rule. Then administer that punishment when the crime is committed. This will save the parent from overreacting in the heat of emotion.

It is helpful to remember that children respond differently to spanking. For some children, spanking will be totally ineffective as a means of correction, which is the purpose of all discipline. Also, the child whose primary love language is "physical touch" will be more deeply hurt when spanked. The parent is using the child's primary love language in a negative way. This child will feel the pain far more deeply than a child who has a different love language.

14. I am having trouble relating to my child. We don't enjoy doing a lot of the same things. How do I relate to a child who is very different from me?

All of us are different. If we don't enter into each other's world of interests, we will never develop a close relationship. In the early stages of life, you must go to the child's interests. When children are in the sandbox, then we enter into the world of sand castles. Later on, we can bring them into our world. But the process must always be a two-way street.

The beauty of all of this is that your own world is enlarged. If your child is interested in sports and you have never been a sports enthusiast, you will discover a whole new world as you explore the world of sports. The goal is to foster the innate interests and gifts of the child, while exposing her to areas of life in which she may have little interest. This is the way all of us grow into well-rounded individuals.

15. My spouse has been offered a job on the other side of the country, and my parents are very angry that we would think about moving away from them. What do we do?

Being a grandparent, I can understand your parents' feelings. It's nice to have the children and grandchildren nearby. However, you must not make your decision based on their desires. Nor should you make the decision simply to prove to them that they cannot control your lives. The decision to take the job or to decline must be made by weighing numerous factors. If you and your spouse conclude that the job is right, then he or she must accept the job.

In that case, I suggest that you express sympathy for your parents' feelings. Assure them that you will visit as often as possible and keep in touch by phone or E-mail. But don't let their tears dissuade you. Remember the Scriptures say that when we marry, we are to "leave our father and mother and be united to each other" (Matthew 19:5).

16. How do I deal with the holiday time when everyone wants us to be in so many places at once.? How do we choose which family to accommodate?

The principle is: Treat both sets of in-laws with equality. This is not always easy to carry out. This may mean Thanksgiving with one set of parents, and Christmas with another; with the understanding that next year you will switch the order. Or if both parents live in the same town, then your family can spend half a day at each place. This assumes that both sets of in-laws want you to visit.

There is also a time to establish your own traditions. As the children get older, it often becomes more difficult to spend the holidays with in-laws. Maybe it is time for the in-laws to start coming to your house. Remember, it may be impossible to please both sets of in-laws. Try to follow the principle of equal treatment, but if one set is unhappy, it is not your responsibility to make them happy. You speak kindly to them, treat them with respect, but you do not let them control your own family decisions.

17. We are supposed to leave our families and cleave to one another but my spouse is so attached to his/her family that I feel left out.

You feel left out because your emotional need for love is not being met by your spouse. You feel that his/her parents are more important than you. However, the answer is not to blast your spouse with angry lectures about being overly attached to parents. When you do that, you drive your spouse away. He or she will want to be with parents even more, because the parents are loving and kind while you are angry and demanding.

A better approach is to focus on meeting each other's need for emotional love. Leave her/his parents out of the discussion. Find out what makes your spouse feel loved, and share what makes you feel loved. Discover each other's primary love language. When each of you is speaking the other's primary love language on a regular basis, your spouse will have positive emotions toward you. You may find that he or she spends less time with parents and more time with you. If not, then you can share your concerns. Your spouse is more likely to hear you because the spouse feels your love so deeply. Without creating this love bond, you will argue endlessly about his or her parents and eventually destroy your marriage.

18. I want to honor my parents, but they are constantly trying to give us advice. How do I let them know that we need to make these decisions on our own?

Three things are important. First, you must understand that your parents' intentions are good. They are not trying to make your life miserable. They are trying to help you avoid making poor decisions. Second, there is a good chance that your parents have more wisdom than you, since they have been around longer and have had more experience. Third, it is true that your parents should not control your life after you are married.

How do you put these three together and get the best of both worlds? I suggest you ask for your parents' advice before they have a chance to give it. You take the initiative in seeking their wisdom. Then pray for God's wisdom. Then discuss the matter with your spouse, and the two of you make the decision you think is best. If your parents object, tell them that you appreciate their input, you found it very helpful, but you are doing what you think is best. And leave it at that. Don't try to argue with your parents. In time, they will come to see you as an adult and respect your wisdom.

If your decision turns out to be a poor decision, admit it and turn it around as quickly as possible. Don't try to make it work just to prove that you were right. For additional information, see my book *Toward a Growing Marriage*, chapter 10, "If You Only Knew My Mother-in-Law."

19. We are having our first child and my mother insists on doing things that contradict our parenting choices. Help!

It always helps to begin by realizing that your mother's intentions are good. Give her credit for trying to help you. In fact, some of her ideas may be excellent. Don't write her off simply because she is your mother. On the other hand, you must not let your mother control your parenting choices. You and your spouse are responsible for raising your child.

I suggest you listen to your mother's ideas. Thank her for sharing. Then you and your spouse do what you think is best for your child. If your mother is upset because you did not take her advice, say, "I can understand that, Mom, and I really appreciate your advice, but we must do what we think is best for our child. That's what you and Dad did, right? And I think you did a pretty good job with me." You mother may not be happy, but she will learn to back off and wait until you ask for her advice—which, incidentally, would be a wise move on your part.

20. The children are gone. Now what? How do we relate to each other after all the children leave the home?

This is when the focus of the past twenty years becomes apparent. If you have focused on the children, then you may have to start back at ground zero and rebuild your marriage relationship. If you have focused on each other while raising the children, then you will climb to new heights of marital satisfaction with the extra time you now have.

Whatever your situation, now is the time to assess the state of your marriage and take steps of growth. I suggest that you attend a weekend marriage enrichment. This will expose you to ideas on how to stimulate growth in your marriage. Also, try sharing a book on marriage by reading a chapter each week and discussing the content. A good book for this stage of marriage is *The Second Half of Marriage,* by David and Claudia Arp.

It is definitely time for the two of you to focus on your marriage. Don't just rock along and think that things will take care of themselves.

Spouse Discussion of the Five Love Languages

As you consider how to express love in your spouse's primary love language, this discussion guide (with mini projects) will help. It also will help you to understand and speak all five love languages (most spouses appreciate hearing love in the other four languages as well) and to recognize your own love language.

The best way to begin this discussion is to fill out the card at the front of the book. It will allow you to name your primary love language and the ways your needs can be met by your spouse. It will also allow your spouse to do the same.

Discovering Your Primary Love Language

1. We often express love in our primary love language rather than discovering our spouse's language. Look back to the times when you felt you successfully communicated love. Did you do so through your primary language or that of your spouse? Are you willing to make a new commitment to speaking your spouse's primary love language?

2. If you still have difficulty with self-understanding as it relates to the love languages, perhaps your emotional tank is either very empty or very full. Take an inventory of your deepest emotions, and evaluate if either case is true. If your tank is empty, say, "Have I ever felt loved in my life?" If you answer yes, indicate when. What made you feel loved? Your answer will reveal your love language.

3. If your love tank is not very full, go back to your courtship and conjure up the memories. That will help you get to the root of what was effective, and solve the mystery. Then you'll better know why the love tank is less than full, and you can work on fine-tuning the relationship.

4. Many of us struggle with making sex a mutual joy. We sometimes focus on technique, frequency, and variety. Yet much of the struggle relates more to

the state of our emotional love tank. Think about your relationship and how you can focus more on the emotional side and thus also improve the physical relationship.

Speaking Love Language #1: Words of Affirmation

1. Take an evening to allow your spouse to share his or her dreams, interests, and talents. Draw out the specifics through empathetic listening. After putting yourself in your spouse's shoes, lovingly and sincerely encourage him/her, and offer to help achieve these goals in any way possible.

2. Familiarity may breed contempt or discourtesy in different forms. Check certain characteristics of your relationship over the past week. Has your tone been harsh, your attitude sarcastic, or your viewpoint judgmental? Have you focused mainly on where your spouse has failed? Resolve these issues and seek forgiveness.

3. Evaluate your relational style in terms of communication patterns. Do your words reflect requests, suggestions, and guidance? Or do they hint at demands, ultimatums, or even threats? Remember that choice, free will, and voluntary service are key aspects of love. How can you improve your verbal approach to your spouse?

4. There are an infinite variety of kind, intimate, and supportive ways of verbally communicating with your mate. As the text in "Glad You Asked" (page 68) suggests, start a notebook in which you record creative and superior ways of building up your spouse even in the smallest ways. Self-help and inspirational reading is especially helpful. Entitle your notebook "Words of Affirmation."

Speaking Love Language #2: Quality Time

1. "My job is so demanding" may be a statement of excuse for not spending quality time with your spouse. Yet success and material provision can't substitute for intimacy. Set up a plan with your spouse to balance your responsibilities to allow for quality time. Be sacrificial in the trade-offs you make.

2. Look back on the last major problem or challenge your spouse faced. Write out ways you could have better achieved the following: (a) less advice and more sympathy; (b) more understanding and fewer solutions; (c) more questions and fewer conclusions; and (d) more attention to the person and less to the problem.

3. Find out how important shared activities are in your marriage. Isolate three experiences that brought you very close and are a source of continuing fond memories. Did these experiences involve quality time in shared activities.? Plan a new event that has strong "memory" potential.

4. Be honest about the role of feelings in your life. When has their proper expression contributed to a healthy resolution of a problem or completed a positive event? Overall, do you repress or fear your emotions? Do you explode or distort them? How do they mesh with your spouse's? How can the emotive aspect of your communication improve?

Speaking Love Language #3: Receiving Gifts

1. The value of a gift is in the eye of the beholder. Perhaps you don't especially value a gift you received. Consider the giver's intent, and reorient your thinking to value the love demonstrated by the giver.

2. Perhaps in your mind, gifts and finances don't mix well at present. Yet if gift giving is your most important "possession," you can view it as a form of savings or security. Review your budget, and sacrificially give more to your spouse.

3. If gifts are your spouse's love language, that may require you to give up your own priorities momentarily. Recall over the last few years situations when a gift or the gift of your presence was highly desired by your spouse and you failed to come through. Consciously plan to make the tough choices the next time around.

4. Remember that the gift of yourself means more than just your physical presence. Attempt for one week to share at least one important event or feeling in your day. Seek the same from your spouse.

Speaking Love Language #4: Acts of Service

1. Even when we wish to comply with our spouse's requests, we like to do it our way on our terms. Loving service means meeting our spouse's expectations. Seek specifics from your spouse on a few new tasks he or she desires of you, and do exactly as instructed.

2. Choose three simple but humble tasks that you don't especially like but know your spouse would be pleased to see completed. Surprise your spouse by doing them without being asked.

3. Many couples feel that they have overcome gender role stereotypes in their relationship but unconscious bias still remains. Discuss your deepest feelings about sharing all activities and your family history in this regard.

4. A lot of problems stem from the myth that we should abandon "courting behavior" after marriage. Try to remember the tremendous love and intimacy resulting from regular acts of service in that period. To retrieve closeness, try some of those early practices to see if there indeed is a connection.

Speaking Love Language #5: Physical Touch

1. Eliminate all negative forms of physical touch. If you've ever harmed your spouse, even in the slightest manner, ask forgiveness and deal with this self-control issue. If other forms of touch have been annoying, discontinue those forms and replace them with positive and pleasing substitutes.

2. Perhaps you and your spouse have never openly shared with one another the types of touching you find pleasurable. Discuss the emotional, sexual, and psychological dimensions related to all these areas of the body.

3. Make a list of all the circumstances, locations, and types of appropriate touch that will enhance your physical relationship. For example, what is the extent and nature of the physical touch you desire as you enter or leave the car? If you each feel differently, come to a compromise resolution, each seeking first to please the other.

4. Crisis situations include death, severe illness, and the like, but can also include the small daily traumas that have a large emotional impact. Devise a method of reaching out with an expression of caring or tender touch, rather than silence or empty words.

Index

How Well Do You Know Your and Your Spouse's Love Language?

THE FIVE LOVE LANGUAGES

- Words of Affirmation
- Quality Time
- Receiving Gifts
- Acts of Service
- Physical Touch

A major element to healthy family relationship are parents knowing their primary love language. So tear out this card and complete this page. Then have your spouse fill out the other side. Do not look at your spouse's response until you have both completed this card.

Answer these questions before choosing your primary love language: What do you request the most? What makes you feel the most loved? What hurts you deeply? What do you desire most of all? These are clues to knowing your own love language.

What is your primary love language? _____

Why do you say that? _____

What do you think is your spouse's primary love language? _____

Why do you say that? _____

_____

List three things you would like your spouse to do or say to communicate love in your own love language. _____

_____

_____

List three things you could do or say to communicate love to your spouse in his/her love language, based on your above guess. _____

_____

_____

Now share your responses with your spouse. Make a commitment to meet needs as he/she expressed them, rather than what you think is the best way.

How Well Do You Know Your and Your Spouse's ʟ... ᴧᴜage?

THE FIVE LOVE LANGUAGES

- Words of Affirmation
- Quality Time
- Receiving Gifts
- Acts of Service
- Physical Touch

Do not look at your spouse's responses (on the other side) until you have completed this card. Answer these questions before choosing your primary love language: What do you request the most? What makes you feel the most loved? What hurts you deeply? What do you desire most of all? These are clues to knowing your own love language.

What is your primary love language? _____

Why do you say that? _____

_____

What do you think is your spouse's primary love language? _____

Why do you say that? _____

_____

List three things you would like your spouse to do or say to communicate love in your own love language. _____

_____

_____

List three things you could do or say to communicate love to your spouse in his/her love language, based on your above guess. _____

_____

_____

Now share your responses with your spouse. Make a commitment to meet needs as he/she expressed them, rather than what you think is the best way.